West Country Cruising

A yachtsman's pilot and guide to ports and harbours from the Exe to Land's End and North Cornwall

Mark Fishwick

Price: £13.95

Published by
YACHTING MONTHLY
IPC Magazines Ltd, King's Reach Tower,
Stamford Street, London SE1 9LS. 1988

Price £13.95
First Edition 1988, revised 1989

ISBN 1 85277 060 0

CAUTION
Whilst every effort has been made to ensure the accuracy of the contents of
this book, readers are nevertheless warned that any of the information
contained may have changed between the date when the author carried out
his research in 1988/1989 and the actual date of publication.

Neither the publisher nor the author can accept responsibility for errors,
omissions or alterations in this book. They will be grateful for any
information from readers to assist in the update and accuracy of the
publication.

Readers are advised at all times to refer to official charts, publications and
notices. The charts contained in this book are sketch plans and are not to be
used for navigation. Some details are omitted for the sake of clarity and the
scales have been chosen to allow best coverage in relation to page size.

West Country Cruising is printed in England by Clifford Frost Ltd,
Wimbledon, London SW19

West Country Cruising

by Mark Fishwick

Preface to the second edition

To my delight, the popularity of *West Country Cruising* resulted in more rapid sales than anticipated, and a revised and enlarged second edition has become a possibility far sooner than I had expected!

Major developments have been relatively few — notably the new marina in Brixham, although I have been surprised at the number of smaller changes. In addition, there is also a whole new, and hopefully, useful section with over 100 extra passage and harbour photographs.

As always, I have tried to ensure accuracy but apologise in advance for any mistakes and omissions that might come to light. Changes are continual, and any assistance, information or comments from readers that will help improve and keep this book up to date will be gratefully received.

Mark Fishwick

3 Gyllyng Street
Falmouth
Cornwall TR11 3EJ
February 1989

Aerial photographs by Patrick Roach
All other photographs by the author

Charts drawn by Mike Collins

Edited by Andrew Bray

Design by Caroline Helfer

Cover
Main picture: Salcombe looking south-west, taken from Scoble Point.
Lower picture: aerial view of Salcombe looking seaward with the Island Cruising Club's Egremont in the foreground and Bolt Head in the distance.
Back cover: St Anthony Light, River Fal.

Contents

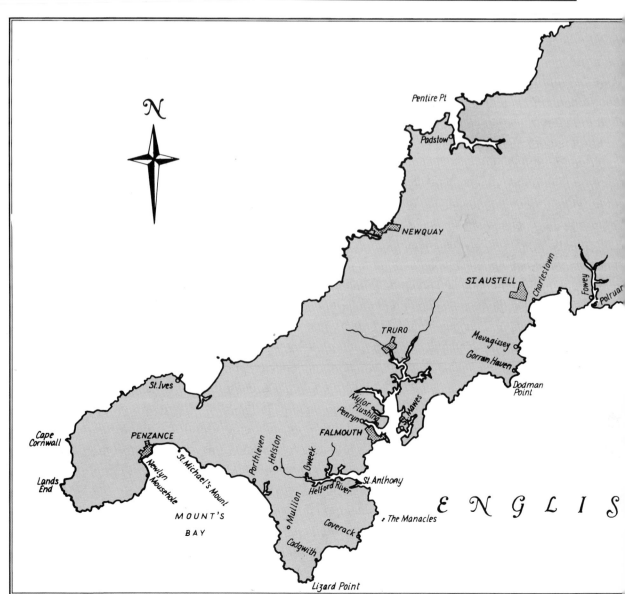

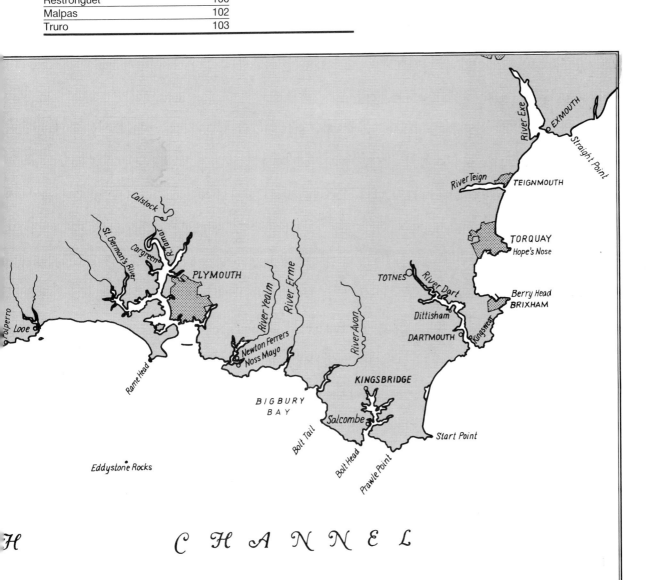

THE AUTHOR: Born and brought up on the River Exe Mark Fishwick began sailing at an early age and soon ventured further to explore the rivers, creeks and harbours of the West Country in his parents 18′6″ Alacrity sloop *Vallette*. He moved to Cornwall in 1973 soon after buying his present boat, the 34 foot 1910 gaff yawl *Temptress*, and since then has enjoyed a varied nautical life involving fishing, charter skippering in the West Indies and yacht delivery. Now based in Falmouth, he divides his time between writing and sailing, and is convinced that there are few places to match the West Country as a cruising ground.

Acknowledgements

Inevitably a book of this sort could not have been completed without a large amount of assistance and help from others, but none of it would have been achieved without Vicki who has not only put up with the disruption to our lives with remarkable calm, but has spent many hours trekking around in search of launderettes and shops open on Sundays, and even more time in the solitude of the darkroom. Above all, organiser supreme, she has managed to keep track of the chaos that I have managed to create!

It would take several pages to mention everyone by name, but, working east to west, thanks to the Harbourmasters and their staff, Jack Nott, Reg Mathews, Captain Cannan, Captain Knowles, Captain Moore, Captain Blazeby, M J Simpson, Pat Marshall, Commander Anthony Dyer, H Butters, Captain Mike Sutherland, P. J. Rafferty, Captain Banks, Jim Stephens, John Vaughan, Captain Martin Tregoning, Andrew Munson, Eric Ward, Captain Sampson, E M Wakelin.

Additional special thanks to my parents, Cliff and Pat Fishwick, Chris, Geoff and Julian Legg, Ian and Rosemary Cowan, Captain Pat McNamara, Danny Murphy, John and Anna Pentecost, Neil Clark, M P Avis, Brian Tankard, Jack Pender, 'Watty', Andrew Bray, Caroline Helfer, Mike Collins, Emma Cussans, Patrick Roach, Chris Hart, Tim Grove, Pete Lucas, Robin Page, Alan Miller, Derek Rowe, Frank Collins, Andy Campbell, everyone at Marine Instruments, Falmouth and all the Club Secretaries, boatyards, marinas and other people who have responded to my requests for information.

Bibliography (further reading and books consulted)
West Country Rivers, D J Pooley, Yachting Monthly 1965
Channel Pilot, Admiralty, Hydrographic Department 1977
**West coast of England and Wales
Pilot,** Admiralty, Hydrographic Department, 1974
Reeds Nautical Almanac, Thomas Reed Publications Ltd, annual
Macmillan & Silk Cut Nautical Almanac, Macmillan, annual
Cruising Association Handbook, Cruising Association
South England Pilot (Vol IV, Start Point to Land's End) Robin Brandon, Imray Laurie Norrie & Wilson 1979
Shell Pilot to the English Channel, Part 1, K Adlard Coles, revised Capt J Coote, Adlard Coles Ltd, 1986
Sailing & Boating guide to the Fal Area, Port of Falmouth Chamber of Commerce, annual
Stanford's Tidal Atlas, English Channel West, Michael Reeve-Fowkes, Stanford Maritime Ltd
AA Illustrated guide to Britain's Coast, Drive Publications Ltd
SW Peninsula Coast Path, Nos 2 and 3, Ward and Mason, Letts & Co 1977
The West Country from the Sea, David and Joan Hay, Stanford, 1972
Cornish Sea Lights, David Mudd, Bossiney Books 1978
Fowey, River and Town, and Rivers of Cornwall, Sarah Foot, Bossiney Books, 1984/85
Sea Stories of Cornwall and Coastline of Cornwall, Ken Duxbury, Bossiney Books, 1984/85
Boats and Boatbuilding in West Cornwall, A S Oliver, Bradford Barton Ltd, 1971
Hevva, K Harris, Cornish Publications, 1983
Smuggling in Cornwall, Cyril Noall, Tor Mark Press
Living History Under Sail, John McDonald, Falmouth Working Boat Association, 1982
Tall Ships in Torbay, John Pike, Ex Libris Press, 1986
Wreck and Rescue Round the Cornish Coast (3 vols) Noall/Farr, Tor Mark Press 1984
Wreck and rescue on the Coast of Devon, G. Farr, Tor Mark Press 1984

West Country Cruising

IF I WAS GIVEN a brief to design a perfect cruising ground the West Country would not fall too far short of it, and I would be little inclined to make many changes. Year after year the magnificent coastline of Devon and Cornwall has attracted more and more visiting yachts with its ports and rivers deep and mostly of easy access, and its rock bound coast steep-to, with few off-lying dangers.

If there could be one major change that we would all agree on it would inevitably have to be the weather, but there again, what would English crusing be without its unpredictability? Generally speaking, well in the track of the prevailing south-westerly air stream and its accompanying depressions, I have noticed in recent years that the early summer can often provide some of the better spells of weather, and also we can be lucky in the early autumn. There does, however, seem to be a tendency for far more unsettled weather, often a blow or two, in August; not in itself a great problem once the long haul across Lyme Bay is astern, for a whole variety of harbours and safe anchorages abound, all within an easy day's sail of each other, and many of the deep wooded rivers threading far inland such as the Dart and the Fal provide days of interesting exploration in themselves.

Way back in 1957 *Yachting Monthly* produced a slim little book called *West Country Rivers* written by D J Pooley, and it proved to be an invaluable guide and a constant companion in my first early explorations of my home waters back in the 1960s. Long since out of print, it was a very pleasant surprise when *Yachting Monthly* invited me to revamp the book, and, including port and passage notes, to expand it into this cruising guide. Inevitably, my researches have revealed that in twenty years much has changed 'down west' for the pastime of sailing has become a big leisure business, and thousands more now enjoy the sport. Once forgotten backwaters and creeks, the haunt of rotting hulks, whispering mud and seaweedy smells, have been cleared and dredged, and marinas have blossomed forth; anchorages that were easy of access under sail no longer exist and moorings have encroached into every available space with their proximity rendering a reliable auxiliary a real necessity.

However, in spite of it all, the essential beauty and atmosphere of the West Country has survived the onslaught well, and the sailing is as good as ever. Ashore, the varied and colourful villages and towns provide all the facilities a cruising yacht might need from essentials like good ale and launderettes to shipwrights and riggers. There is much of historical interest, and with vast areas fortunately preserved by the National Trust, many lovely walks. There can be few who visit these waters that sail away disappointed, and hopefully, this guide will help to make *your* cruise just that bit more enjoyable . . .

Mark Fishwick

General information

Cellar Bay at the mouth of the beautiful River Yealm is a favourite daytime anchorage for many

Buoyage: All buoyage within the area of this Pilot falls for the most part into IALA System A. **LATERAL MARKS,** defining extremities of channels, are red cans, with square red topmarks and red light to be left to port; green or black conical buoys with triangular topmarks and green lights, to be left to starboard, when proceeding in the direction of the main **FLOOD** stream. **CARDINAL MARKS** are used in conjunction with the compass, placed N, S, E, or W of a hazard, usually pillar buoys coloured with a combination of black and yellow, (see abbreviations) with quick flashing white lights, the significant feature being the double cone topmark. Two cones pointing up means the best water lies to the North, two cones pointing down, pass to the South, two points up and down (diamond) pass to the east, and two points together (wineglass) pass to the west. Other marks likely to be encountered include **ISOLATED DANGERS,** black double spheres topmark, as on Black Rock, Falmouth. **SPECIAL MARKS,** yellow buoys, sometimes with a yellow X topmark, often marking limits of danger zones such as the firing ranges at the entrance to the River Exe. Note, however, in the upper reaches of some of the rivers that some buoys

are privately maintained and do not necessarily conform to these shapes or colourings. Narrow creeks are marked with a variety of beacons from simple poles or stakes in the mud, to complicated perches with wire stays and topmarks.

Abbreviations: Colours of buoys, lights and their frequency is as follows:

R	. . .	Red.
G	. . .	Green.
Y	. . .	Yellow.
B	. . .	Black.
W	. . .	White.
RW	. . .	Red and white.
YB	. . .	Yellow and black (South cardinal).
BYB	. . .	Black, yellow, black (East cardinal).
BY	. . .	Black and yellow (North cardinal).
YBY	. . .	Yellow, black, yellow (West cardinal).
BR	. . .	Black and red.
FR	. . .	Fixed red light.
FG	. . .	Fixed green light.
Fl	. . .	Flashing light, period of darkness longer

than light. If followed by a number, indicates a group of flashes, e.g. Fl(3). Colour white unless followed by a colour, e.g. Fl(3) R. Timing of whole sequence, including light and darkness flash indicated by number of seconds (sec or secs), e.g. Fl(3) R 15secs.

L.Fl . . . Long flash, of not less than two seconds.

Occ . . . Occulting light, period of light longer than darkness.

Iso . . . Isophase light, equal periods of light and darkness.

Q . . . Quick flashing light, up to 50/60 flashes per minute.

VQ . . . Very quick flashing light, up to 120 flashes per minute.

Soundings: Are all in metres and tenths of metres reduced to Chart Datum, the level of the lowest astronomical tide, LAT.
HEIGHTS: are in metres, above mean high water springs, MHWS. Drying heights, underlined are above LAT.

Charts: Are of necessity simplified to show the main basics a visitor will require and should always be used with caution. A back up of current Admiralty Charts is strongly recommended.

Bearings: Are True from seaward. Magnetic variation should be applied as shown on current Admiralty charts. Variation in most of the West Country lies between 07.00 degrees W and 05.30 degrees W, 1989, decreasing about 8′ annually.

Marine Radio Beacons: Marine and Aero Radiobeacons for the area covered by this book are as follows:

No	Name	Lat/Long	Ident	Freq kHz	Mode	Range
1	Round Island	49.58.7N 06.19.3W	RR (— · · — ·)	308	A2A	100nm
5	Lizard	49.57.6N 05.12.1W	LZ (· — · · — — · ·)	298.8	A2A	70nm
A2	Penzance Heliport	50.07.7N 05.31.0W	PH (· — — · · · · ·)	333	NonA2A	15nm
9	Penlee Point	50.19.1N 04.11.3W	PE (· — — · ·)	298.8	A2A	50nm
A6	Plymouth	50.25.4N 04.06.7W	PY (· — — · — · — —)	396.5	NonA2A	20nm
13	Start Point	50.13.3N 03.38.5W	SP (· · · · — — ·)	298.8	A2A	70nm
A10	Berry Head	50.23.9N 03.29.6W	BHD (— · · · · · · · — · ·)	337	NonA2A	25nm
A190	St Mawgan	50.26.8N 04.59.6W	SM (· · · — —)	356.5	NonA2A	50nm

Tides: The maximum rate at Springs is used throughout this book to give an indication of the worst (or best, if you're going with it!) rate you will encounter. Generally, along the coast of the West Country, streams run parallel to the shore, but set in and out of the bays, and allowance should be made for this when crossing them. Within the bays, and

In settled weather Gorran Haven, near Mevagissey is an attractive daytime stop, where bilge keelers can dry out on the sandy beach

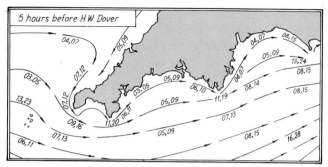

5 hours before HW Dover

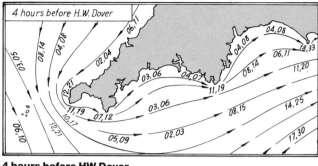

4 hours before HW Dover

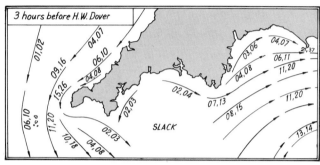

3 hours before HW Dover

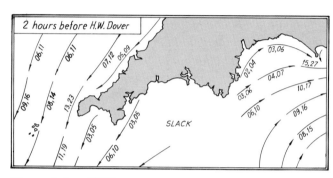

2 hours before HW Dover

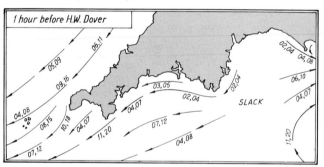

1 hour before HW Dover

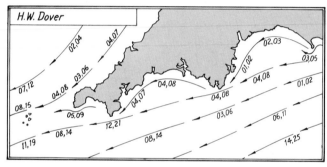

HW Dover

inshore, streams are generally weak but increase considerably in the vicinity of headlands where overfalls are often found. Streams are also much stronger within the confines of the rivers, and here it should be remembered that these are fed by the large gathering basins of the inland moors, Dartmoor, Exmoor, and Bodmin, and after any period of rain, the amount of flooding fresh water can noticeably increase the rate of streams at up to 2 knots, particularly in the upper reaches. Barometric pressure will also affect predicted tidal heights; explore the upper reaches of rivers only on a rising tide, and do not push your luck too close to high water at Springs, or you risk being neaped for a considerable time!

Rise and fall of the tide is not at a constant rate, and the old 'rule of twelfths' is always a good guide.:

Rise or fall during the 1st hour .... $1/12$ of range.
Rise or fall during the 2nd hour .... $2/12$ of range.
Rise or fall during the 3rd hour .... $3/12$ of range.
Rise or fall during the 4th hour .... $3/12$ of range.
Rise or fall during the 5th hour .... $2/12$ of range.
Rise or fall during the 6th hour .... $1/12$ of range.

Spring tides occur a day or so after the full and new moon, approximately every 15 days. High water is usually 50 minutes later each day; low water approximately six hours after high water.

Weather and forecasts: As in most places in the British Isles the weather in the West Country can be very changeable, and can deteriorate fast. However, with comprehensive forecasting available, and ports within easy reach of one another, there is little excuse for getting caught out, and it should be remembered if you do, due to the exposed nature of a lot of the coastline, and ground swell, the seas will be a lot larger than elsewhere in the Channel, particularly with wind against tide.

If it is possible to generalise, the weather in the early summer May and June can often provide a fine spell, ideal for fitting out and usually giving rise to all sorts of hopeful predictions that this one is going to be the long hot summer! July, alas, has a tendency to dispel such promise, and can often be very mixed. Although summer gales are rare, August can be a poor month, and I have noticed a distinct tendency for there to be at least one bad blow during it, such as

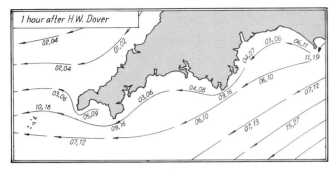

1 hour after HW Dover

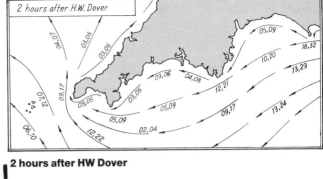

2 hours after HW Dover

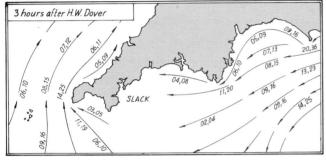

3 hours after HW Dover

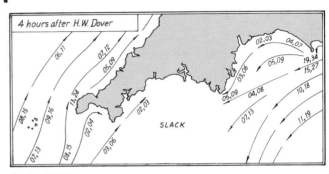

4 after HW Dover

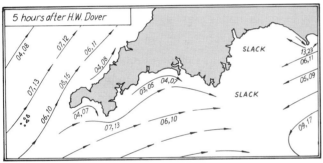

5 hours after HW Dover

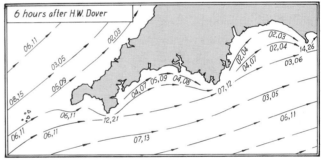

6 hours after HW Dover

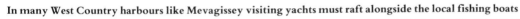

In many West Country harbours like Mevagissey visiting yachts must raft alongside the local fishing boats

In Torbay, Paignton is a crowded drying harbour where smaller boats can sometimes find a berth

the Fastnet disaster in 1979, and the tail of Hurricane Charley in 1986. September, too, can be very unsettled although occasionally, the much vaunted Indian Summer can occur, if only briefly.

The dominant feature of the weather is the prevailing south-westerly air stream, across the warm waters of the Gulf Stream which touches the far west, and the depressions it creates usually pass to the north of the area with associated trailing warm and cold fronts creating an unsettled but fairly predictable sequence of events, drop in barometer, wind backing to the south or south-east, increasing, light rain becoming heavy for several hours, and wind freshening further before veering more to the west when rain becomes steadier with poor visibility in the warm sector. With the passage of the cold front, the rain will stop, skies clear, barometer begins to rise, and the wind will then veer north-westerly and often blow quite hard with blustery showers. As these die out, if another frontal system is in the offing, the wind will start to back, but there is usually a good chance of at least 6-12 hours of reasonable weather before it arrives.

The alternative, when the Azores High manages to push far enough north to keep the depressions at bay, and deflect them much further to the north, should theoretically result in the fine weather. Often it does, ashore, but the easterly airstream has a tendency to be fresh at sea, and creates very hazy conditions, blowing hard during the day, but dying down more at night. In fine weather, localised land and sea breezes are far more frequent, often blowing fresh out of the river approaches in the late afternoon, but generally the winds ease considerably by evening.

Rain is likely at any time! June, however, is often one of the driest months, and although the skies may be overcast and grey a lot of the time, heavy prolonged rainfall is a lot less than in some parts of the country.

Fog, fortunately, is not very frequent this far west, but in warm weather sea mist can occur without warning, often towards the end of a fine warm day. In fine, settled weather, usually when high pressure prevails, early morning mist in rivers will often be thick but clears within a couple of hours. However, poor visibility associated with the passage of fronts is far more frequent, misty rain, good old Cornish 'mizzle'. Thunderstorms can occur but not particularly frequently, tending to generate over the continent and drift over the channel further to the east.

Approaching Turf Lock, the upper reaches of the Exe provide an interesting contrast to some of the deeper, wooded rivers further west

Boats dry out on the foreshore at Newton Ferrers and Noss Mayo just across the creek, well tucked away up the River Yealm

Forecasts can be obtained from a variety of sources:

BBC Radio 4 (198kHz) Shipping Forecasts at 0033, 0555, 1355, 1750 daily, particularly for sea areas Portland, Plymouth, Sole, Lundy Fastnet.
BBC Local Radio Stations also issue Coastal waters forecasts:
BBC Radio Devon (Exeter 990kHz, Torbay 1458kHz, Plymouth 855kHz)
Daily: 0633, 0733, 0833, 1310, 1733
Sat: 0733, 0833, 1310
Sun: 0833, 1310.
BBC Radio Cornwall: (630kHz)
Daily: 0605, 0745, 0845, 1245, 1710, 1740.
Sat: 0715, 0745, 0815, 0845.
Sun: 0915, 0945, 1015.
BBC Radio 4 Inshore Waters Forecast at end of daily broadcasting.
By telephone:
Marinecall, Area 8, Hartland to Lyme Regis (0898 500458).
Plymouth Weather Centre: (0752 402534).
RNAS Culdrose: Helston (4121).
RAF St Mawgan: Newquay (2201).
In addition, the following local Coast Radio Stations issue VHF bulletins at 0803 and 2003 hours GMT, and on request:
Start Point Radio, VHF Channel 26.
Pendennis Radio, VHF Channel 62.
Land's End Radio, VHF Channel 27.

Yacht Clubs: The traditionally stuffy image of many Yacht Clubs has fortunately changed much in recent years and most are only too happy to welcome genuine cruising yacht crews on a temporary basis to use their facilities. However, this normally only applies to members of other recognised clubs, although some, such as the Salcombe Yacht Club and Dartmouth Yacht Club extend a welcome to all. Whatever the situation, it is a privilege that visitors should not abuse, and on arrival at any new Club immediately introduce yourself to the Steward, Secretary or a member, ascertain if you are indeed welcome and ask for the visitors' book which should be signed not only by yourself but also your crew. For two or three nights, this will be sufficient, but should you wish to use the Club facilities for a longer period check with the secretary as to the arrangements for temporary membership which is often available. Remember at all times, you are their guest and behave accordingly.

Customs: Sadly, the menace of drug-smuggling has been increasing along the British coast and the West Country is no exception. Any suspicious activity, such as gear being unloaded from boats in isolated bays, or small craft alongside each other at sea, should be reported immediately to the Customs, dial 100 and ask for 'Freephone Customs Drugs'. As increasing numbers of sailing boats are being used in this insidious trade ultimately it can only bring the name of genuine cruising yachtsmen into suspicion and disrepute so it is very much in our interests to do anything we can to help assist in stamping it out. It may be irksome at times to be asked, often frequently, who you are and where you have come from by Customs patrols; try not to forget that they are only doing their job.

Passages
Straight Point to Start Point

Favourable tidal streams	
PORTLAND BILL	Bound West: HW Dover
	Bound East: 5 hours after HW Dover
START POINT:	Bound West: 1 hour before HW Dover
	Bound East, 5 hours after HW Dover

'Going West?' said the skipper of the pilot cutter.

'Yes,' we answered, and felt like adventurers. 'And you?'

He shook his head. We'd have a head wind, he reminded us, all across the bay. We knew it, but we had a good ship, too.

The west wind still blew. When we were clear of the harbour we backed the jib and let the boat lie while we hoisted the dinghy on deck, and lashed it. That done, we let draw, set the foresail and mizzen, and stood away for the Shambles Light.

Our voyage had begun. We were bound west, to visit a new country beyond the Bill . . .

FROM PORTLAND BILL to Berry Head it is exactly 40 miles, and 47 to the Start. It never seems less, and usually feels like a lot more. The opening lines were written by Aubrey de Selincourt in 1948, and nothing has changed — the odds are still just as much in favour of being on the wind most of the way, plodding into the prevailing south-westerlies. There is always a certain nervous relief at watching Portland drop safely astern, but for many, the long haul across Lyme Bay, often in normal visibility, is the first opportunity to make a passage out of sight of land.

There is at first, the anticipation of the new cruising ground ahead, but as the hours pass, and there is still nothing to be seen, those first niggling doubts begin to set in. Is the compass really accurate? Did I allow for the tidal set, and leeway? And always, the anxious eye on the weather, the slight greyness to windward, and the hint of an increase in the wind. And underlying it all, that hollow awareness that there are now no safe harbours under your lee.

But then, at last, there it is, no longer a figment of wishful thinking but unmistakeably, the land again, and looking, of course, not the least bit as you imagined. A featureless, thin, low line, and no sight of Berry Head and Start Point, the two bold headlands you expected to see for they will be indistinguishable until much closer — Berry Head distinctively square and flat topped, and the Start, an unmistakeable jagged cockscomb, with a conspicuous white lighthouse and two very tall radio masts close by. In practice it is invariably much easier to make a landfall on a strange coastline at night, ideally just before dawn, for then the lights will take away the doubts. Start Point (Fl 3 10secs) has a 25-mile range, and Berry Head (Fl 2 15secs) has an 18-mile range. For first timers across the bay, the prospect of a night passage is probably not very appealing and it is more likely that your approach will be a race against daylight, which is no real drawback, as your probable first ports-of-call, Torquay, Brixham or the River Dart are all well lit and

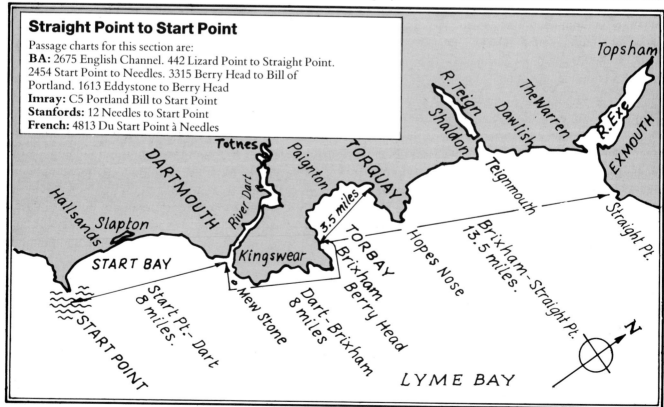

Straight Point to Start Point

Passage charts for this section are:
BA: 2675 English Channel. 442 Lizard Point to Straight Point. 2454 Start Point to Needles. 3315 Berry Head to Bill of Portland. 1613 Eddystone to Berry Head
Imray: C5 Portland Bill to Start Point
Stanfords: 12 Needles to Start Point
French: 4813 Du Start Point à Needles

Approximate distances — nautical miles

Approaching the Exe, Straight Point from the west

easy to enter and, though tired, the excitement of landfall and arrival in the West Country should carry you through.

The coastline you will now be cruising is varied, spectacular in places, and very different from that to the east of Portland. The last prominent chalk headland is at Beer, 15 miles east of the River Exe, and from here onwards, the high cliffs of deep red Devon sandstone begin, broken only by the seaside towns of Sidmouth and Budleigh Salterton, where beaches of large round pebbles rise steeply from the sea. Inland, Woodbury Common, an area of heathland and forestry plantations rises to nearly 200m in height.

The Exe estuary

Straight Point, (Fl R 10secs) forms the eastern side of the entrance to the **River Exe**, a low lying sandstone promontory, with two prominent flagstaffs used to indicate when the rifle ranges are in use. Two yellow DZ buoys just under a mile SW of the point mark the seaward limit of this range. Straight Point light is only of 7 miles range, visible from 246-071°T.

The River Exe, is a broad, drying estuary, navigable for 6 miles inland to Topsham, but little frequented by visitors, who tend to be put off by the presence of the bar. Although dangerous in onshore winds, in favourable conditions it is worth a visit, and the entrance channel is well-buoyed, leading inwards from the Fairway Buoy just under half a mile SSW of Straight Point. Although lit, it should not be attempted at night.

The high red cliffs of Orcombe Point lead in to the beach and town of **Exmouth** on the eastern side of the entrance. Opposite, the Warren, a long sandy promontory closes off the greater part of the wide mouth of the Exe and shallow banks extend nearly a mile to seaward. To the west, the red sandstone cliffs

Radio beacons

Beacon	Range (NM)	Frequency (kHz)	Call Sign
Marine beacons			
Portland Bill	50	291.88	PB
Start Point	70	298.8	SP
Aero beacons			
Exeter airport	15	337	EX (cont)
Berry Head	25	318	BHD (cont)

Coastal Radio

Start Point Radio, working channels 22, 65, 60.
Traffic lists usually broadcast at 3 minutes past the hour.
Weather forecasts at 0803 and 2003.

reappear between the resort towns of Dawlish and Teignmouth, and beneath them the main London/Penzance railway line enjoys a spectacular run along the coast. Inland, the land rises to over 250m again into the Haldon Hills. There are no offlying dangers except Dawlish Rock, covered 2.1m LAT ½ mile ESE of the town, and a course ½ mile from the shore can safely be followed if you wish to admire the scenery, weathered cliffs, and sandstone pinnacles like the Parson and Clerk.

Inshore, the tidal streams along this stretch of coast are generally weak, and run parallel to the coast, the NNE going flood beginning 5 hours after HW Dover, and SSW ebb beginning just after HW Dover, attaining a maximum of 1 knot at springs. Channelled in the closer approaches to the rivers, however, rates increase considerably, attaining up to 5 knots at springs.

The Teign estuary

Immediately to the west of **Teignmouth,** which is easily located by the prominent church tower, and long pier on the seafront, there lies the narrow entrance to the River Teign, bounded on the western side by the prominent high sandstone headland of the Ness (QWRG) a sectored approach light with 7 mile range, not that any approach should be made at night by strangers. Here, too, a bar renders the entrance dangerous in onshore winds. Facilities for visitors within the river are severely restricted by a bridge which cuts off the upper reaches half a mile above the entrance.

The coast remains steep from the Ness for the next four miles westwards, with no dangers except within a few boat's lengths of the shore. Topped with fields, trees, and isolated houses, the red sandstone gives way to pale grey and ochre limestone off Babbacombe Bay, where there is a reasonable anchorage in westerly winds, and Anstey's Cove to the west of the quarry scarred Long Quarry Point is another good temporary anchorage, although care must be taken to avoid three drying rocks near the southern entrance point to the cove.

Torbay

In contrast to the high cliffs to the east, Hopes Nose, the eastern boundary of **Torbay,** slopes gently down to the sea, grassy turf, with low rock ledges and cliffs at its base, the home of the largest kittiwake colony in Devon. Just under four miles away, the distinctive flat topped line of Berry Head marks the western limit of the bay, which takes a deep, sheltered bite into the Devon coast. Well protected in westerly winds it was a traditional anchorage for the Navy prior to the development of Plymouth, and it has always been a popular venue for yacht racing, graced by the magnificent 'Js' during their brief heyday, and more recently, by large multihulls, and powerboat racing, with the punishing Cowes/Torquay a long standing event.

To seaward, the low, flat Lead Stone and the 32m high Ore Stone, ½ mile offshore, are popular with the seabirds, too and white with droppings. There is a deep passage between the two islands, but do not pass too close to the south-west of the Ore Stone where the 'Sunker' lurks awash at LAT. In calm weather, with an absence of swell, it is possible to land on the Ore Stone, anchoring just north of the island on the rocky ledge which has 3m LAT. Pick anywhere on the rocky shore, but an inflatable is best for the job as this can then be lifted clear on to the rock platform. I would not, however, recommend leaving your mother ship entirely unattended.

The last of the Hopes Nose islands is Thatcher Rock, south-west of the point, a jagged pyramid rising to 41m. Behind it, the concave sweep of the large hotel high on the cliffs is a foretaste of what will emerge as **Torquay** opens beyond the next point. Just under ½ mile west of Thatcher Rock lies Morris Rogue, a shoal with a least depth of 0.8m LAT. Keep the Ore Stone open of Thatcher Rock and you will clear this hazard, otherwise deep water extends safely right to Torquay Harbour entrance.

Although the actual harbour mouth is not easy to spot until close, Torquay is unmistakeable, a proliferation of large buildings, tower blocks, and the large façade of the Imperial Hotel high on the cliffs just to the south of the harbour. Facilities in Torquay are excellent. It is easy of entry, day and night, and a large part of the outer harbour is now a marina with ample berthing for visitors.

The whole of the coast backing Torbay is one large urban sprawl, the 'Riviera of the South-West', an unbroken line of busy beaches, promenades, resorts and holiday camps in the hinterland, comprising Preston sands, Paignton sands, Goodrington sands and Broad sands. Along their length yellow speed limit buoys are positioned about two cables offshore during the summer, with 5 knots on square topmarks, restricting the areas for swimming, and inside these controlled areas you should proceed with extreme caution.

Paignton, just under half way across the bay is a popular resort with a traditional pier; west of this, is the sandstone bluff of Roundham Head, and a small drying harbour is situated on its northern side. Given over completely to local moorings, and busy with tripper boats, the harbour is not recommended for visitors, except for very small boats which can sometimes find room to dry out against the walls. Rocky ledges extend eastwards from the south wall, marked by a red beacon, and an approach should be made from a northeasterly direction, close to HW. On arrival berth on the south-east wall and seek out the Harbourmaster to see if space is available. As there are heavy mooring chains across the harbour do not

attempt to anchor. Facilities are limited, but there is a restaurant and pub beside the harbour and a small chandlery.

The once-peaceful anchorage of Elberry Cove in the extreme southwestern corner of the bay is now marred by water skiing activity. East of it, the houses give way to the large expanse of Churston golf course, beneath it the cliffs, broken with many disused quarries, fall steeply into the sea with no dangers at their foot. Just west of the wide entrance to Brixham outer harbour is Fishcombe Cove, a quiet secluded anchorage in westerly winds. **Brixham,** a busy fishing port, is well sheltered by the long breakwater except in north-west winds when Torquay is the obvious alternative; facilities are good, and berths are available for visitors in the outer harbour.

Brixham to Dartmouth

With the exception of rocks extending a cable to the north of Shoalstone Point, the coast between Brixham and Berry Head is steep to. The headland, 55m high, is an impressive sight, rising steeply with its northern side heavily quarried. A coastguard lookout with latticed radio mast stands beside the lighthouse at the eastern end which drops almost vertically into the sea, and though not recommended, you could sail to within a boat's length of the foot of the cliffs. Off the point the tide attains a rate of 1½ knots at springs, the north going flood begins 5½ hours after HW Dover, south going ebb 1 hour before, the streams running parallel to the coast.

Half a mile to the south of Berry Head, off Oxley Head which has a ruined fort and car park on its top, there are the Cod rocks, two steep islands, the larger of the two, East Cod 19m high. Between them lie the drying Bastard Rocks, and although it is quite safe to enter the bay to the north to admire the impressive limestone cliffs overhanging a large cave, keep well to seaward when leaving, and do not attempt the inshore passage between the rocks.

Various dangers and shallows extend for about half a mile to seawards for the rest of the four mile passage along this stretch of coast, and a sensible offing should

The Exe fairway buoy

Berry Head, flat topped and sheer

be maintained. Mostly high, rolling turfy hills, sloping to low irregular limestone cliffs, it is interspersed with several beaches and coves in steep valleys. Mag Rock, drying 0.3m, lies 1½ cables east of Sharkham Point, and to seaward, Mudstone Ledge, safe enough, with a least depth of 5.4m does, however, kick up an uncomfortable sea at times. It is also a popular spot for pots, and markers and buoys, the scourge of the whole Devon and Cornwall coastline, will be found in abundance from here on. Many are barely awash, and a careful lookout must be kept at all times, which renders inshore passages at night particularly wearisome if under power.

A course at least half a mile from the coast will clear both Druids Mare, a group of rocks drying 2.1m 1½ cables SSE of Crabrock Point, and Nimble Rock, a particularly insidious outcrop with 0.9m over it LAT, which lurks nearly two cables SSE of Downend Point. Start Point lighthouse open of Eastern Blackstone will clear the Nimble.

Eastern Blackstone, steep and 16.5m high, is not difficult to miss, nor too, the much larger, 35m high jagged outcrop of the Mewstone beyond it to the south-west. Do not be tempted to cut the corner from here into **Dartmouth** as submerged rocks extend nearly three cables to the south-west of the Mewstone. Inshore, high on Froward Point is the prominent Dartmouth day beacon, a tower with a wide base that is particularly valuable for locating the Dart when approaching from the south or south-west, as the narrow entrance to the river is very difficult to distinguish in the high folds of the coastline.

Start Bay

The wide sweep of Start Bay extends nearly 8 miles south-west from Dartmouth to Start Point, and inshore the high cliffs undergo a dramatic transformation into Slapton Sands, a long low beach enclosing the fresh water lake of Slapton Ley, a valuable wildlife sanctuary. During the War, this area was used extensively by the American forces practising for the D-Day invasions. There are no inshore dangers, and with an offshore breeze a fine sail in calm water can be enjoyed along its length close to the shore.

West of Torcross, the cliffs begin to rise again, with the tiny fishing village of **Beesands** at their foot, and its less fortunate neighbour the ruined village of **Hallsands.** During the latterpart of the nineteenth century nearly 700,000 tons of shingle were removed from this corner of the bay to build the new docks in Devonport — vital natural defences for the small fishing village, which met its fate on 26 January 1917 when an easterly gale and high tide destroyed the entire village, leaving just the one ghostly ruin that remains today. In settled offshore weather, if time permits, or waiting for the tide west around the Start, this is a handy anchorage, and a trip ashore has a distinctly ghoulish fascination.

Ironically, it is further offshore than Start Bay poses more problems, for it is here that you encounter the only real offshore bank in the West Country, the Skerries, which extends 3½ miles in a NE direction from a position 6 cables NE of Start Point. Although the depths over the bank are adequate for most small craft, the shallowest point being the SW end with a depth of 2.1m LAT, its biggest danger is the breaking seas it can produce in bad weather, at which time it should be given a wide berth, and an approach to Dartmouth from the south not attempted until the red Skerries can is passed at the NE end of the bank.

Deriving its name from the Anglo-Saxon meaning, a 'tail', **Start Point,** is one of the more distinctive West Country headlands with five grassy hillocks topped with rocky outcrops about 60m high along its prickly spine, and two very high 264m BBC radio masts. Built in 1836, the white buildings and lighthouse (Fl 3 10secs) perch neatly above the low cliffs at the eastern end, and a fixed red sector covers the Skerries Bank visible 210-255°T.

Although weak in Start Bay, tidal streams now have to be reckoned with again, becoming much stronger off Start Point and attaining up to 4 knots at springs, creating a race which extends about a mile to seaward from the lighthouse. Three miles south of the point the streams are weaker, just over 2 knots at springs, the ENE flood beginning 5 hours after HW Dover, and the WSW ebb about 1½ hours before HW Dover. Closer inshore the tide turns about half an hour earlier. There is no inshore passage as such but in fair weather less turbulence can be found closer to the point, taking

Above and below, Start Point

Torbay, the Ore Stone and Hopes Nose

The Mewstone

care to avoid Start Rocks, and the numerous pot markers. In bad weather, especially wind against tide, the race should be taken seriously as it produces heavy overfalls, and the point should be passed at least two miles to the south. As ships bound down channel for Plymouth and Fowey close the land at this point there is a noticeable increase in traffic.

In fog or poor visibility, audible aids to navigation are restricted to the 60 sec foghorn on Start Point, the bell on the Skerries Buoy, and the bell on the Exe Fairway Buoy.

River Exe

Tides
HW Dover −0445. Range: Exmouth
MHWS 4.6m — MHWN 3.4m, MLWN 1.7m — MLWS 0.5m.
(HW Topsham approx 20 mins after HW Exmouth.)
Spring ebb can attain 5 knots off Exmouth docks.

Charts
BA: 2290. **Stanford:** 12. **Imray:** Y43, Y45.

Waypoint
Exe Fairway Buoy, 50.36.00N. 3.21.87W.

Hazards
Pole Sands, Maer and Conger Rocks (lit by fairway buoys). River approach dangerous in strong east and southerly weather. Strong tidal streams in entrance. Large part of river dries.

THE LITTLE VISITED estuary of the **Exe** differs greatly from its deep, wooded companions further west, for it has a character far more in keeping with one of the rivers of the East Coast, and could easily be dubbed the 'Blackwater of the West'. Flat, and wide it forms an open expanse over six miles long at HW, which dries for the most part into banks of mud and sand. Inshore of the normal track across Lyme Bay — most yachts heading west tend to make a landfall on Berry Head or Start Point — this, and the unsavoury reputation of the entrance tend to deter most visitors. However, the channel is well-buoyed and in the right weather a visit to the Exe can provide a very pleasant diversion from the better known cruising haunts. For many years this was my home patch, and although a lot busier than it used to be there are still several peaceful anchorages and interesting places to explore; it is unlikely that you will sail away disappointed with what you have found.

Approaches

The entrance to the river is formed by a long, narrow channel running parallel to the beach and foreshore at **Exmouth,** flanked to seawards by the Pole Sands, an extensive area of shallow water that dries considerably. The tides can run hard, particularly on the ebb at springs, and in winds of any strength from the south or south-east a first time visit to the Exe should not be considered, as a confusing area of breaking sea soon builds up in the approaches, and the run in is along an uncomfortable lee shore, which leaves little room for mistakes. Ideally an approach should be made from the south-west, in favourable weather, and not long after local LW, when most of the drying banks can be seen, providing a lee in the fairway. Although well lit, it is not recommended at night without local knowledge.

Exmouth Bar is two miles to the east of the town, which is best located by the conspicuous tower of Holy Trinity Church, and, approaching from the south-west, the Exe Fairway buoy (spherical RW vertical stripes, Fl 10secs) marking the entrance to the buoyed channel lies just under half a mile SSW of Straight Point. This low headland lies just south of the

Peaceful Topsham — reeds and tidal mud

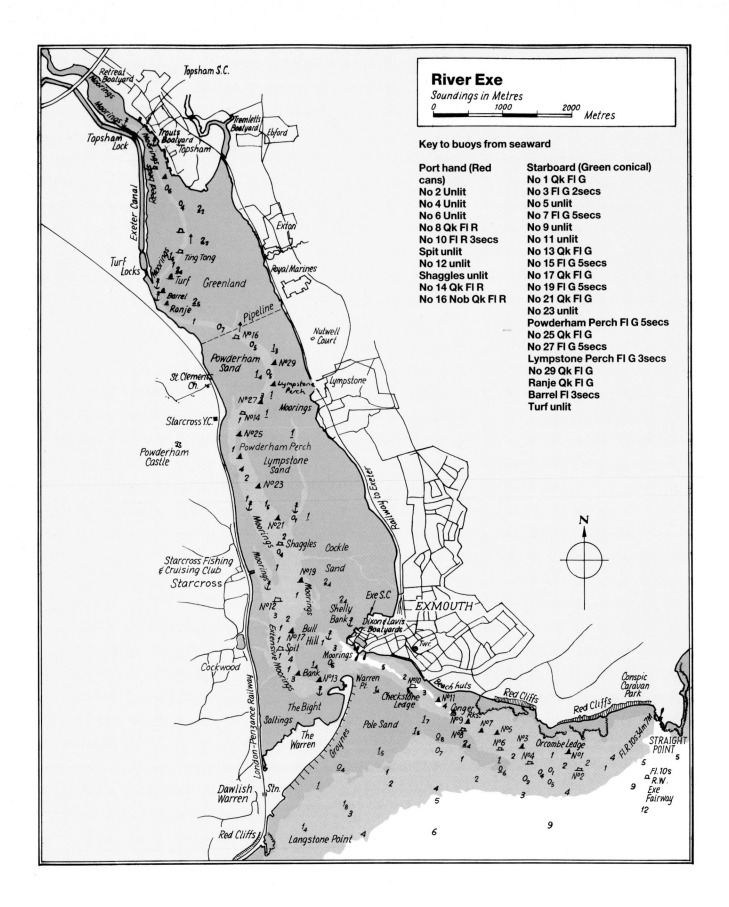

River Exe

Soundings in Metres

0 1000 2000 Metres

Key to buoys from seaward

Port hand (Red cans)	Starboard (Green conical)
No 2 Unlit	No 1 Qk Fl G
No 4 Unlit	No 3 Fl G 2secs
No 6 Unlit	No 5 unlit
No 8 Qk Fl R	No 7 Fl G 5secs
No 10 Fl R 3secs	No 9 unlit
Spit unlit	No 11 unlit
No 12 unlit	No 13 Qk Fl G
Shaggles unlit	No 15 Fl G 5secs
No 14 Qk Fl R	No 17 Qk Fl G
No 16 Nob Qk Fl R	No 19 Fl G 5secs
	No 21 Qk Fl G
	No 23 unlit
	Powderham Perch Fl G 5secs
	No 25 Qk Fl G
	No 27 Fl G 5secs
	Lympstone Perch Fl G 3secs
	No 29 Qk Fl G
	Ranje Qk Fl G
	Barrel Fl 3secs
	Turf unlit

prominent white diamond shape of Sandy Bay caravan park with high red cliffs beneath it. There are two flagpoles on the headland, and in its vicinity there are invariably large numbers of small local angling boats. Straight Point is used by the Marines as a firing range and its seaward limits are marked by two yellow DZ buoys to the south, the western Fl Y 5secs, and the eastern Fl·Y 3secs. These buoys are convenient for positioning your approach; however, from March to October shooting can take place on weekdays between 0800 and 1600, and the danger area should be avoided. When firing is in progress a safety boat patrols the area, and red flags are flown from the flagstaffs on the point. No flags mean no firing, a flag on each pole indicates firing in progress, and two flags on each pole means firing temporarily ceased. The range can also be

The upper reaches of the Exe — Retreat Boatyard fuel pontoon and moorings at HW

contacted on VHF Ch 8, call sign Straight Point Range.

From the Fairway buoy, the channel is marked with even numbered red cans to port and odd numbered green conical buoys to starboard, the first of which is red No 2. The shallowest water, the bar proper, lies between Nos 3 and 4 buoys south of the high red sandstone cliffs that form Orcombe Point. Here, there is a depth of 1.4m LAT, but once inside the channel there is a minimum of over 2m at all times. Exmouth beach and promenade run parallel close on your starboard hand, rows of brightly painted beach huts give way into a long row of typical Edwardian seaside hotels as you close the real mouth of the river, between the Warren, a long, low, sandy promontory, and the entrance to Exmouth Docks. Do not be tempted to stray from the channel at LW, there is little room outside of it. Although for the most part bounded by the hard sand of the Pole Sands which is steep to, rocky ledges do extend southwards between Nos 5 and 9 buoys, forming Maer and Conger rocks, a notorious grounding spot. Little more than 100m wide, the channel is at its narrowest at this point. Checkstone Ledge, a rocky outcrop inside No 10 buoy is also one to avoid, and at LW do not be tempted to cut the corner towards the low sandy promontory of Warren Point as this is continually extending south-east, forming a large area of gravelly shallows. Hold a course close to the dock end before turning west across the river.

Exmouth

Here, the tidal streams run strongly, reaching up to 5 knots on the ebb at springs, creating a confused tidal lop in the narrows. Beware of the frequent passenger ferries that run out of the hidden entrance to the dock, and also the possibility of coasters emerging. Entered through a swing bridge, Exmouth Dock is a privately owned commercial port that has seen a noticeable increase in trade in recent years, importing animal feed, and exporting scrap metal. The dock is closed to yachts, which is no great loss as it has nothing to recommend it, being dirty, muddy and mostly drying.

The pool to the north-west of the dock entrance is completely taken up with local moorings, and the Exmouth Lifeboat is also moored here. Anchoring is not recommended due to the risk of fouling moorings and the strong run of the tide. With sufficient water, a boat capable of taking the bottom comfortably can always anchor 'round the back' past the colourful jumble of bungalows and beach houses that line The Point. Here, out of the main stream, and clear of the moorings, you can dry out on Shelley Bank, hard sand, just off the Exe Sailing Club, and visitors from other clubs are welcome to use the showers, clubhouse and bar when open. This large new building was built several years ago after the previous clubhouse on the north side of the dock entrance was spectacularly destroyed when the quayside collapsed.

The main shopping centre of Exmouth is about half a mile from the dock area and all normal facilities can be found. There is fresh water at the Sailing Club, but fuel is not easily obtained except in cans. There are several small boatyards all in the vicinity of the docks; engine and electronic repairs can be arranged through them.

The Bight

Exmouth, in reality, does not have a lot to offer a visiting yacht, and I would not recommend a stop unless absolutely necessary. The essential attraction of the Exe is getting away from the crowds and they certainly abound in Exmouth, a busy holiday resort since the 1750s . . . Just a short distance across the water the eastern end of the Warren provides a peaceful contrast, but sadly the deeper anchorage off it is now very restricted by moorings which run parallel to the beach along the curve of the river known as the **Bight,** opposite No 13 buoy. However, shoal draught boats capable of drying out can still creep inside the moorings where the Warren turns back on itself to form Salthouse Lake, and here you will lie in an eddy comfortably out of the fast main stream, just grounding or drying out at LW on firm sand. In the evenings, and mid-week this delightful spot, one of

Coasters regularly use the port of Exmouth and yachts must take care to avoid them in the restricted channel into the Exe.

my particular favourites, is very quiet and you will probably have it all to yourself. In the 1930s this end of the Warren was covered with a large number of bungalows and holiday homes, but the winter storms and shifting sands allow no such permanence. As a boy, I can remember the last few houses high on the dunes on the seaward side of the beach, and the fascination of seeing their broken remains after they had been undermined and began to collapse. The sea broke right through the **Warren** in the 1960s during a winter storm, but the massive repair works and new groynes on the seaward side have resulted in a steady growth ever since. The western end of the Warren is a popular golf course, but the lonely eastern end is now a 500 acre nature reserve. Once again, there is nothing more than the low sweep of the beach, and the low dunes behind, a wilderness of lupins and marram grass. At dusk it becomes the silent haunt of the rabbits and birds; just across the water, the cheerful glare of the fairy lights along Exmouth seafront somehow emphasise the pleasant isolation of the place; there is nothing, except perhaps, the rumble of the main line trains along the western shore to disturb its peace.

In complete contrast, if you decide to walk the mile or so along the beach to the village of **Dawlish Warren,** you will find an unsightly sprawl of amusement arcades, gift shops and even a betting shop, catering for the large holiday chalet villages. There is also a grocery, newsagent, Post Office and pub if you're desperate. Fortunately, the attractions and the long walk tend to concentrate the masses at that end of the Warren, and it is easy to escape back to its real delights.

Starcross

To avoid the encroaching edge of Bull Hill Bank do not steer directly for No 15 buoy but keep out towards the large mooring buoys in mid-channel. These are primarily for commercial vessels but can be used if you are not too worried about your topsides; however, just to the NW there is a single yellow Harbour Authority visitors' buoy for up to 40 feet, marked 'ECC Visitors' available at £2.50 per day, call 'Port of Exeter' VHF Channel 12 during normal working hours to check availability.

At the red 'Spit' buoy just upstream a channel branches away to the mass of moorings off **Starcross**, where there are limited provisions, a Post Office, petrol and diesel at the garage, banks in the morning, and a chemist. The Starcross Fishing and Cruising Club has a visitors' mooring off the village, although more are often available if members are away cruising, and visitors are welcomed to their fine clubhouse at Regent House just opposite the railway station. Note, however, that the ferry pier is private and a charge is made for landing.

The main channel continues between Nos. 12 and 19 buoys, a line of moorings to port marking the edge of the drying Shaggles Sand, and to the east of the larger moorings to starboard the whole area of Cockle Sand dries completely at LW.

Lympstone

Past the red Shaggles can above Starcross keep close to both Nos 21 and 23 buoys. The drying channel to **Lympstone,** nestling between two red cliffs on the eastern shore branches off just below No 21 buoy, and this can provide an interesting diversion sounding in on a rising tide, for a quick dinghy run ashore to this pretty, former fishing village, where thatched cottages mingle with more elegant and substantial Georgian houses. A number of local boats have drying moorings off the village but here the bottom is mud, and it will be a messy walk ashore if you stay to dry out.

Back in the main channel, opposite the green buoy marked Powderham Perch the extensive estate behind the railway embankment is **Powderham,** an elegant deer park, and through the trees you can just glimpse Powderham Castle, the seat of the Courteney family since the fourteenth century and home of the present Earl and Countess of Devon. For many years there was a perch at this point but as the long spit of sand is continually extending downstream from the next buoy, No 25, a buoy is obviously easier to move. Somewhat ironically, from here on the buoyage in the Exe is better than it has ever been, although the coasters using the upper reaches have virtually ceased, with the exception of the South West Water's sludge disposal vessel *Countess Wear* which sails a round trip near high water.

At No 14 buoy, where the channel turns to the north-east, the buildings and slipway on the wooded promontory are Starcross Yacht Club which has the distinction of being one of the oldest in the country, formed in 1773. The moorings off the Club mostly dry at LW.

Next, steer for Nutwell Court, a large Georgian house completely set among trees on the eastern shore. From No 14 buoy keep to the starboard side of the channel, close to Nos 27 'Lympstone Perch' and 29 buoys following the curve of the channel, and do not cut across the shallow edge of Powderham Sand to port. During the summer months, as in several of the other West Country rivers, these upper reaches are frequently used by salmon fishermen who shoot long seine nets from small rowing boats, usually on the last of the ebb and first of the flood when they are likely to be encountered anywhere between here and Topsham. The few licences granted for these fisheries are jealously guarded and passed down from father to son, but disease and pollution have seen a dramatic decline from the days when up to 99 prime fish were caught in one shot of the net. Nor, too, has a monster salmon like the one caught by netsman Dick Voysey close to this spot in March 1924 ever been seen again.

Weighing a staggering 61¼ pounds this was no fisherman's tale as it was preserved and can still be seen in Exeter's City Museum.

The large incongruous blocks of flats on the eastern bank are accommodation blocks for the famous Marine Training Camp at **Lympstone,** so don't be too alarmed if you hear the sound of gunfire along the shore. Just beyond the beacon with triangular topmark opposite the red No 16 Nob buoy, a pipeline carrying North Sea Gas runs across the river east-west, and anchoring should not be attempted near it. Also at this point the tributary of the River Clyst enters the Exe, winding away through the mudbanks to the distant railway bridge on the northern shore. Just upstream, at Odhams Wharf there has been an inconveniently located boatyard for many years, where masts had to be removed below the bridge alongside an old barge with a derrick. It still sits there in the mud but the yard is now the home of Tremletts, builders of high speed powerboats, and their kind of low profile vessels are far more suited to the location.

Exeter Ship Canal

The channel, much narrower at this point, leads close to the western shore, under the high flood embankment past the green Ranje and Barrel buoys and right ahead, the building half hidden in the trees with a tall isolated pine, is Turf Hotel, at the mouth of the **Exeter Ship Canal.** The entrance lock is to the left of the buildings and the canal, which runs five miles inland to Exeter has the claim to fame that it is the oldest pound lock canal in England, opened in 1566, after the river passage to Exeter was blocked with a weir by the Countess of Devon in an attempt to force vessels to use her own port at **Topsham.** The canal was originally entered opposite Topsham but larger vessels resulted in the extension to Turf in 1831, but as ship sizes continued to increase it always restricted the growth of the port of Exeter. Now sadly, it is a thing of the past and the coasters carrying petrol, timber and coal no longer pass incongruously above the reed beds opposite Topsham, and create havoc with the holiday traffic on the once notorious Exeter by-pass, when the swing bridge was opened. For that has all changed, too, and sweeping across the wide Exe Valley just

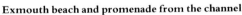
Exmouth beach and promenade from the channel

above Topsham is the M5 motorway bridge. Although its arrival ended the traffic jams, the 11m clearance also finally sealed the fate of Exeter's waterborne commercial trade.

Today the canal is being rejuvenated for fishing and pleasure boating, and the trip to Exeter is quite feasible either by dinghy, outboard and a bit of portage, or in boats not restricted by the height limit, although for them the locking charge of £9 each way, and another £12.60 each way (inc. VAT) for the transit is not exactly cheap. However, if a number of boats make the trip together there are favourable discounts, providing a fascinating excursion through a wetland conservation area with alongside berthing close to the centre of Exeter for sightseeing and shopping. Arrangements to enter the Canal can be made by phone (0392 74306) or by calling 'Port of Exeter' on VHF channel 12.

At the City Canal Basin you will find the excellent Exeter Maritime Museum, where junks, dhows, Fijian outriggers, and the steam tug *St Canute* make up one of the largest collections of full sized working craft in the world. Created in 1968 by retired army Major David Goddard it is not merely a static display and it is quite likely that you will encounter some of their fascinating craft out sailing in the West Country enthusiastically crewed by supporters of the International Sailing Craft Association (ISCA) which runs the museum.

Open daily throughout the year 1000-1700, the Museum should not be missed, and it is easy to reach by bus from Topsham, too.

Turf Hotel is a favourite local watering hole, and a popular evening trip down river from Topsham. Anchor south-east of the pier on the edge of the channel clear of the local moorings where there is about 1m LAT and a soft mud bottom. Do not anchor in the approach to the lock as this is used a couple of hours either side of HW by the sludge vessel which often sails in the middle of the night from the sewage works further up the canal.

Landing is easy at the steps and pontoon at the end of the jetty and a lawn leads up to the old slate hung Georgian building, now a pub open during normal licensing hours when bar food and fresh water can also

be obtained. It is possible, but not cheap, to lock into the adjoining basin, a tranquil spot, popular for laying-up where there is invariably an interesting assortment of boats. From here, the tow path along the canal provides a pleasant walk of just over a mile to Topsham Lock where a ferry runs across to the town, and during the summer the pub also runs a water taxi along the canal as far as Countess Wear.

Topsham

The final stretch of the river from Turf to **Topsham** is very shallow at LW, with less than a metre in many places. However, on the flood, a few groundings are no problem in the soft mud, and the channel is not difficult to follow, with buoys and one perch. Ting Tong is a red can just upstream of the moorings, and as the channel curves northwards again, there is the perch with triangular topmark to starboard, traditionally knows as Black Oar, now a yellow pole with square red topmark to port, and then a red can buoy. Topsham lies ahead to starboard, and there are many local moorings in the approaches, with a fairway between them, and the last two buoys, green No 37, then a red No 18.

Beyond the large modern block of flats that unfortunately dominates the waterfront, Topsham Quay is easily located by the square brick lager warehouse, and for a visitor this is the best overnight berth, alongside where you will dry out on soft mud, unless there is space at the extreme northern end where you can just remain afloat. The only possible anchorage off Topsham town is just upstream of the quay opposite Trout's Boatyard in mid-stream, clear of the moorings and their all-tide landing pontoon, which is private but can be used by visitors by arrangement with the yard. There is about 1m here at LAT, but the bottom is gravel and the holding not good, particularly on the ebb when the current can run quite fast. Topsham Sailing Club might be able to provide a mooring if members are cruising. Alternatively, to get away from it all, continue upstream beyond Topsham Lock and find a spot clear of the moorings among the extensive reedbeds, where you will dry out completely. Technically, there is a small charge for lying alongside the Quay which is

Topsham, looking upstream at LW

M5 Bridge · Topsham Sailing Club · Public landing · Anchorage · Trout's Boatyard · Topsham Quay · Fairway

Anchored at the 'back of the Warren' shoal draught boats can edge inshore and ground at LW

administered by Exeter City Council, who are slowly upgrading the facilities. Water and electricity are available, but unless someone appears to collect your dues the odds are in favour of a free night or two.

'. . . not so small a Town as I find it represented in some Accounts,' wrote an observer in 1754, 'It has not only one pretty long Street to its Kay (where there is a Custom House) and another below it to a fine Strand, the latter adorn'd with diverse handsome Houses, but several good Bye-Streets branching out several ways; and is, in short, a very pleasant, a considerable, and flourishing place, inhabited by many Persons of good Fashion and Politeness, as well as Ship-masters, Ship-builders &c, &c . . . Its chief Market, Saturdays, is well supply'd not only with Shambles Meats of all sorts, but Poultry and other Fowls, Butter Cheese and Fruits, and here being Butchers and Fishermen resident, there's seldom a total Lack of Provisions of either Kind, neither of very good Bread, nor as good Beer, Cyder, Wine, Spirit, Liquors . . . It may be concluded that 'tis no despicable or mean Town . . .'*

Two hundred and fifty years on, you can say just about the same, with just a few additions to the facilities. Topsham is an attractive little town, relatively quiet but once an important Roman and medieval port, and a particularly prosperous place in the mid-seventeenth and early eighteenth centuries when it flourished as a shipbuilding centre. During the Napoleonic wars no less than 27 warships were built here for the Royal Navy by Davy's yards, and in 1850 John Holman opened a new yard with a plan to rejuvenate Topsham as a major port. Wooden vessels up to 600 tons were built, and a dry-dock capable of handling 1,000 ton ships was opened. But within 15 years Holman died and there the dream ended, the silting river finally sealing Topsham's fate. The link with the name remains, however, for John Holman's great granddaughter Dorothy established a unique museum of Topsham's history in her house on the Strand which she left to the town on her death. It is now run by volunteers and open on Mondays, Wednesdays and Saturdays, 1400-1700.

Facilities are good, with all provisions available, including a convenient grocery store on the main road towards Exeter that is open 0845-1830, and 0930-1800 Sundays, a well-stocked chandler in the main street that is also an Admiralty Chart agent; there are branches of Lloyds and Natwest banks, a launderette on the Exeter road, and a Saturday morning market. No shortage of restaurants and bistros, there are no less than ten pubs most of which do food, several cafés and a fish and chip shop. The attractive cathedral City of Exeter is well worth a visit, either by a fifteen minute ride on the regular mini buses or the train which connects with the main line at Exeter.

Topsham Sailing Club was founded in 1885 and today has a particularly active cruiser fleet, one of the largest in the West Country. Visitors are welcome, and those two cruising essentials, showers and a bar, are available on Wednesday evenings and at weekends. There is a convenient fresh water tap on their slipway.

Water is also obtainable from a tap in Trout's Yard, and Dan Trout is the local Cruising Association boatman.

By far the biggest problem in all of the Exe is fuel. Petrol can be obtained in cans from the garage at Topsham, but the only place where diesel is available alongside is, perversely, just about as far upriver as you are likely to go at the **Retreat** Boatyard, half a mile beyond Topsham. Nestling almost beneath the motorway bridge the yard is accessible two hours either side of HW for an average draught boat. In spite of its tidal location, the yard has grown rapidly in recent years, and apart from all the usual services, there is a 36 ton crane, two marine engineers, electronic engineer and sailmaker all on site. There is the largest chandler in the area, and they are also agents for Avon inflatables, Autohelm, Volvo inboards, Yamaha Outboards, International Paints, with full Interspray facility, Westerly, Moody and Sadler yachts. In addition to diesel, water is available alongside, Calor and Camping Gaz.

To reach the Retreat, continue upstream through the moorings past the Sailing Club, and beyond the old lock entrance on the port hand, leaving the outfall beacon with green triangular topmark to starboard. Keeping a few boat lengths off the shore, pick your way through the large number of local moorings beyond which the river mostly dries at LW leaving a large area of mud and reedbeds, and a narrow channel which follows the reed fringed edge of the playing field on the starboard hand. The next beacon with triangular topmark off a dinghy park is also left to starboard. From here, the channel bends tightly to the right hand shore, overlooked by a number of substantial detached modern houses, and there is a large shallow bank to port, so don't be tempted to cut the corner. It is then a straight run past Retreat House, the large white Georgian building, towards the group of moorings and the pontoon off the boatyard. Do not try to anchor as the bottom is foul, but berth alongside the pontoon, rafting if necessary, as this is only used for short stay visitors. If you wish to stay longer, drying moorings are sometimes available off the yard; it would be a very safe spot to leave a boat if forced to return home for a while.

The main channel runs between the Warren and the moorings off Exmouth before turning upriver past Bull Hill bank

Port guide — River Exe

Harbourmaster: Exeter, City Canal Basin (Tel: 0392 74306). Exmouth Dockmaster, The Docks (Tel: 0395 272009)

VHF: Port of Exeter Channel 12, Retreat Boatyard Channel 37 (M)

Emergency services: Lifeboat at Exmouth. Brixham Coastguard, Brixham (Tel: 080 45 58292). VHF Channels 16, 10, 67, 73

Customs: Exeter, Custom House, The Quay, Exeter (Tel: 0392 74021). Exmouth (Tel: 0395 263177)

Anchorages: Off the Warren. Turf. Topsham. Various possibilities within river

Mooring/berthing: Drying alongside quay at Topsham. Drying moorings at Retreat Boatyard. Lock into Exeter Canal

Dinghy landings: The Point, Exmouth. Starcross Pier. Turf. Public slipways at Topsham, ladders on Quay. Topsham SC. Trout's Pontoon

Marinas: None

Charges: Alongside Topsham and Exeter Canal based on 23p per foot per week (inc. VAT). Visitors' mooring £2.50 per night. Exeter Canal locking £9 each way transit, £12.60 each way (inc. VAT). Discounts for convoys.

Phones: Dock entrance, Exmouth. High Street by Church, Topsham

Doctor: Exmouth (Tel: 0395 273001). Topsham (Tel: 039287 4648)

Hospital: Exmouth (Tel: 0395 279684). Exeter (Tel: 0392 77991)

Churches: Exmouth, Topsham, most denominations. C of E, RC, Baptist, Methodist, Gospel

Local weather forecast: None

Fuel: Diesel at Retreat Boatyard, Topsham (Tel: 039287 4720) Diesel and Petrol in cans from Wills Garage, Starcross. In cans from WW&AD Pretty, Garage, High Street, Topsham

Gas: Calor and Camping Gaz, Hancock and Wheeler, Exmouth (Tel: 0395 263485). Calor and Camping Gaz, Wills Garage, Starcross. Calor and Camping Gaz, Retreat Boatyard, Topsham

Paraffin: Westaways, Fore Street, Topsham

Water: Exe Sailing Club, Exmouth. Turf Hotel. Topsham SC. Trout's Yard, Topsham. Retreat Boatyard, Topsham, Topsham Quay

Banks/cashpoints: Exmouth: all main banks have cashpoints. Starcross: Lloyds and Natwest, mornings only. Topsham: Lloyds, Natwest. Cash point: Lloyds, Topsham, and all banks in Exeter

Post Office: Exmouth, Starcross, Topsham

Rubbish: No specific facilities

Showers/toilets: Exe Sailing Club, Exmouth. Starcross Fishing & Cruising Club, Starcross. Topsham Sailing Club, Topsham. Retreat Boatyard, Topsham. Also public toilets

Launderette: Exmouth and Topsham

Provisions: All facilities, Exmouth, EC Weds. Limited shops, Dawlish Warren. Provisions/chemist, Starcross. Good selection shops, Topsham, EC Weds. Mortimores general store open 0845-1830, Sundays 0930-1800

Chandler: Peter Dixon, Docks, Exmouth (Tel: 0395 2630630). Lavis & Son, Camperdown Terrace, Exmouth (Tel: 0395 263095). Foc'sle, Fore Street, Topsham (Tel: 039287 4105). (Admiralty Chart Agents), Trout's Boatyard, Topsham (Tel: 039287 3044). Retreat Boatyard, Topsham (Tel: 039287 4720)

Repairs: Dixon & Son, Dock Road, Exmouth (Tel: 0395 263063). Lavis & Son, Camperdown Terrace, Exmouth (Tel: 0395 263095). D. J. Trout & Son, Topsham (Tel: 039287 3044). Retreat Boatyard, Topsham (Tel: 039287 4720)

Marine engineers: Dixon & Son, Exmouth (Tel: 0395 263063). Wills Garage, Starcross (Tel: 0626 890225). Retreat Boatyard, Topsham (Tel: 039287 4720). Grimshaw Engineering, The Quay, Topsham (Tel: 039287 3539)

Electronic engineers: DS Electrics, Exmouth (Tel: 0395 265550). Retreat Boatyard, Topsham (Tel: 039287 4720). Grimshaw Engineering, Topsham (Tel: 039287 3539)

Sailmakers: Michael McNamara, Camperdown Terrace, Exmouth (Tel: 0395 264907). Sails and Canvas, Retreat Boatyard, Topsham (Tel: 039287 7527)

Transport: Regular bus and train connections from Exmouth via Lympstone and Topsham to Exeter. Buses and trains to Exeter from Starcross. M5 Motorway at Topsham. Exeter Airport 15 mins

Car hire: Exmouth and Exeter

Yacht clubs: Exe Sailing Club, 'Tornado', Estuary Road, Exmouth, Devon EX8 1EG (Tel: 0395 264607). Starcross Fishing & Cruising Club, Regent House, Starcross, Exeter, Devon (Tel: 0626 890582). Starcross Yacht Club, Powderham Point, Starcross, Exeter, Devon (Tel: 0626 890470). Topsham Sailing Club, Hawkins Quay, Ferry Road, Topsham, Exeter, Devon (Tel: 039287 7524)

Eating out: Pubs, restaurants, cafés and fish and chips, Exmouth. Pubs at Starcross. Good selection pubs, restaurants, fish and chips at Topsham

River Teign

Tides
HW Dover −0450. Range: MHWS 4.8M — MHWN 3.6m
MLWN 1.9m — MLWS 0.6m. Spring rates can attain 5 knots
in entrance.
Charts
BA: 26. **Stanford:** 12. **Imray:** Y43.

Waypoint
SW end Den Point 50.32.38N. 3.29.98W.
Hazards
Shifting bar, dangerous in east or southerly winds and swell,
particularly on the ebb. Strong tidal streams in river. Large
part of harbour dries. Low bridge across river ½ mile from
entrance.

JUST OVER FIVE MILES west of the Exe, and in many ways similar, the river **Teign** is, unfortunately, of very limited appeal from a visitor's point of view, suffering from two distinct disadvantages. Not only does it have a bar, but, sadly, the pleasant wide and drying upper reaches of the estuary are effectively closed to all but small boats by the 3.5m clearance of the road bridge just above the town of **Teignmouth.** A large part of the harbour also dries, space is at a premium, and within the main channel and the entrance the tides run fast, between 4 and 5 knots at springs. However, in spite of the difficult entrance, a considerable amount of commercial shipping uses the docks, exporting clay, around which the harbour developed during the nineteenth century, and importing pulp and animal foodstuffs, and vessels up to 2,000 tons regularly berth.

Very much a working port, visitors are left to look after themselves. There is only one official fore and aft visitor's mooring available off the town where you will remain afloat, and anchoring in deep water is impossible due to the number of local moorings, and the fairway which must be left clear. However, for a bilge-keeler, or boats able to dry out, the river is a more attractive proposition, as space can usually be found somewhere on the 'Salty', the large bank in the centre of the harbour adjoining the Shaldon shore.

The Bar has a justifiably unpleasant reputation and in fresh winds from the south or east, especially on the ebb, it can become a treacherous area of steep breaking seas and surf. In offshore winds, however, and after half-flood, with no likelihood of southerly or easterly weather in the offing, the river is not particularly difficult to enter, and once inside, perfectly sheltered. Although lit, including floodlights on the Ness during the summer, it is definitely not recommended at night.

Approaches
Easily located by the high red sandstone headland of the Ness, topped with trees, on the south side of the entrance, and the conspicuous tower of St Michael's church in the centre of the town on the northern shore, the approach should be made from a position east of

Flanked by shifting sands — the approach to the Teign, showing the Ness, Den Point and the Salty

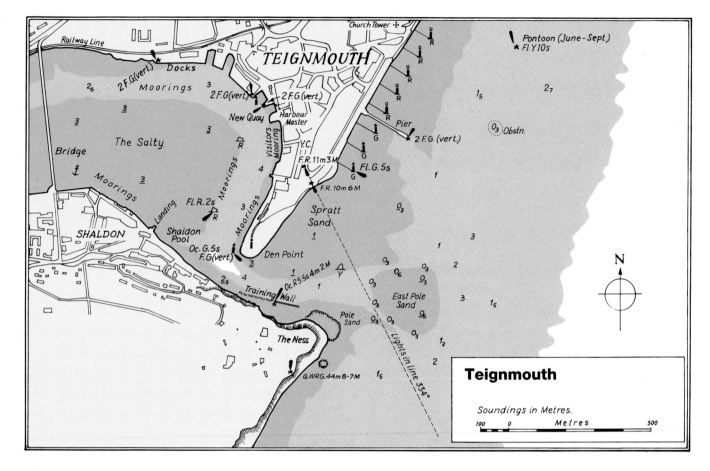

The Salty

SHALDON

Bridge

Shaldon Pool

Landing

Fl.R.2s

Oc.G.5s F.G(vert.)

Training Wall

The Ness

Q.WRG.44m 8-7M

TEIGNMOUTH

Church Tower

Railway Line

Docks

2 F.G.(vert.)

Moorings

New Quay

Harbour Master

Visitors Mooring

Y.C.

F.R.11m3M

F.R. 10m 6M

Spratt Sand

Den Point

Oc.R.5.5s 4m 2M

Pier

F.L.G. 5s

2 F.G. (vert.)

Pontoon (June-Sept.)
Fl.Y 10s

Obstn.

East Pole Sand

Pole Sand

Lights in line 334°

Teignmouth

Soundings in Metres.

100   0   Metres   500

N

the Ness. Two marks on the Teignmouth seafront, a very tall black pole with a grey stone tower in front of it provide a transit of 334°T which clears the Ness Rocks. There is a long row of terraced hotels immediately behind the marks, and they lie closest to the second gable of the building. This line leads between the isolated East Pole Sand to seaward and across the tail of the Pole Sand, a spit extending from the Ness. Do not be confused by the small orange buoys with square topmarks in the vicinity — these are used by the local Pilots, and frequently moved. A rocky ledge extends north-eastwards from the Ness, and the shore is littered with large boulders, so don't be tempted to cut the corner but steer towards the conical yellow buoy marking the edge of Spratt Sand leaving it close on your starboard hand before turning west towards the river entrance. Philip Lucette, a white beacon, marks the south side of the channel, standing on a training wall just off the shore which dries 2m; leave it several boat lengths to port, and steer towards the beacon with triangular topmark which marks the end of the low sandy spit, Den Point. **Shaldon,** and a large group of moorings in the 'pool' lie ahead, but the main channel turns sharply to starboard, the moorings and waterfront of **Teignmouth** opening before you.

Here, the tide runs strongly, and do not cut the corner, keeping in midstream. The eastern edge of the 'Salty' which dries 3m is marked by three red can buoys which should be left to port, and the fore and aft visitor's mooring lies on your starboard hand; two large red buoys capable of accommodating up to four boats at a time.

The Harbour Office does not maintain a constant VHF watch, and can only usually be contacted when a ship is expected when they use working channel 12, and would be able to advise as to the visitor's berth availability. New Quay, where the Harbour Office is situated, lies a bit further upstream on the starboard hand, and it is possible to berth here temporarily if space is available on arrival to make enquiries if contact has not already been made. If you have decided to anchor and dry out, make your way through the moorings off Shaldon and sound into a suitable spot off the village, clear of the many local moorings. The bottom is sandy shingle, hard, and holding is not particularly good, especially when the tide is running at strength.

A recorded port for nearly 1,000 years, today Teignmouth is rather a mixture. It's a typical beach resort, with reddish sands which were developed early in the 1800s with a traditional pier and elegant seafront, and the usual modern accoutrements, novelty golf, a seafront theatre, children's rides and just a few amusement arcades. In marked contrast, behind the town, the jumble of brightly painted fishermen's beach huts, slipways, alleyways, and small quays along the shingly waterfront has its own particular charm. Salmon fishermen work the river in season, often shooting nets right across the river mouth at low water. The famous Morgan Giles Shipyard was located here until it closed in 1969, once employing over 150 local people, designers and builders of many fine yachts that are still sailing today.

Teignmouth from Shaldon
waterfront at LW

All usual facilities can be found in the town with water on the quay, but fuel is only available in cans from local garages. There is no shortage of pubs, restaurants and cafés and there are branches of all main banks, and regular main line rail connections.

Shaldon

Shaldon is a much quieter place, an unspoiled waterside village, with a delightful central square surrounding a bowling green. There is less of a choice for facilities, but all the basics are obtainable, including branches of Lloyds and Midland banks, open 1030-1230 Mon-Fri during July and August, and Mon-Wed-Fri the rest of the year. There is a general store open daily 0800-2100, 1000-1300 Sundays. There are two chandlers, *Mariners Weigh* specialising in motorboat gear, and the extremely well-stocked *Brigantine* on the foreshore, which has just about everything, including Calor and Camping Gaz, but fuel is not obtainable. There are pubs, fish and chips, and several restaurants and tea-rooms. A small ferry runs regularly to Teignmouth if you wish to avoid the row, and for the energetic the coastal footpath up to the summit of the Ness and beyond provides good exercise and fine views. There is also a curious tunnel through the Ness to Ness Cove and, by its entrance, the Shaldon Wildlife Collection.

Port guide — The Teign

Harbourmaster: R G W Mathews, Harbour Office, New Quay, Teignmouth (Tel: 06267 3165). Office open weekdays 0900-1230, 1400-1700. VHF Channel 16 and 12, call sign Teignmouth Port Radio

Mail drop: None

Emergency services: Lifeboats at Brixham and Exmouth. Brixham Coastguard VHF Channels 16, 10, 67, 73. Brixham (Tel: 08045 58292)

Customs: HM Custom House, Old Quay, Teignmouth (by commercial docks) (Tel: 06267 2234)

Anchorages: None floating. Drying only on the Salty

Moorings: One fore and aft mooring for up to 4 boats, maximum 13m

Dinghy landings: On foreshore at Teignmouth, at Polly Steps and foreshore at Shaldon

Water taxi/boatman: None. Small passenger ferry from Shaldon to Teignmouth

Marinas: None

Charges: £3 plus VAT per night up to 8m; £5 plus VAT up to 13m

Phones: Behind old Morgan Giles yard

Doctor: (Tel: 06267 4355)

Hospital: Teignmouth Hospital (Tel: 06267 2161)

Churches: All denominations

Local weather forecast: None

Fuel: Petrol in cans from Central and Bobbetts Garages behind waterfront. Diesel (taxed) in cans from Bobbetts

Gas: Calor and Camping Gaz from *Brigantine,* Shaldon

Water: Tap on New Quay. Ask at *Brigantine,* Shaldon

Tourist information office: Centre of town

Banks/cashpoint: Branches of all main banks in Teignmouth have outside cashpoints except Barclays and TSB. Lloyds and Midland, limited opening in Shaldon

Post Office: In both Teignmouth and Shaldon

Rubbish: No specific facilities

Showers/toilets: No showers. Public toilets behind old Morgan Giles yard, and in Shaldon

Launderette: *Jaxwash,* Brunswick Street, Teignmouth

Provisions: All facilities. EC Thursday

Shops on Sunday: Newsagents. Off-licence and provisions, Teignmouth, just by bridge, 0800-2000, 1000-1300 Sunday. Shaldon *Spar* 0800-2100, 1000-1300 Sunday

Chandler: *Brigantine,* Shaldon (Tel: 06267 2400). *Mariners Weigh,* Shaldon (Tel: 06267 3698)

Repairs/boatyards: Chris Humphrey, Riverside, Teignmouth (Tel: 06267 2324).

Marine engineers: J & C Engineering, Gales Hill, Teignmouth (Tel: 06267 78633). Teignmouth Engineering (Tel: 06267 2302). Chris Humphrey (Yanmar diesels) — see above. Sleeman & Hawken Ltd, (Lister/Petter), Bridge Road, Shaldon (Tel: 06267 872750)

Electronic engineers: PFB Electronics, Teignmouth (Tel: 06267 6845/6772). DCS Electrics, Teignmouth (Tel: 06267 5960)

Sailmakers/riggers: None

Transport: Main line rail. Bus. M5 motorway 15 minutes. Air at Exeter Airport

Car/bike hire: None

Car parking: Limited

Yacht club: Teign Corinthian Yacht Club, Eastcliff, Dawlish Road, Teignmouth (Tel: 06267 812734)

Eating out: Pub food, cafés, restaurants and fish and chips in both Teignmouth and Shaldon

Museums/things to do: Small museum close to railway station. Cinema, seaside theatre in Teignmouth. Wildlife Collection, Shaldon

Beaches: Teignmouth seafront. Swimming dangerous inside river

Torquay

Tides
HW Dover −0500. Range: MHWS 4.9m — MHWN 3.7m
MLWN 3.7m — MLWS 0.7m. Tidal streams weak.

Charts
BA: 26. Stanford: 12. Imray: C5. Imray: Y43.

Waypoint
Haldon Pier Head 50.27.40N. 3.31.67W.

Hazards
Narrow harbour entrance, often busy. Harbour closed for arrival/departure Channel islands ferry. Approach poor in strong SE winds. Inner harbour dries.

CENTRE OF THE SELF-STYLED 'Riviera of the southwest' **Torquay** is the nearest thing to Cannes or Nice you're likely to find on a West Country cruise. Once described by Tennyson as the 'loveliest sea village in England' he would see some considerable changes today from the small fishing village that he knew as a fledgling resort.

Torquay's inhabited existence has a definite pedigree, with the famous underground caves at Kent's Cavern nearby, where spectacular stone age remains dating to *circa* 35,000 BC were found. However, its real growth and prosperity came much later, beginning during the Napoleonic Wars, when Torbay was much used by the Royal Navy as an alternative to Plymouth, being accessible and better sheltered in south and south-westerly weather before the breakwater was built in Plymouth Sound. With the Fleet often anchored in Torbay for months at a time, the town found favour among naval officers, with smart lodging houses rising beside the old thatched medieval cottages. The full transformation to a fashionable resort came with the arrival of the Great Western Railway in 1848, and the unusually mild climate soon established it as the West Country's premier watering place. Large hotels began to rise on the surrounding hills, palms and other sub-tropical plants flourished in the parks and gardens and, as the harbour was enlarged, elegant Georgian terraces began to grow around it.

Torquay developed early as a yachting centre; the Royal Torbay Yacht Club was founded in 1875, and with the addition of the large outer harbour completed in 1880, the fashionable resort soon became a firm favourite in the grand era of Edwardian yachting popularity. The regatta was a tradition dating back even earlier, a major event that continues today. Then, with only the drying inner harbour, it was customary for vessels to lie at anchor offshore, and it was here that R T McMullen wrote of a close shave with his 16 ton cutter *Orion* in August 1868, when he joined the fleet of boats anchored in the bay for the regatta.

'. . . *Awakened at 2am by the uneasy motion of the vessel, I immediately struck a match over the barometer, and, perceiving that its state was unsatisfactory, hastily dressed myself and called up the men to make snug, as a precaution . . . we first stowed the boat, then housed topmast, and hove*

Torquay

the bowsprit short in. Meanwhile the rain was pelting down, and the wind gradually backing to the SE, throwing in a nasty sea. The mainsail in very short time became so thick and heavy with the rain, that the labour of reeving the earrings and taking reefs down was very great indeed. At 4am it blew a heavy gale SE . . . 5am there was a terrible sea, all the yachts were pitching bows under, and most of them beginning to drag home. I was glad to see three or four yachts that lay in our way slip and run for the harbour, although it was only half-tide. Having unshackled our chain at 30 fathoms and buoyed it, we set mainsail with four reefs down, reefed foresail and storm jib and slipped at 5.30am.'

However, they survived the rest of the blow which fortunately veered southwesterly.

Although the outer harbour provided better shelter than the open roadstead, it still suffered from an uncomfortable surge in southeasterly weather. Amazingly, the short extension to Haldon Pier that has eliminated this problem was not built until 106 years later.

A reputation for overcrowding and high harbour dues did much to discourage visitors in the 60s and 70s, but since then, the 1985 opening of Torquay Marina has radically improved matters, and with excellent facilities, Torquay is enjoying renewed popularity.

Approaches

There are no immediate hazards in the approach to Torquay, and there is deep water to the harbour mouth, but as this is narrow, it is not recommended in strong south-easterly winds when there is a considerable backwash, and Brixham is by far the easiest place to enter. It is, however, not particularly easy to make out the overlapping entrance until quite close. A large blue and white Torbay Seaways ferry to the Channel Islands operates from Haldon Pier and when the ship is berthed the entrance lies just west of her. Closing the entrance, which is only just under 50m in width, care must be taken as it is invariably busy. If closed due to navigational hazards, such as the ferry entering or leaving, three vertical red balls are displayed on the pierhead — three vertical red lights at night, and no vessels are allowed to enter or leave. To direct vessels into the harbour mouth between May and September a green conical buoy (QG) is situated approximately 70m west of the end of Haldon Pier — leave this to starboard, and keep to starboard between the pierheads. The yellow buoy situated to seaward marked 5KTS is one of the limits of the controlled inshore swimming areas around Torbay, within which the speed limit of 5 knots must not be exceeded.

Entry at night is not difficult, Haldon Pier displaying a quick flashing green light, and Princess Pier a quick flashing red, both of 6 miles visibility, although it is not at times easy to pick them out against the blaze of lights from the town. Once inside, two

Map

Torquay

Soundings in Metres.

100   50   0   Metres   200

Town Centre

Pavilion

Old Harbour

Marina Office

Moorings

Torquay Marina

Fuel Berth

2 F.G. (vert.) South Pier

Visitors Berths

North Hard

Local Moorings

Harbour Master

South Hard

Beacon Quay

Royal Torbay Y.C.

Visitor's Pontoons

Princess Pier

Q.R.9M 6m

Q.G.9m 6M

Ferry Berth

Haldon Pier

Q.G. May-Sept.

N

31

vertical fixed green lights mark the end of the south Pier, the entrance to the inner — old — harbour, which is totally given over to local moorings, drying 1.2m LAT.

The outer harbour has an average depth of 2m LAT, except in the north-eastern corner, to the east of the fairway leading to the Old Harbour where there are a number of local swinging moorings. Anchoring is prohibited anywhere within the inner and outer harbours and, note, too, that there are heavy penalties for discharging marine toilets within the harbour.

The marina

The 500 berth marina occupies most of the western side of the outer harbour, and this includes 60 berths for visitors adjacent to the fairway clearly indicated by a large notice giving berthing directions. Tie up, and report to the marina office. On a par with other marinas, charges can hardly be described as cheap — £1.10 per metre per night plus VAT including harbour dues, based on overall length, including bowsprits, davits, etc, and there is a 25% surcharge for multihulls. This includes the use of showers and toilets and fresh water and 24-hour security. Telephones, refuse disposal, a launderette and 240 volt shore power are all available, and a large car park. Dating from 1912 the extravagant Art Deco Edwardian pavilion adjoining the marina has been completely refurbished and transformed into an elegant shopping centre, which includes a chandler. A 24-hour watch is kept on VHF Channel M (37).

For visitors with more austere requirements, the Torquay Harbour Authority can sometimes provide moorings, subject to availability, or berthing alongside the pontoons on the inner end of Haldon Pier. However, much of this space is used by local trip boats with frequent comings and goings. It is best to make VHF contact with the Harbour Authorities; otherwise, berth, and check immediately with the Harbour Office on Beacon Quay.

Facilities

Facilities in Torquay are excellent, as might be expected in a major holiday resort, and it is a particularly convenient spot for fuelling with diesel, petrol and water all available alongside South Pier. There is a vast selection of hotels, pubs, restaurants, and although lacking the restful charm of the peaceful rivers, the bustling contrast can make an interesting change, with plenty of nightlife for the younger members of the crew, although the older hands will probably prefer the more comfortable surroundings of The Royal Torbay Yacht Club. Open daily, visitors are welcome to use the bar, restaurant, and showers.

Port guide — Torquay

Harbourmaster: Captain J. B. Cannan, Harbour Office, Beacon Quay, Torquay. (Tel: 0803 22429). Office manned Mon-Fri 0900-1300, 1400-1700, and May-Sept. 1800-2000 daily

VHF: Harbour Office, when open, Channel 16, working channel 14. Torquay Marina Channel M (37) monitored 24 hours

Mail drop: Marina will hold mail and messages for customers. Royal Torbay Yacht Club will hold mail

Emergency services: Lifeboat at Brixham. Coastguard Brixham (Tel: 08045 58292)

Customs: Custom House, Beacon Quay, Torquay (Tel: 0803 22137)

Anchorages: In offshore winds, Torquay Roads, 3 cables west of harbour entrance. Anchoring prohibited within harbour

Mooring/berthing: Occasionally available on application to Harbour Office, pontoon berthing alongside Haldon Pier

Dinghy landings: Beacon Quay slipways

Marinas: Torquay Marina, 9 Vaughan Parade, Torquay (Tel: 0803 214624/5, 213721). 500 berths, 60 visitors

Charges: Harbour Authority, 16p per foot per day plus VAT. Torquay Marina, £1.10 per metre per day plus VAT

Phones: Beacon Quay. Torquay Marina

Doctor: (Tel: 0803 212489) or (Tel: 0803 28441)

Dentist: (Tel: 0803 211646)

Hospital: Torbay Hospital (Tel: 0803 64567)

Churches: All denominations

Local weather forecast: At Harbour Office daily. Marina 24 hrs

Fuel: Petrol and diesel alongside South Pier. Paraffin available from Carlton Hardware (Tel: 0803 37711)

Water: Alongside South Pier. Torquay Marina

Gas: Calor and Camping Gaz available from Carlton Hardware (Tel: 0803 37711) — will deliver to Marina customers. Queen Anne Marine, Beacon Quay

Tourist information office: Opposite Marina

Banks/cashpoints: All main banks have cashpoints

Post Office: Centre of town

Rubbish: Skip in Marina car park. Bins on quays

Showers/toilets: Public toilets on quayside. Showers and toilets in Marina for customers. Showers available at Royal Torbay YC

Launderette: In town and at Marina

Provisions: Everything available, including basics on Sundays

Chandler: Queen Anne Marine, Beacon Quay (Tel: 0803 24509)

Repairs: Torquay Harbour has 6 ton crane on South Pier, Torbay Seaways 20 ton mobile crane

Marine engineers: Enquire at Marina

Electronic engineers: Enquire at Marina

Sailmakers: Enquire at Marina

Transport: Branch line with regular service to main line at Newton Abbot. M5 motorway 20 mins. Exeter Airport 45 mins

Car hire: All major rental firms

Car parking: Many public car parks. Large Marina car park

Yacht club: Royal Torbay Yacht Club, Beacon Hill, Torquay TQ1 2BQ (Tel: 0803 22006)

Eating out: Vast selection from fish and chips to top restaurants

Things to do: Torre Abbey — art gallery. Kent's Cavern, underground prehistoric remains. Torbay Royal Regatta, last week in August

Brixham

Tides
HW Dover −0505. Range: MHWS 4.9m — MHWN 3.7m
MLWN 2.0m — MLWS 0.7m. Tidal streams weak.

Charts
BA: 26. **Stanford:** 12. **Imray:** Y43.

Waypoint
Victoria Breakwater Head 50.24.29N. 3.30.70W.

Hazards
Busy fishing and pleasure boat harbour. Inner harbour dries.

BRIXHAM AND TRAWLERS are synonymous. Today, a large fleet of sizeable steel vessels are graphic evidence of the remarkable reversal of the port's commercial fortunes; twenty years ago, the fishing fleet was struggling to survive. This remarkable turn around came with the formation of the Brixham and Torbay Fishermen's Co-operative and, with a united effort, new, much larger vessels were introduced, and the fish quays extended to accommodate them. Since then the port has flourished to become, once again, one of the most prosperous in the country, a success story that is impressive when compared to the recession that has dogged so many other places.

With the expansion of the port of Brixham in recent years much has changed since I first began to visit it twenty years ago when there was far less commercial activity, and always plenty of room to anchor; frequently, we used to nose our way in and find space to dry out in the inner harbour alongside the wall. Today, first and foremost, Brixham is a busy fishing port, secondly it is an important pilotage station with large vessels regularly entering Torbay to take on or land Channel Pilots, and there is also a busy fleet of

Above: Brixham is a busy fishing port which still retains much of its charm. Below: wide and easy to enter. The outer harbour from the yacht club, showing one of the visitors' pontoons.

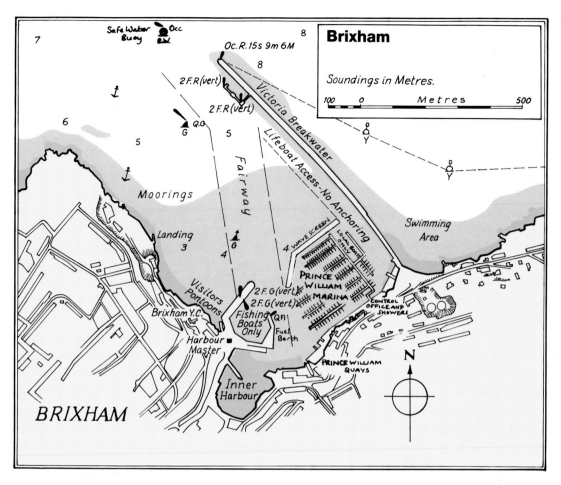

pleasure trip and angling boats. However, as long as you keep out of the way of the more important business in hand, apart from harbour dues, you will be pleasantly left to look after yourself.

Approaches

Brixham's half-mile long Victoria breakwater has a white lighthouse at the outer end (Occ R 15 secs) and is easy to locate about a mile west of Berry Head. However, keep clear of the breakwater end as there is often a lot of fishing boat movement in the vicinity and there is an IALA Safe Water buoy, spherical with vertical red and white stripes (Occ) radar reflector and bell about 200m north-west of the breakwater light to mark the beginning of the harbour fairway. Entering, this buoy should be left to port, and vessels should then keep to the starboard side of the 75m wide fairway which is clearly marked by port (FlR) and starboard (FlG) buoys right up to the fish quays and the marina. Anchoring is prohibited in the fairway, and the only feasible spot is to seaward of the moorings on the west side of the harbour which is sheltered in all but north-westerly winds, and it can also be uncomfortable in north or north-easterly conditions when a ground swell runs in. The bottom is foul in places and a trip line is essential. Anchoring is also prohibited in the fairway along the inside of Victoria Breakwater which is kept clear for the lifeboat. An alternative anchorage, less convenient for the town, but a delightful spot, is **Fishcombe Cove** just to the west of the harbour, sheltered and peaceful in southerly and westerly weather, and also free.

Most visitors to Brixham, however, will probably opt for the convenience of the new 535 berth 'Prince William Marina', a major facility due to open in the late spring of 1989, which now fills the greater part of the south-eastern corner of the harbour, and is well-protected by a wave screen wall. At least 30 visitors' berths will be available, ideally call ahead on VHF Channel M 'Prince William Marina' for berthing instructions, otherwise approach along the fairway, and once past the western end of the outer wall, the reception berth will be seen immediately inside it on your port hand; tie up here and proceed to the Marina Control for further instructions.

All services will be available at the marina, fuel, water, electricity, showers, toilets, launderette, telephones and 24 hour security. Charges, ex-VAT but including Harbour Dues will be 30p per foot daily, with reduced rates for longer stays. In addition the Harbour Authority now have three pontoons moored off the Brixham Yacht Club during the season in the south-western corner of the harbour for visitors to berth on. Charges are 16p per foot per night plus VAT. Although the pontoons are not linked to the shore it is a short row to land at the Yacht Club, where you are made very welcome, with a bar and showers available. Established in 1937, the Club's burgee includes a crown and an orange in the hoist which is derived from the historical landing of Prince William of Orange in Brixham in 1688, supported by a Dutch invasion force of nearly 15,000, to restore the throne of England to Protestantism, and be crowned as William III. A statue at the head of the inner harbour

Brixham's outer harbour is wide and easy to enter. The piling for the new Prince William Marina (due to open Spring 1989) can be seen in the top right hand corner

commemorates the event.

Retaining the fishing village atmosphere, the colourful town climbs around steep hills surrounding the drying inner harbour which is given over to local moorings, repair work, and pleasure boat activity. A popular but unsophisticated tourist spot, it has a distinctive character, surrounded with pubs, cafés, excellent fish and chips, local artists painting on the quay where, in the Old Market House, there is the fascinating British Fisheries Museum.

The busy main shopping centre, Fore Street, follows the valley leading inland from the harbour, and most facilities can be found. There are branches of all main banks, but only Lloyds and Natwest have cashpoints. Apart from the pubs, cafés, and fish and chips there are several more up-market restaurants, a couple of bistros, and the Yacht Club has a very good restaurant with magnificent views over the harbour.

Port guide — Brixham

Harbourmaster: Captain R. Knowles, The Harbour Office, New Fish Quay, Brixham (Tel: 08045 3321). Office manned daily May/Sept. 0900-1300, 1400-1700, 1800-2000. Oct/Apr, Mon-Fri 0900-1300, 1400-1700

VHF: Channel 16 monitored during office hours; working Channel 14

Mail drop: Brixham Yacht Club

Emergency services: Lifeboat. Brixham Coastguard (Tel: 08045 58292), VHF Channels 16, 10, 67, 73

Customs: Custom House, King's Quay (Tel: 08045 2130)

Anchorages: To seaward of moorings on west side of harbour, 4 to 5m LAT. Fishcombe Cove, west of harbour

Mooring/berthing: Prince William Marina. Harbour Office has 120 feet of visitors' pontoon berths off Yacht Club in SW corner of harbour

Dinghy landings: At Yacht Club, and public slipways/steps west and east side of outer harbour

Marinas: Prince William Marina, Berry Head Road, Brixham, Devon TQ5 9BW (Tel: 0803 882711). 535 berths, 30 visitors.

Charges: 16p per foot per night plus VAT. Prince William Marina, 30p per foot per night plus VAT

Phones: At Yacht Club. Public phones by Harbour Office and at head of inner harbour. At Prince William Marina.

Doctor: (Tel: 08045 2731)

Hospital: Torbay Hospital, Torquay (Tel: 0803 64567)

Churches: All denominations

Local weather forecast: At Harbour Office

Fuel: Diesel from fuel berth, eastern arm fishing boat basin. Petrol in cans from garage. Prince William Marina

Water: From fuel berth if fuelling. Taps at Yacht Club and New Pier. Prince William Marina

Gas: From chandlers

Tourist information office: In Fisheries museum

Banks/cashpoints: Lloyds and Natwest have cashpoints. Barclays and Midland do not

Post Office: New Road, centre of town

Rubbish: Bins on quay and Marina

Showers/Toilets: In Yacht Club. Public toilets on New Pier, and Fishcombe car park. Prince William Marina

Launderette: Bolton Street, centre of town at Marina

Provisions: Everything available. EC Wednesday but many shops open in season

Chandler: Brixham Boating Centre (Tel: 08045 51888). Brixham Yacht Supplies, 72 Middle Street (Tel: 08045 2290). Brixham Net Co Ltd, Pump Street (Tel: 08045 6115)

Repairs: Bearman and Wilson (Tel: 08045 2221). Drying grid in inner harbour by arrangement with Harbour Office

Marine engineers: BMT Engineering Co, (Tel: 080 428 240). Dart Auto and Marine Services (Tel: 08045 3887). E G Hubbard & Co (Tel: 08045 6115).

Electronic engineers: Lawrence & Rae Marine Electronics Ltd (51202). Quay Electrics (Tel: 08045 3030)

Sailmakers: Nearest in Dartmouth

Transport: Bus to Paignton to connect with branch line to main line. Ferries to Torquay

Car hire: None

Car parking: Multiple storey car park in centre of town

Yacht club: Brixham Yacht Club, Overgang Road, Brixham TQ5 8AR (Tel: 08045 3332)

Eating out: Good selection from fish and chips to restaurants/bistros

Things to do: British Fisheries Museum on quay. Brixham Museum, including Coastguard Museum in centre of town. Aquarium. Walks to Berry Head

River Dart

Tides
HW Dover −0510. Standard Port.
Range: MHWS 4.7m — MHWN 3.5m MLWN 2.1m — MLWS
0.6m. Streams attain over 3 knots in entrance at springs.

Charts
BA: 2253. **Stanford:** 12. **Imray:** Y47.

Waypoint
Castle Ledge Buoy 50.19.96N. 3.33.05W.

Hazards
Rocks to SW of Mewstone, Homestone Ledge, Western
Blackstone (all unlit). Castle Ledge, Checkstone (lit).
Approaches rough in strong southerly weather/ebb tide.
Fluky winds in entrance. Ferries between Kingswear and
Dartmouth. Chain ferry below Dart Marina. Large part of
upper reaches dry.

'A shipman was ther, woning fer by weste:
For aught I woot, he was of Dertemouthe . . .'

STEEPED IN A SEAFARING tradition stretching back way beyond Chaucer's time when the Shipman's goodly barge *Maudelayne* plied her trade from *'Gootland to the cape of Finistere, and every cryke in Britayne and in Spayne,'* the deep, natural harbour of the **Dart** is, as ever, a must on any cruising itinerary. Often the first port of call after the long haul across Lyme Bay, its steep wooded shores and peaceful upper reaches provide a welcome contrast, and a classic introduction to the area. Epitomising the essential character of West Country cruising, it is a foretaste of the further delights to come.

Approaches

Approaching the river from Berry Head and the east it is not difficult to find with the jagged Mewstone providing a distinctive seamark. From further offshore, to the south and the south-west, however, this island is lost against the shore, and the entrance to the river completely hidden in the folds of the 170m high cliffs. It would still be a notoriously elusive haven if our predecessors had not bothered, in 1864, to build a 25 metre high column with a wide base high above Inner Froward point to the east of the entrance, a fine daymark that is easy to spot. On the west side of the entrance, the row of white coastguard cottages about 100m above Blackstone Point, are very conspicuous against the green hillside. However, once located, there are few other problems. Although the entrance is relatively narrow it is extremely deep with the few hazards close to the shore.

Take care, though, in strong south-east to south-westerly winds and an ebb tide. This can run out at over three knots at springs, after heavy rain, or strong northerly winds. Confused seas will be found in the immediate approaches, and the high surrounding shore tends to create rapid and baffling shifts of wind direction, a factor that should be considered if entering under sail alone. Once inside, the shelter is excellent.

From the east, give the Eastern Blackstone and the Mewstone a wide berth as there are a number of drying rocks extending to the west, and hold a course

Looking seawards to the entrance of the Dart, Darthaven Marina is a prominent feature within the river

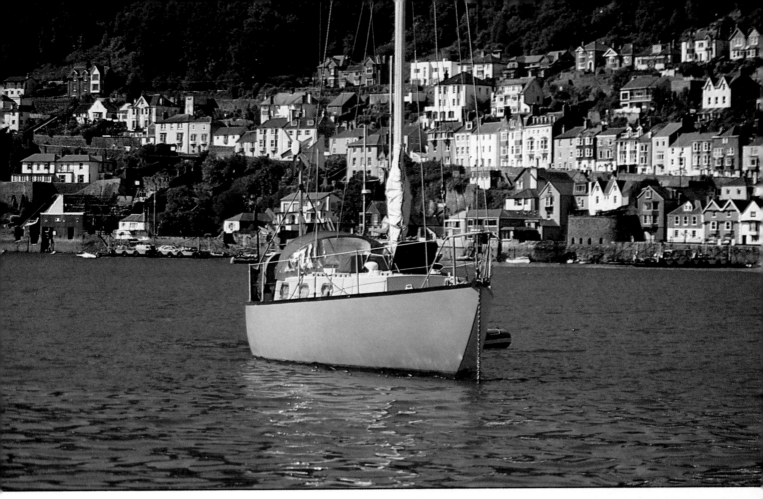

From the anchorage, the houses of Dartmouth form a colourful backdrop to this deep and sheltered river

for the conical green Castle Ledge buoy (Fl G 5sec) which should be left on your starboard hand. Approaching at night, keep both Start Point (Fl (3) 10sec) and Berry Head (Fl (2) 15sec) visible until Castle Ledge buoy is located. This will bring you into the sectored light on the **Kingswear** shore (Iso WRG 3sec) which covers the entrance to seaward, an area known as the Range, the red sector just clearing hazards to the west, and the green sector hazards to the east. Keeping in the central white sector you have a safe and easy run in, leaving the Checkstone buoy (Fl (2) R 5sec) on your port hand. Through the narrows, wait until the white sector of the inner light low down by Bayards Cove (Fl WRG 2sec) is open before turning north-west into the harbour, keeping in midstream and taking care to avoid the large unlit mooring buoys in the centre of the channel just beyond Kingswear. There are usually larger vessels lying on these which makes them easy to spot.

Although straightforward at night, the whole approach should really be timed for daylight, the imposing scenery, St Petrox Church and the two castles guarding the narrow entrance are a sight not to be missed, certainly on a first visit. Kingswear Castle is privately owned, but Dartmouth Castle to port dates from 1481, and at one time a 750 foot chain resting on six barges was stretched from here to the opposite shore to protect the port from raiders. It is now administered by English Heritage and open daily during the summer (1400–1830 Sundays), with a small charge. The walk out from the town is well worth the effort with fine views of the entrance and there is a

Boats raft alongside at the Dart Marina

pleasant continuation through woods along the cliffs to Compass Cove, a shingly beach safe for bathing.

In daylight a closer approach can be made from the south-west, keeping close to the Homestone a red can buoy marking a rocky ledge with a least depth of just under 1m LAT to the north-west, and a course can then be laid along the shore, keeping clear of the two Western Blackstone Rocks off Blackstone Point, and the red Checkstone buoy just south of Dartmouth Castle and St Petrox Church, perched on the western shore. Once past the Castle keep to starboard and

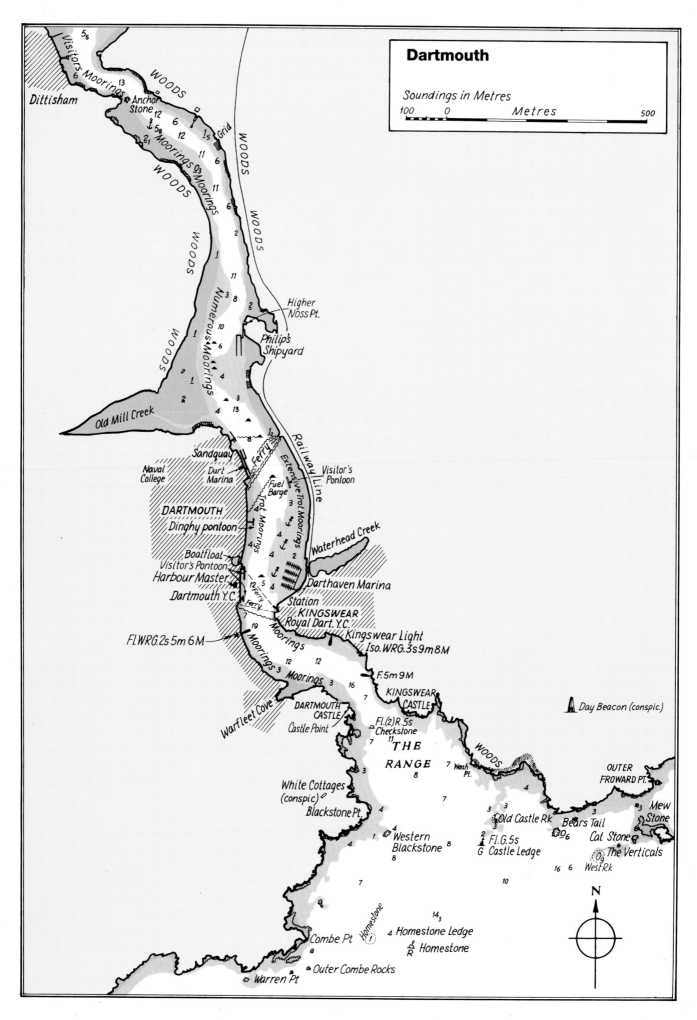

Dartmouth

Soundings in Metres

100   0   Metres   500

Dittisham

WOODS

WOODS

WOODS

WOODS

Visitors Moorings

Anchor Stone

Moorings

Numerous Moorings

Grid

WOODS

Higher Noss Pt.

Philip's Shipyard

Old Mill Creek

Ferry

Railway Line

Sandquay

Naval College

Dart Marina

Extensive Trot Moorings

Visitor's Pontoon

Fuel Barge

DARTMOUTH

Dinghy pontoon

Trot Moorings

Waterhead Creek

Boatfloat

Visitor's Pontoon

Harbour Master

Dartmouth Y.C.

Ferry

Ferry

Darthaven Marina

Station

KINGSWEAR

Royal Dart. Y.C.

Fl.WRG.2s 5m 6M

Moorings

Moorings

Kingswear Light
Iso.WRG.3s9m8M

F.5m 9M

Moorings

Warfleet Cove

DARTMOUTH
CASTLE

Castle Point

KINGSWEAR
CASTLE

Fl.(2)R.5s
Checkstone

**THE
RANGE**

Wash Pt.

WOODS

Day Beacon (conspic.)

OUTER
FROWARD PT.

White Cottages
(conspic)

Blackstone Pt.

Old Castle Rk

Bears Tail

Mew
Stone

Cal Stone

Fl.G.5s

Western
Blackstone

G Castle Ledge

The Verticals

West Rk

N

Combe Pt

Homestone

Homestone Ledge

R Homestone

Outer Combe Rocks

Warren Pt

follow the eastern shore and the line of moorings below the Royal Dart Yacht Club, a gabled red brick building with a flagstaff and dinghy pontoon. Immediately beyond the Yacht Club frequent passenger and car ferries run between Kingswear and Dartmouth, the latter manoeuvring with difficulty. They have priority at all times and care should be taken to keep clear even if under sail, and always pass astern. Also, do not exceed the 6 knot speed limit.

Don't be too taken aback if you hear a loud whistle and the sudden puffing of a steam train close by; right on the Kingswear shore there is the old railway station, now the terminus for the Torbay and Dartmouth Steam Railway, a sight guaranteed to send most overgrown schoolboys into instant nostalgia.

Dartmouth and Kingswear

Stretching before you the large, virtually landlocked harbour is an impressive sight. **Dartmouth** and **Kingswear** overlook it from their respective steep hillsides in a colourful profusion of pastels, intermingled with the odd contrast of black and white half-timber, and upriver, dominating the view, the large building of the Britannia Royal Naval College has taken pride of place since 1905 when it replaced the old wooden walled ship HMS *Britannia*. Dartmouth has been the Royal Navy's primary officer training establishment since 1863, a proud association with the town which has, in its time seen several Kings of England, and the heir to the throne among the cadets.

At first glance the harbour is one large mass of moorings, but though crowded in the season, you will always be able to find a berth somewhere in the Dart — even during the very popular Dartmouth Royal Regatta which runs for three days at the end of August. If anything, you are spoiled for choice, but one thing is certain, wherever you go, it will cost you something, for the whole river as far as Totnes is administered by the Dart Harbour and Navigation Authority (DHNA) and dues are payable throughout at a rate of just under 9p a foot per day plus VAT.

The cheapest options, therefore, are still the traditional anchorages, with the main one off Kingswear, between the line of large mooring buoys in midstream and Darthaven Marina and the trot moorings. The holding ground is good, but the ebb can run at up to two knots at springs, and it is a good row across to Dartmouth. If the anchorage is crowded, conditions of wind against tide can also produce quite a few unpredictable antics, and a sudden glut of neighbours in embarrassingly close proximity. The other disadvantage with anchoring is that the Harbour Authority does not allow boats to be left unattended at anchor except for short periods, for shopping or meals. Local fishing vessels work in and out of the moorings and an anchor light is advisable.

There are always moans and groans about harbour dues, but it is probably worth reflecting that the DHNA is a totally independent and self-financing body that maintains the facilities in the river, including the buoyage, and it has been trying in recent years to upgrade the facilities for small craft in the Dart, such as

their pontoons on the Dartmouth waterfront. Very convenient for the town, a berth on the lower pontoons (max. 35′ LOA) works out at around £7 per night plus VAT for a 30 footer. Larger craft can lie inside the lower end of the Town Jetty and between 1700 and 0900 visitors can also berth outside it when the passenger boats close down. The very friendly Dartmouth Yacht Club on the embankment extends a welcome to visitors, with excellent showers, a good bar and meals, including breakfast. The Royal Dart YC also welcomes members of recognised clubs, and they, too, offer showers, bar, light lunches and evening meals. There is a fresh water tap, a very convenient dinghy pontoon and they also have a number of fore and aft moorings, for up to 15 tons, available just downstream for visitors to hire. In addition, the DHNA have a number of visitors' moorings, a pontoon off Kingswear, and also visitors' moorings further up river, below and off Dittisham, at a slightly cheaper rate. These are all allocated by the 2-3 River Officers on the water during working hours who monitor VHF Channel 11. Advance booking of moorings is also possible with a non-refundable charge of £5.00 which is deducted from your mooring fees if you take up the reservation. Temporary berthing is also possible alongside the north and south embankment in available space when the tide permits, which is handy for a quick shopping expedition. The north embankment upstream of the ferry pontoon dries on most tides; the south embankment below the pontoon dries at springs. Quay dues are applicable for anything more than a short stay. Note, too, that there is a very good scrubbing grid on the embankment which can be booked through the DHNA. Both water and electricity are available here and along the Quay.

Finally, there are also the two private options, the old established Philip & Son's Dart Marina, above the higher ferry, and Upham's newer Darthaven Marina off Kingswear. Dart Marina can accommodate up to 36 visitors, unless there are more permanent berths vacant, and rafting is necessary, sometimes up to twelve boats deep. Long bow and stern lines are essential. The nightly charge is 25p per foot, plus VAT and harbour dues, and this includes use of shower and toilet facilities and launderette at the adjoining Marina Hotel. There is a chandler and diesel. Water and Calor Gas are also available and the fuel pontoon is open from 0730, seven days a week. Dart Marina monitors VHF Channel M, call sign 'Dart Marina Control'.

Darthaven Marina, with slightly fewer facilities is cheaper, at 22p per foot, with showers, toilets, a chandler and the advantage of finger pier berths but space is limited, and visitors' berths subject to availability. Advance booking is not possible. Call on VHF Channel M when in sight, or berth in an available space and check immediately with the office. Late arrivals will find vacant overnight berth numbers chalked up on the noticeboard by the office, and if your berth is not shown as vacant, move to one that is.

Dartmouth

Ashore, Dartmouth has plenty to offer. A busy and popular holiday town, its fortunes were founded around the export of cloth in the middle ages, and the magnificent Butterwalk, a half-timbered row of former merchants' houses with their upper storeys perched on granite columns which date from 1640, its size and fine carvings are an indication of its importance. The fascinating Dartmouth Borough Museum is now part of this fine building, and a foray into the steep winding back streets will reveal several other splendid examples of seventeenth century architecture.

A grumpy E E Middleton passed this way in 1869, early on in his *Cruise of the Kate,* an epic single-handed circumnavigation of England in a 21ft yawl. Weatherbound in a south-westerly gale, true to his gentlemanly form, he slept on board and *'went to the Castle Hotel for meals'.* He could still do it today, and in surroundings that have probably not changed a lot, a good meal can be found, overlooking the Boatfloat which is the focal point of the town's waterfront. This enclosed dinghy harbour entered under a bridge is full of local boats but is not the ideal place to leave your dinghy as it dries completely. There are ample landing steps along the embankment — but remember to pull your dinghy clear so that others can get alongside — or berth on the inside of the lower visitors' pontoon. In addition, just below the higher ferry, dinghies may be left on the outer end of the long low tide pontoon off the embankment.

The most popular attractions in Dartmouth are undoubtedly the river trips but, amazingly, a close second, the crowds still come to stare at, and photograph the attractive cobbled quayside of Bayard's Cove, used for a brief part of its life by the BBC for filming the *Onedin Line,* and now, it would seem, immortalised forever as a tourist attraction.

Mudbanks and steep wooded shores, the unspoiled beauty of the upper Dart

Facilities

Facilities are excellent, with all normal provisions, a good delicatessen, many pubs, good restaurants and cafés and a launderette. There is, however, no branch of Barclays Bank; both Lloyds and Natwest have outside cashpoint facilities. There are several chandlers, and all repair facilities available, from rigging to divers. Diesel is available from both the Dart Marina and also the convenient fuel barge moored in mid-river. Petrol is not available alongside, but can be obtained in cans from the handy garage, Dartmouth Motors, close to the embankment, which sells paraffin, too. Water is in plentiful supply from taps on the embankment, all marinas, and the fuel barge. One other facility worth mentioning is the large converted Dutch barge *Res-Nova* moored in the centre of the river just upstream of the fuel barge. This is the home of the Dart Sailing Centre, and open to visiting yachts with berthing available alongside, and facilities include a friendly bar, and showers. There is also a water taxi service to the shore. *Res-Nova* monitors VHF Channels 37/M/P1.

Kingswear

Kingswear, by way of a contrast, is a much quieter place. There is a general store, several pubs and bistros, a launderette and, of course, the Royal Dart YC. The steam trains run regularly to Paignton and back: a great way to keep the kids occupied for an afternoon and father, too.

'I grudged the delay at Dartmouth,' continued Middleton, *'but was recompensed in some measure by the natural beauty of the place, which gains its greatest charm, to my way of thinking, from the entrance to the harbour. I pulled some little distance up the river in the dinghy, but the scenery appeared much tamer, not nearly so beautiful as at the mouth.'*

Sadly, the poor chap did not pull quite far enough;

Kingswear showing the Marina, trots, and Royal Dart YC pontoon, bottom left

that runs across the river on wires and berths just downstream of the Dart Marina. Always pass astern and give it a wide berth, as the wires close to it are well up in the water.

Beyond Dart Marina, to port, the jetties and moorings all belong to the BRNC, and a wary eye should be kept out for the numerous small Naval craft running around with lively crews of Midshipmen under training. The wide mouth of Old Mill Creek dries completely, and the hulk on the northern shore is the remains of one of the last Irish three-masted trading schooners, *Invermore,* abandoned after an abortive attempt to sail her to Australia. Opposite, the famous shipyard of Philip & Sons at Noss has, apart from a tradition in building larger vessels since 1858, produced a number of famous yachts, notably Claud Worth's lovely *Tern IV* and Chay Blyth's *British Steel.* In recent years, the expansion of the trawling fleet in Brixham has generated a lot of work; there is a large yacht repair facility and, fronting the yard, the Kingswear Marina, an offshoot of Dart Marina but reserved totally for permanent berth holders with no visitor facilities.

From here on, the shores are steep and wooded, the trees brushing the high tide mark, a wide reach which narrows as you approach the Anchor Stone, a 3.7m drying rock with a beacon and squarish orange topmark, which should be given a good berth, and left on your port hand. The passage between the rock and the western shore is not to be recommended; as its many victims will confirm it is a spectacularly embarrassing spot to get stranded.

Dittisham

Sadly, anchoring is no longer allowed off *Dittisham* because of the extensive moorings and the anchorage just downstream of the Stone is the nearest, if not the most convenient for the village. Sound in just to the edge of Parsons Mud, upstream of the local moorings, where you will lie out of the main strength of the tide. It's a brave row against the ebb; an outboard puts the Ferry Inn within a much more tenable reach. If you are merely looking for a peaceful anchorage in delightfully sylvan surroundings and wish to go nowhere else you have found it — at least, when the numerous river trips wind up for the day.

There are a number of DNHA visitors' moorings available off Dittisham, subject to availability, and during the season you will invariably have to raft up.

the real delights of the Dart, are definitely to be found upstream. The name 'Dart' is derived from the Old English word for 'oak' of which there are plenty upstream as the river is navigable for ten miles inland to Totnes; at springs, coasters up to 1,000 tons and 4m draught still discharge timber just below the town, although less frequently than in recent years. The channel is well-buoyed, and well worth exploring on a rising tide if time permits, and a number of secluded and peaceful anchorages can be found in the upper reaches.

The first section of the river as far as **Dittisham** is quite straightforward, wide and extremely deep, with over 5m throughout the channel at LAT. The only real hazard is the upper ferry, a large blue and white vessel

The Anchor Stone and Dittisham beyond, just after LW

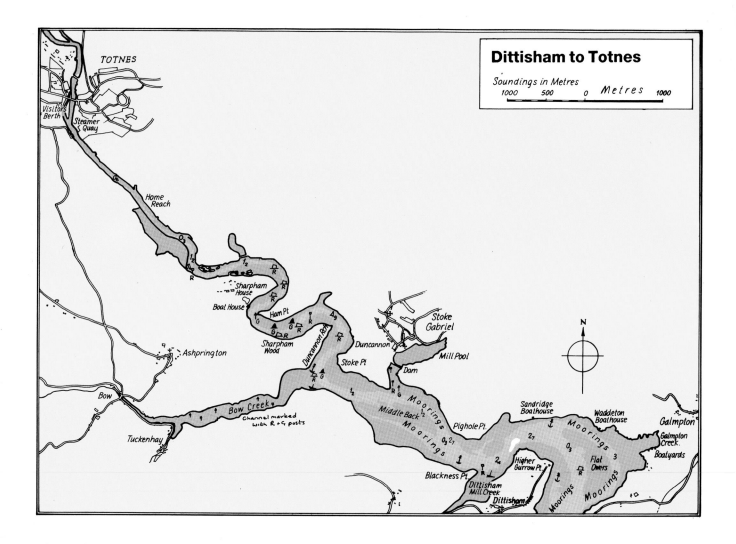

Landing is easy at all states of the tide at the long dinghy pontoon but do not obstruct or leave your dinghy on the end as this is used by the passenger ferry to Greenway Quay, opposite.

Dittisham, pronounced locally as 'Ditsam' straggles up the steep hill. It is a hotch-potch of pretty thatched stone and cob cottages from the foreshore to the village centre, with limited provisions, Post Office and phone. Water is available from a public tap opposite the Ferry Boat Inn, a convenient distraction in itself, right by the waterside where a varied selection of food is available, with fine views upriver. Widening into a shallower tidal lake, thick with moorings, the water stretches for a mile towards the distant buildings of the boatyard in Galmpton Creek, and the steep wooded shores fall away into gently rolling fields.

Above the moorings, the large area of Flat Owers Bank dries at LW, and the main channel keeps close to the wooded south shore, swinging round across the entrance to Galmpton Creek, where the Dartside Quay and Dolphin Shipyard are both situated at the head of the drying creek. A number of moorings lie along the deep water, but care should be taken to avoid the Eel Rock (dries 1.5m), on the eastern edge of the channel south of the gabled boathouse on Waddeton Point. With sufficient water, there is a short cut to the west of Flat Owers, and from Greenway Quay steer straight for Waddeton boathouse, a course of about 020°T, until abeam of the port hand No 1 Flat Owers

buoy, before altering slowly towards the second boathouse, Sandridge, and steering about 310°T. There are a few shallow patches but with a couple of hours of flood you should get across.

From Sandridge boathouse, the channel deepens again and swings back close to Higher Gurrow Point, steer for the port hand beacon ahead at the entrance to Dittisham Mill Creek, keeping close to Blackness Point, and then working back across the river to the delightfully named Pighole Point on the eastern shore. This wide reach of the river is known locally as the

Peaceful creeks and villages — Tuckenhay, Bow Creek, can be reached a couple of hours either side of HW

The channel to Stoke Gabriel dries completely at LW

Lake of the Dart as it is impossible to see a way out from the centre at high water. It is not, however, a deep lake for Middle Back, a large drying bank extends right up its centre. Keep close to the line of moorings along the eastern shore and the beacon with a green triangular topmark which marks the entrance to the drying **Stoke Gabriel** creek. A channel marked by two port hand beacons with square orange topmarks leads to a dinghy pontoon and a tiny quay where it is possible to land, but beware, do NOT proceed any further than the quay; there is a tidal dam right across the creek, submerged at high tide.

Stoke Gabriel

A picturesque Devon village, with three pubs, a hotel and limited provisions, its claim to fame is the massive yew tree in the church yard reputedly the oldest in England. A fleet of salmon seine boats lies here in the creek, and during the season 16 March–16 August, the netsmen can be encountered anywhere in these upper reaches, and should be given a wide berth if fishing.

Bow Creek

The channel bears back to the western shore above Stoke Gabriel, and at the mouth of **Bow Creek,** passes between No 2 port hand and No 3 starboard hand buoys, turning sharply to the east and narrowing towards the tiny hamlet of Duncannon. Bow Creek is accessible for shallow draught boats a couple of hours either side of HW, but is probably best explored by dinghy. A convenient anchorage is just under the northern shore by Langham Wood Point, or further into the creek, beyond the low promontory, where you will just ground on a muddy bottom at LW. The channel follows the north shore, then crosses to the south bank, and is marked beyond the entrance by red and green posts with topmarks right up to the cluster of buildings at **Tuckenhay.** You are now as deep as you are likely to get by boat into the depths of rural Devon. The shoreline is a mixture of overhanging trees, and rough pasture right to the water's edge where cows graze and silently watch as you slip past over the brown, soupy water.

Tuckenhay is a forgotten, sleepy place, and today it seems amazing that in 1806 it was the ambition of Mr Abraham Tucker to develop it as a major port. His plan never came to much, but the gas house he built did put the village on the map as one of the first places in England to receive gas lighting, and for many years the nearby paper mill produced paper for banknotes. There was, when I first visited the creek, a fine cider factory on the crumbling quayside but developers of a different kind to Abraham Tucker have since moved in and converted the fine stone buildings into homes. The Maltster's Arms, close by, is a popular local pub with good food, and convenient if the high tide coincides with opening time.

Beyond **Duncannon** the river remains narrow and, generally, shallow on the inside of the bends. A large number of quite sizeable pleasure boats run regularly between Totnes and Dartmouth as soon as the tide permits and in the restricted water passing can be tricky at times. They are plying their trade, and you are there for fun so pull in to let them pass; it is a courtesy they will greatly appreciate.

Totnes

Leaving No 4 buoy to port, keep close to the rocky east shore until the 'Six Knot Speed Limit' sign is abeam, and leave the beacon with red topmark to port, to enter Ham Reach, where the shores are once again steep and wooded. Keep can buoys Nos 5 and 7 to port, and Nos 6 and 8 conical buoys to starboard, then remain close to the west shore, under Sharpham Woods, and leave the starboard hand beacon well to starboard as this is inshore of the edge of the bank. Sharpham House, an impressive Georgian mansion standing high above the trees, was reputedly built with 365 panes of glass in its windows, and many other calendar features.

Steer back to the eastern shore beyond Ham Point, leaving the next three can buoys Nos 9, 10 and 11 to port, and into Fleet Mill Reach, avoiding the saltings to port, as the channel lies closer to the starboard bank

At Totnes, visitors can dry out alongside the old quay

past the remains of the old paddle steamer *Kingswear Castle* on the shore, then edges back to the western side, passing near to the next port hand beacon. Swinging back starboard, hold a course close to the rocky outcrop on your starboard hand, then turn to port into Home Reach, with the buildings and distant tower of **Totnes** church in sight at last beyond the flat marshy fields and saltings. The deeper water lies along the centre of the river for the first 200m, then closer to the stone wall to port, then back to the starboard bank up to Baltic Wharf, the timber quay, and passing the boatyard of Totnes Marine Services on Seymour Wharf to port, you will reach Mill Tail, where the river divides. The starboard channel leading to the bridge is full of local moorings, and the Steamer Quay to starboard is in constant use by the pleasure boats. Visitors should berth in the port arm, on the western wall, where it is possible to dry out in soft mud.

Although not the most attractive berth at low water, Totnes more than compensates for it — a very attractive and unspoiled mediaeval town, which rises up a steep main street, to a hilltop surmounted by the remains of the Norman motte and bailey Castle. It is a bustling shopping centre, with all normal facilities available, pubs, restaurants and banks. It is situated on the main railway line with regular connections to London and the north. Fuel is, however, not available so make sure you fill up at Dartmouth.

Finally, on Tuesday mornings throughout the summer, be warned — there is a special market when the locals dress in Elizabethan costumes, so don't be too surprised when your shopkeeper emerges in ruff and pantaloons.

Port guide — River Dart

Harbourmaster: Captain C J Moore, Dart Harbour & Navigation Authority, The Old Post Office, South Embankment, Dartmouth (Tel: 08043 2337). Weekdays 0900-1730. Three harbour patrol dories during season

VHF: Channel 11

Mail drop: Harbour office will hold mail, also Royal Dart YC

Emergency services: Lifeboat at Brixham. Brixham Coastguard Brixham (Tel: 08043 58292)

Customs: Custom House, Bayards Cove, Dartmouth (Tel: 08043 9440)

Anchorages: Between large ship buoys and moorings on Kingswear side of river. Below Anchor Stone. Various possibilities upriver. Vessels not allowed to be left unattended at anchor for any length of time

Moorings: Harbour Authority pontoons and fore and aft moorings off Kingswear and visitors' pontoons on Dartmouth waterfront, also visitors' moorings off Dittisham. Check availability with River Officers. Royal Dart YC fore and aft moorings on application. Berthing alongside Dart Sailing Centre barge *Res-Nova*

Dinghy landings: At pontoons. Steps on embankment and low tide pontoon

Water taxi: Two. Contact on Channel 16 or M

Marinas: Dart Marina, Sandquay, Dartmouth (Tel: 08043 3351). Visitors' berths available. Kingswear Marina, Noss (Tel: 08043 3351) no visitors' berths. Darthaven Marina, Kingswear (Tel: 080425 545) visitors' berths available.

Charges: Harbour dues payable throughout river to Totnes. Average charge for 30 footer: £6.45-£7.45 per day plus VAT on pontoons; £3 per day at anchor. Dart Marina 25p per foot per night plus VAT and harbour dues. Darthaven Marina 22p per foot per night plus VAT and harbour dues

Phones: By Boatfloat, opposite the Butterwalk

Doctor: (Tel: 08043 2212)

Hospital: Dartmouth and Kingswear Hospital (Tel: 08043 2255)

In mid–season the popularity of Dittisham invariably means having to raft on the visitors'
moorings off the Ferry Boat Inn

Churches: All denominations

Local weather forecast: Darthaven Marina

Fuel: Diesel from Dart Marina; River Dart Fuel Barge (24 hour service (Tel: 08043 4136) or VHF Channel 6). Petrol in cans from Dartmouth Motors, Mayors Avenue

Paraffin: Dartmouth Motors

Gas: Calor and Camping Gaz — Battarbees Ltd, Lower Street (Tel: 08043 2272). Also Dart Marina and Darthaven Marina

Water: Free taps on embankment. At both marinas. Free tap at Dittisham, in front of Ferry Boat Inn. Public tap on slipway at Stoke Gabriel

Tourist information office: In park by Boatfloat

Banks/cashpoints: Lloyds and Natwest have cashpoints. Midland. No Barclays

Post Office: Victoria Road

Rubbish: Bins on embankment. Floating skip off Dittisham. It is an offence to throw rubbish into river

Showers/toilets: Available at Royal Dart YC. Dartmouth YC. At Dart Marina and Darthaven Marina for customers only. Dart Sailing Centre Barge, *Res-nova*. Public toilets on embankment

Launderette: Dartmouth Launderette, Market Street. Launderettes at Dart and Darthaven Marinas

Provisions: Everything available. EC Wednesday, but most shops open six days a week during season. Shops on Sundays: Mace, Lower Street. Mr Sam's Supermarket, Ivatt Road (on hill out of town — taxi ride) open 0900-2100 seven days a week

Chandler: Yacht Parts, Newcomen Road, (Tel: 08043 5222). Dartmouth Yacht Services Ltd, Mayors Avenue (Tel: 08043 2035). The Bosun's Locker, Lower Street (Tel: 08043 2595). Battarbees Ltd, Lower Street (Tel: 08043 2272). Dart Marina (Tel: 08043 3351). Darthaven Marina, Kingswear (Tel: 080425 545). Coopers Sailing and Boating Centre, Totnes (Tel: 0803 862255)

Repairs: Philip & Son Ltd, Noss Works (Tel: 08043 3351). Creekside Boatyard, Old Mill Creek (Tel: 08043 2649). Dartmouth

Yacht Service Ltd, Mayors Avenue and floating workshop off embankment (Tel: 08043 2035). Western Approaches Ltd, Hauley Road (Tel: 08043 2137), floating workshop upstream of Darthaven Marina. Dittisham Marine Services, Dittisham (Tel: 080422 375). Dartside Quay, Galmpton, Churston (Tel: 0803 845445). Dolphin Shipyard, Galmpton, Churston (Tel: 0803 842424)

Marine engineers: BMT Marine Engineering Co. Stoke Gabriel (Tel: 080428 240). Also through most of yards above

Electronic engineers: Western Ocean Yachts, Old Mill Creek (Tel: 08043 2649). Burwin Marine, Mayors Ave (Tel: 08043 5417). Also through yards above.

Sailmakers: Dart Sails, Foss Street (Tel: 08043 2185) (24 hour in season). Dart Textiles (Tel: 08043 3901)

Riggers: Peter Lucas Rigging, Foss Street (Tel: 08043 3094). Proctor S.W. (Tel: 08043 3322)

Divers: South Hams Divers, Lower Contour Road, Kingswear (Tel: 080425 581). VHF Channel 6

Bus/train connections: Main line at Totnes; irregular bus connections but regular ferry connections in season. Torbay and Dartmouth Railway, Kingswear, connections to British Rail at Paignton

Car hire: Dartmouth Motors, Mayors Avenue (Tel: 08043 2134)

Car parking: Off Mayors Avenue behind embankment

Yacht clubs: Royal Dart Yacht Club, Kingswear TQ6 0AB, Kingswear (Tel: 080425 272). Dartmouth Yacht Club, South Embankment, Dartmouth TQ6 9BB (Tel: 08043 2305)

Eating out: Very good selection of restaurants, and good pubs too

Museums/things to do: Dartmouth Borough Museum, Butterwalk. Newcomen Engine House, Mayors Avenue. Dartmouth Castle/St Petrox Church. Friday Market. Torbay Steam Railway. Good walks on both sides of harbour entrance

Regatta/special events: Dartmouth Royal Regatta, three days at end of August. South Western area Old Gaffers Race around end of July

Passages

Start Point to Rame Head

Favourable tidal streams

START POINT Bound West: 1 hour before HW Dover
Bound East: 5 hours after HW Dover
RAME HEAD: Bound West: 2 hours before HW Dover
Bound East: 4 hours after HW Dover

WITH A CERTAIN romanticism, Frank Carr summed it up.

'West of the Start one begins to have the feeling that one is at last getting to deep seas and blue water; and although the mouth of the Channel is no more from Ushant to Scilly than thirty-nine leagues, it is quite wide enough and deep enough for small craft to be able to be caught out pretty badly . . .'

After the gentle, protected sweep of Start Bay, the rock fringed coast beyond Start Point can often feel exposed, and almost inhospitable, which, in poor weather, it most certainly is. Here, Devon projects its southernmost point far into the English Channel, prey to the weather and the full strength of the tidal streams in a combined assault on the coastline that is clearly reflected as you move further west to the high cliffs between Bolt Head and Bolt Tail. In the prevailing south-westerlies a long ground swell, and much larger seas will be encountered once clear of Start Point; carrying a fair tide westwards, the odds are certainly in favour of the wind being against it, and this can often produce an exaggerated impression of wind and sea conditions.

From **Dartmouth, Salcombe,** six miles west of Start Point, is the most likely destination for most cruising boats — a particularly unspoiled estuary with excellent facilities for yachts. It does, however, have a bar which is extremely dangerous in southerly weather, and combinations of ground swell and ebb tide. With a least depth of 0.7m LAT it is always best crossed after half flood. **Plymouth,** the next real port of refuge, accessible in all weather, lies almost 25 miles west of Start Point and these are factors that should be considered before setting out from the Dart, or making a landfall on the South Devon coast.

However, in fair weather, Salcombe presents no problem and, ideally, leave Dartmouth towards local LW which will bring you to the Start with the main ebb running westwards. By the time you reach Salcombe the local inshore flood should ensure ample water over the bar.

Assuming that you pass over a mile to seaward of

Radio beacons

Beacon	Range (NM)	Frequency (kHz)	Call Sign
Marine beacons			
Start Point	70	298.8	SP
Penlee Point	50	298.8	PE
Aero beacons			
Plymouth airport	10	396.5	PY

Coast Radio

Start Point Radio, working channels 22, 65, 60.

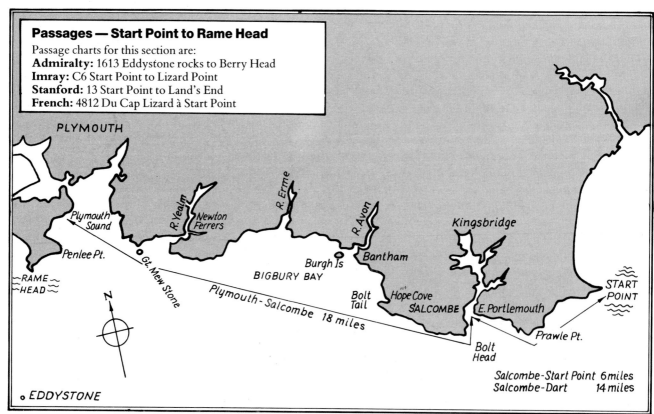

Passages — Start Point to Rame Head
Passage charts for this section are:
Admiralty: 1613 Eddystone rocks to Berry Head
Imray: C6 Start Point to Lizard Point
Stanford: 13 Start Point to Land's End
French: 4812 Du Cap Lizard à Start Point

Salcombe-Start Point 6 miles
Salcombe-Dart 14 miles

Approximate distances — nautical miles

Approaching Plymouth or the Yealm, the Great Mewstone is an unmistakable sight

the Start to avoid the race your course will take you well clear of any inshore dangers such as the isolated Blackstone and Cherrick rocks, and the Sleaden rocks extending about 400m south of Peartree Point. In calm weather, it is possible to pass much closer inshore where the tidal streams turn approximately half an hour earlier, but attain considerably greater strength, up to four knots at springs. For this reason the fisherman's passage inside the Blackstone is not recommended.

Beyond Start Point the coast is lined by low cliffs, ledges and small rocky bays backed with steep, higher land, a mixture of fields and heathland, with extensive gorse and ferns, and just a few isolated houses. There are no dangers more than three cables offshore except the large numbers of pot buoys which can turn the passage into a slalom at times.

Prawle Point, three miles west, is not particularly spectacular, a Coastguard lookout prominent on its flat, grassy top, with cliffs falling away to a rocky outcrop which forms a natural arch when viewed from the west. Just to the east there is a line of coastguard cottages. In contrast, Bolt Head is a dramatic sight as it emerges in the distance, over 100m high, steep to, and very distinctive, with jagged rocky ridges and pinnacles. The tide runs at up to two knots at springs, and can kick up another small race off Prawle Point which can be uncomfortable at times, and it is best to keep a good half mile offshore.

Salcombe lies at the head of the bay formed between Prawle Point and Bolt Head, and a course should be held towards the western side before turning north towards the entrance, which is not easy to spot from a distance. At night, Start Point light is obscured north of a line extending from the Start through Prawle Point; keep the light open across the bay until the leading light into Salcombe is located before turning north.

Off Bolt Head there are two isolated rocks, the Mewstone (19m) and the Little Mewstone (5m), close to the shore. Overfalls extend to seaward in their vicinity, and this can often be an uncomfortable corner. The high, dramatic cliffs between Bolt Head and Bolt Tail for the next four miles have a particularly rugged and rather grim appearance, an uncompromising lee shore, which should ideally be given a good offing, not only to avoid the dangers, but also the severe squalls that the high cliffs can generate, a phenomenon described with suitable drama by Hilaire Belloc in his *Cruise of the Nona*.

'As for the spill off Bolt Head, it fell after a clear midnight . . . and it was more than a spill; for it blew for the best part of an hour then ceased. But like its brother off Beachy, it was peculiar to the high land, for it came due northerly whereas the main wind had east in it. I was watching the morning star burning like a sacred furnace on the edges of the black hills when Satan sent that wind and tried to drown three men. But we reefed in time — there were three of us, one for the helm and two to reef; and when dawn broke, and the blessed colours of the east renewed the day, strange! — one end of the boom had three reefs down, and the other only two!'

The main hazards are the Gregory Rocks, least depth just under 2m, half a mile south-east of the Ham Stone, an isolated rock (11m) off Soar Mill Cove, the only major break in the line of the high cliffs, where a grassy valley runs down to the shore. This rock is infamous for sinking one of the last great Finnish grain barques, *Herzogin Cecilie,* when she went ashore in thick fog on 25 April 1936. After seven weeks, the vessel was refloated and towed to Starhole Bay, at the entrance to Salcombe, her rotting and fermenting cargo unwelcome in the harbour. It proved to be her final resting place, for soon afterwards a summer gale from the south-east broke her back, and her remains can still be dimly seen today.

Herzogin Cecilie was wrecked with no loss of life; in contrast the disaster of HMS *Ramillies* in 1760 was catastrophic. A 74 gun ship of the line, set to the east before a severe south-westerly, she mistook Bolt Tail for Rame Head, and realised her mistake too late when steep cliffs, rather than the entrance to Plymouth appeared through the murk. Unable to claw off the lee shore, she anchored, only eventually to drive ashore with 26 survivors from her complement of 734. Few ships have survived once ashore on this particular stretch of coast; it has an uncomfortable feel about it, and I, for one, invariably feel a certain relief once it is safely astern.

The cliffs remain steep right to Bolt Tail, and west of Soar Mill Cove there is a group of three tall radio masts (50m), and then two radio towers (25m) on the grassy plateau along the clifftop. The final hazard just east of Bolt Tail is Greystone Ledge (1.8m) which extends a quarter of a mile to seawards. At Bolt Tail, a precipitous cliff with an isolated rock at its foot, the coast falls suddenly back into **Bigbury Bay.** The cliffs are steep to, and if followed 200m offshore the small village and harbour of **Hope Cove** will appear, tucked snugly behind Bolt Tail, where it is possible to anchor in the centre of the bay in offshore winds in settled weather.

From here the Devon coastline bears away to the north-west, and the large indention of Bigbury Bay, seven miles wide, is usually passed by most cruising boats, as it lies inside the direct course for the Yealm or Plymouth. Although normally a lee shore, in easterly or northerly weather it can be explored further, visiting the little frequented rivers of the Avon and Erme.

About a third of the way across the Bay, off the holiday resort of Bigbury-on-Sea, is the distinctive hump of Burgh Island which lies just to the west of the hidden entrance to the drying **River Avon,** bounded on the east by the beach and sand dunes, and a line of low rock strewn cliffs below the golf course at Thurlestone Links. Further east, isolated Thurlestone rock (10m) is a conspicuous feature, rather like a large boat aground on the beach.

Accessible near HW in favourable conditions the Avon is a particularly beautiful small river, and ideal for shoal draught boats capable of drying out, with excellent shelter once inside. There is a temporary anchorage to the east of Burgh Island if waiting for the tide.

The **River Erme,** three miles to the north-west, although attractive, is very open and only really feasible as a daytime anchorage. Wells Rock and several other shoal patches extend half a mile south of Erme Head, the eastern side of the river mouth. Within Bigbury Bay the tidal streams are considerably weaker, attaining a maximum of 1kt at springs on the flood which rotates in an easterly direction, beginning HW Dover +0415, the ebb, weaker, runs to the west-north-west, beginning HW Dover −0200.

On passage across Bigbury Bay, the East Rutts, a spherical yellow DZ buoy with radar reflector (Fl.Y 2.5 secs) will be seen to seaward. This marks the easternmost edge of the HMS *Cambridge* gunnery range at Wembury; full details are in the Plymouth Port Guide, but the normal course to the Yealm is outside of its limit, and presents no problems if you remain inshore. However, if gunfire is heard and you are intending to pass to seaward of Plymouth, if you have VHF, it is worth calling 'Wembury Range' on Channel 16 to find out what is happening and advise them of your whereabouts.

Closing the western shore, Hillsea Point, rounded and grassy with low cliffs has a Coastguard lookout and flagstaff just to the east. Hillsea Rocks and a number of shallow patches lie up to half a mile offshore. Do not close the land if bound for the Yealm, but hold a course off the shore towards the Great Mewstone, an unmistakeable large pyramid shaped island, until the marks into Wembury Bay can be located, which will lead into the hidden delights of the **River Yealm,** one of the least physically spoiled West Country rivers, but inevitably popular and crowded in the season.

Dominating Wembury Bay, the Great Mewstone (59m), is an impressive lump of rock, with sparse sea turf and ferns on the steep slopes that are now just the haunt of the sea birds that give it its name. At one time, however, it was inhabited and the ruin on the eastern side, a single storey circular stone building with an unusual conical roof was possibly built with the remains of a small medieval chapel that is recorded as being sited there. The last known inhabitants of the Mewstone were Sam Wakeham and his wife, in the 1820s, a rent free domicile in return for protecting the island's rabbits during the off-season for its owners, the Calmady family, and shooting them when required. Today, the island is owned by the Ministry of Defence, and lies within the HMS *Cambridge* danger area, the gunnery ranges situated just inshore on Wembury Head. A wildlife conservation area, and subject of a special study, the island is closed to the public in general.

Shoals extend nearly half a mile south-west and east from the Mewstone, and the passage between it and the mainland is rock strewn. However, once past it, the huge bay enclosing the large Royal Naval and commercial port of **Plymouth** opens to the north and, with the exception of the Shagstone, an isolated rock on the eastern shore well marked with a beacon, there are no hazards for small craft, and deep water is carried right into Plymouth Sound, the large outer harbour enclosed by a central breakwater, with an entrance to the east and west. Tidal streams in the approaches to Plymouth are complicated by a clockwise rotation; at the eastern entrance, however, the main flood commences half an hour after HW Dover; the ebb, HW Dover −0530. Streams in the entrances can attain just over a knot at springs; within the harbour they can be considerably greater in the Narrows.

The approach to Plymouth is easy at night, being well lit, with plenty of water, and the only real problem is likely to be distinguishing the navigation lights from the huge mass of the City lights which can be seen from a very long way off. Care should be taken, too, to keep a careful watch on other shipping, as the harbour and approaches are invariably busy.

Penlee Point on the western side of Plymouth Sound is a wooded and rocky headland with white buildings low down on the point. Draystone shoals extend two cables to the south-east, and are marked by a red can (Fl (2)R 5 sec). A mile and a half west, Rame Head, the western extremity of Plymouth Sound, is distinctively cone shaped, its grassy slopes climbing to

Prawle Point with the distinctive profile of Bolt Head to the west

Crossing Bigbury Bay, Burgh Island lies close to the little visited river of the Avon

From east and west Rame Head is easy to identify from its pyramid shape and the ruin at the summit

the conspicuous ruins of a chapel on the summit. It is steep to, and can be approached to within two cables, although rocks extend from the western side, and in conditions of wind against tide overfalls will be encountered for about half a mile south of the headland.

In good visibility, eight miles south of Rame Head, the thin pencil of the Eddystone lighthouse rises incongruously from the sea. A lurking nightmare for ships running into Plymouth, a light on this curious isolated reef was first established in 1698 by an aggrieved shipowner, Henry Winstanley, who had lost two vessels. His distinctly Heath Robinson structure somewhat akin to a Chinese pagoda survived a mere five years before it was washed away, taking, by chance, the luckless Winstanley and some workmen with it. In 1709 John Rudyerd erected a wooden lighthouse with considerably more success,

but this was destroyed by fire, not water, after 47 years. Four years later, John Smeaton's fine granite column began a vigil that was to last for 120 years, his design setting the pattern for many others, and were it not for the rocks crumbling beneath it, it would probably still stand there today. Instead, when the present lighthouse designed by Sir J N Douglas replaced it in 1882, Smeaton's dismantled tower was re-erected on Plymouth Hoe.

Just awash at HWS, the rocks extend in a radius of about three cables around the lighthouse, a grey tower with a helicopter pad. The major light in this section of coast, it has a 24 mile range, (Fl (2) 10 sec), and a fixed red sector 112-129°T covers the paradoxically named Hand Deeps — in reality a shoal with least depths of 7m 3½ miles north-west of the Eddystone, which breaks heavily in bad weather; this and the Eddystone are both very popular with sea anglers and in fine weather there are invariably a number of boats in the vicinity.

In fog, this passage area is not easy, with few aids, and although most of the dangers lie inshore of the 10m line particular care should be taken to avoid being set into Bigbury Bay, the hazards approaching Yealm Head, and the Great Mewstone and surrounding rocks; generally, it is always the best policy to maintain a good offing. Apart from Start Point (Horn 60 sec), the Eddystone (Horn (3) 60 sec) and Plymouth West Breakwater end (Bell (1) 15 sec) there are no other sound signals. As an alternative to feeling your way into Plymouth, where the shipping movements continue in spite of fog, if conditions are suitable, the western anchorage in Cawsand Bay, of safe and easy access, is worth consideration.

Salcombe Estuary

Tides

HW Dover −0535. Range: MHWS 5.3m — MHWN 4.1m
MLWN 2.1m — MLWS 0.7m. Spring ebb attains up to 3
knots off town.

Charts
BA: 28. **Stanford:** 13. **Imray:** Y48.

Waypoint

Wolf Rock Buoy 50.13.49N. 3.46.48W.

Hazards

Bar, dangerous in southerly weather, and ebb tide. Bass
Rock, Wolf Rock and Poundstone (all unlit). Blackstone (lit).
Harbour very crowded in season. Large part of upper
reaches dry.

> *Sunset and evening star,*
> *And one clear call for me!*
> *And may there be no moaning of the bar,*
> *When I put out to sea . . .*

SO BEGINS Tennyson's famous *Crossing of the Bar*, inspired by the sound of the sea upon Salcombe Bar as he lay there, a guest aboard Lord Brassey's yacht *Sunbeam* in 1889, for even then this estuary was a popular, if somewhat exclusive, haunt of the wealthy, who were attracted by the romantic beauty and the beneficially mild, almost Mediterranean climate.

Not a lot has really changed since, except the numbers of visiting boats, and today Salcombe is one of the most popular stopovers for boats cruising the West Country. Away from the main tourist track through Devon, the small town has managed to resist any attempts to over-develop the area, relying totally on its natural attractions. There are several smart hotels, but a limited amount of accommodation ashore, and no amusement arcades or similar diversions to pull in the masses. Apart from the local fishing boats, mostly crabbers, and the Kingsbridge ferry there is no commercial traffic within the river and it is totally committed to pleasure boating in all its forms. As harbours go Salcombe is super efficient, managing the ever increasingly large numbers of visitors with a polite but necessary authority, for at times, particularly during the regatta weeks at the beginning of August — a tradition dating back to 1857 — the numbers have to be seen to be believed.

As an estuary Salcombe is rather an anomaly as there is no Salcombe River flowing out of it, merely a number of small streams from the eight large creeks inland known locally as Lakes. Navigable for four miles to Kingsbridge, a large area of the upper reaches dries, but within the lower half of the estuary there is plenty of deep water, extremely attractive scenery and a number of superb clean sandy beaches. That it never developed as a major port is partly due to its remote position right at the southernmost tip of Devonshire's South Hams, but also because of the Bar which has a least depth of 0.7m LAT, and becomes very dangerous in onshore winds or swell, and ebb tide, when an approach should never be attempted.

Approaches

The approach is memorable, the dramatic steep jagged profile of Bolt Head forming a succession of pinnacles and gullies rising 100m to a flat grassy top. If arriving from the east, keep a good half mile off the shore to avoid the Chapple Rocks, least depth 2.7m, and close the steep western shore to within 1½ cables of the Eelstone, before turning northwards, but be ready for very strong gusts, and fluky winds beneath the cliffs.

From the west, the Great Mewstone (19m) and Little Mewstone (5m) are large prominent rocks several cables to the south of Bolt Head. They can be passed within a cable and the harbour will then begin to open.

The Bar extends in a south-westerly direction from the rounded fern-covered Limebury Point, footed with low sloping cliffs on the eastern shore, and a leading line is formed by the beacon on the Poundstone, a red and white striped pole with red

Approaching Salcombe, leading marks in line from the vicinity of the bar

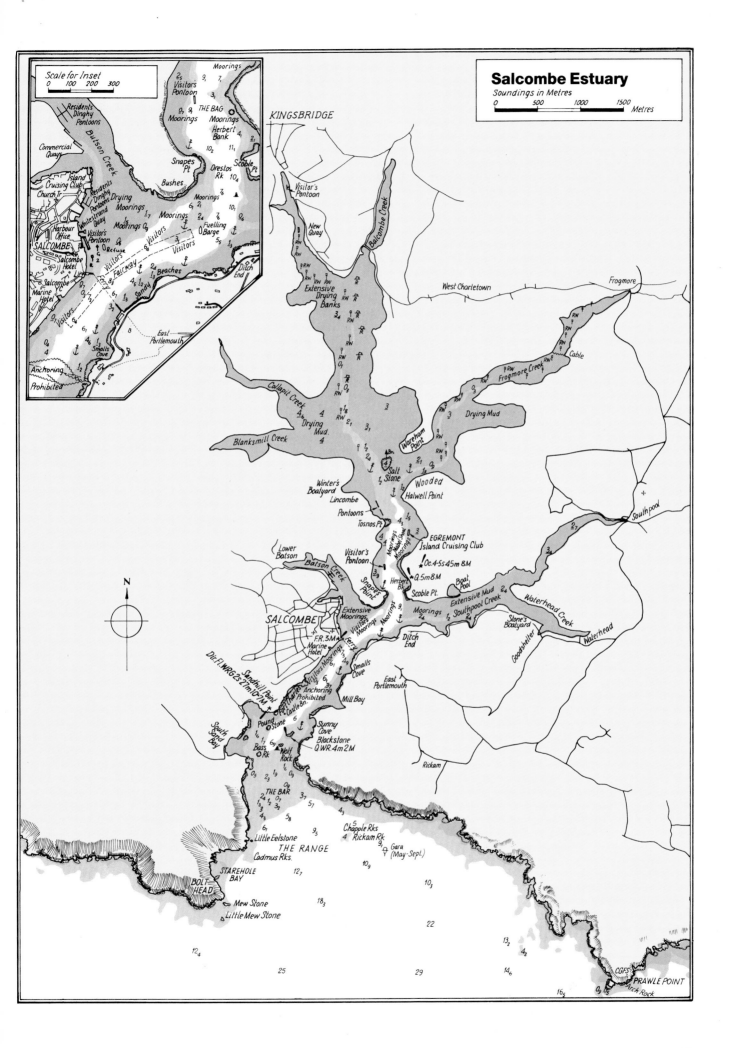

Very busy during the season, rafting is normal on the visitors' buoys just off the town

topmark, and another beacon higher behind it on Sandhill Point, white with a horizontally striped red and white diamond topmark, which displays a Directional Flashing light, WRG 2 sec, the white sector 357-002°T indicating the leading line. It is, perhaps, almost easier to enter at night, as in daytime the beacons are not easy to spot from a distance. Sandhill Point appears as an evenly rounded hill, its wooded slopes dotted with detached houses. Prominent in the centre there is a large red brick house with two white dormer windows in the roof and ivy covered gables at each end — the beacons lie exactly below the left hand gable.

Normally, in offshore winds, and preferably after half flood with an absence of ground swell, Salcombe Bar will present no problem. However, if you have any doubts about the conditions or it seems from seaward that water is breaking do not take a chance. A number of boats have been lost here and it is a place to be taken very seriously.

In 1916 the Salcombe lifeboat *William & Emma* capsized returning to port in a south-westerly gale with a loss of 13 lives, and among the many unwary yachtsmen who have suffered some notably hair-raising moments here, myself included, the young, and then inexperienced, Eric Hiscock relates a more typical encounter sometime in the 1930s . . .

'No sensible person who has studied the chart or read the sailing directions would be fool enough, one would think, to run for Salcombe in a strong onshore wind; but that was the very thing I did. There was absolutely no excuse, even though I was in a hurry to get in out of the wet, for Dartmouth, safe to approach in any weather, was not so much very further on.

'The seas could not have been properly breaking on the bar, or I would not have survived; but one crest broke with sufficient force to fill Wanderer's large open cockpit, and bursting open the cabin doors, flooded everything below. Fortunately we were through the worst of it by then, for if another crest had come aboard, I think it would have been the end of us . . .'

Once inside the Bar, Bass Rock, which dries 0.8m off Splat point can be avoided by steering up to pass close to the conical green Wolf Rock buoy, which is not lit at night, and should be left to starboard. The

Salcombe is wide and deep once inside the bar and the few dangers are clearly marked

Blackstone, a large rocky shoal drying 1.5m is marked by a black and white beacon on its western extremity (QWR), and the channel lies between this and the line of red and white beacons on the western shore off the remains of Fort Charles. At night, a pair of leading lights situated just west of Scoble Point, upper (Occ 4.5sec), lower (Q) give a transit that will take you up the centre of the harbour in clear water with a least depth of 5m right up to the town.

Anchorages and moorings

In settled weather there is a pleasant anchorage just north east of the Blackstone off the sandy beach at Sunny Cove, with a little under 2m at LW. Because of underwater cables, anchoring is prohibited in the area below and above Mill Bay, the next sandy cove of the starboard shore, Smalls Cove, just upstream, is a popular spot. Sound in to the edge of the beach shore where there is about 2m at LW. On the opposite side of the channel the first of the visitors' moorings lie off the large Marine Hotel; orange buoys marked *Visitor*. In season it is likely that one of the four harbour patrols will meet you in the vicinity and allocate a berth if you have not already contacted them on VHF channel 14. Just upstream of the Marine Hotel the Salcombe Yacht Club, a large red brick building with a tower and veranda is set up on the hillside; their landing and starting line is on the waterfront below the Club. Here a line of small yellow buoys with burgee like topmarks run parallel to the shore, marking a fairway that must be used when races are starting, as the centre of the river gets very congested.

The Ferry Inn, beside the ferry steps, is a waterside pub with a beer garden and bars overlooking the river and inevitably, a popular spot for the pundits to gather and critically watch everyone else's mistakes from behind the safety of a pint. Batson Lake is wide and mostly drying but a clearly marked channel (G/W and R/W poles with topmarks) dredged to 1m CD leads to a convenient daytime visitors' pontoon which is linked to the shore by a bridge — ideally, vessels over 40 feet and 2m draft should check with the harbour patrol first. This is for short stays only, up to 2 hours, for shopping or topping up water and overnight use is prohibited. Just beyond it, the main dinghy landing pontoon is off Whitestrand Quay where the Harbour Office is located. From here, the dredged channel continues along the creek to an all-tide small craft launching slip at Batson.

The main fairway which must be kept clear runs up the centre of the river, and most of the visitors' moorings lie along its edge on both sides; anchoring is not really recommended on the Salcombe side of the channel except just below Snapes Point because of the large number of local moorings. By far the best spot is opposite, off East Portlemouth's sandy beach, upstream of the ferry, towards Ditch End along the edge of the bank which drops off steeply. The tide can

A favourite anchorage is off the sandy beach at Ditch End

Below: the main Salcombe waterfront follows the shoreline of Batson Lake where there are many local drying moorings

run fast however, so don't skimp on the cable, as many a relaxed drink at the Ferry has been prematurely terminated by the sight of a boat dragging resolutely out to sea.

Salcombe

Historically Salcombe was not always the smart, respectable town that it is today. In 1607 the harbour was a much busier place and the justices reported that the town 'was full of dissolute seafaring men, who murdered each other and buried the corpses in the sands at night.'

The forlorn remains of Fort Charles at the harbour mouth date from the mid 1600s, the last garrison in England to hold out for Charles I, which endured six rather uncomfortable months while the Roundheads bombarded them from the Portlemouth shore. As a commercial port, the peak came in the mid-1880s, with a large number of schooners built here to engage in the curious salt cod trade with Newfoundland and Labrador, particularly by the famous yard of William Date in Kingsbridge. After buying the fish, these small British vessels regularly crossed the Atlantic to sell their cargoes in Spain, Portugal and the Mediterranean and, through this, in turn, a new trade developed bringing citrus and soft fruit to England. Speed was the essence of this financially precarious activity, and it produced a small but extremely fast type of schooner, that was able to set large amounts of sail, synonymous with the ports of South Devon, and Salcombe in particular.

By the beginning of this century, the port had lapsed into total decline, and it was then that its new popularity as a select holiday resort was established. However, apart from the bombardment of Fort Charles, undoubtedly the most dramatic event to engulf the town was the arrival in 1943 of 137 officers and 1,793 men of the US Naval Construction Battalion in preparation for the D Day landings. The Salcombe Hotel was requisitioned as well as many other properties, several rows of old cottages were bulldozed to make a loading ramp which has since become Whitestrand, and the large concrete slipway was built in Mill Bay. A large fleet of landing craft was assembled in the estuary and practice landings carried out on nearby Slapton Ley. On 4 June 1944, 66 vessels sailed from Salcombe; for the small town its invasion had ended, and in Europe, it was about to begin.

Facilities

Nowadays, the invasion is annual, and although not swamped with the trippers that choke some of the West Country holiday spots, it is probably a good guess that in Salcombe's case 90 per cent of the people walking the narrow streets in mid-summer are doing something with some kind of boat. The town is compact, and rather chic; really just one main shopping street where most normal requirements can be obtained, and, very much a holiday place, a large number of restaurants, pubs and bistros abound.

From a family point of view the attraction of Salcombe has to be the number of beaches. South Sands, one of the safest at the entrance can be reached by a regular ferry, and from here the walk up through the woods on to Bolt Head, all National Trust land, is quite magnificent with spectacular views, and if the tide is very, very low, you might just glimpse the ghostly outline of the ill-fated barque, *Herzogin Cecilie,* in her last resting place far below in Starehole Bay.

Greatly favoured by dinghy sailors, the harbour's large area of sheltered, clean water provides excellent sailing, and is one of the reasons that the famous Island Cruising Club has been based here since 1954. An RYA recognised sailing school, members sail a varied fleet of vessels, from their lovely 72ft 1909 gaff schooner *Hoshi* right down to dinghies. The Club's name was derived from the Island, the area to the south of Shadycombe Creek, 'round the back of the town' where their clubhouse and bar can be found, and in addition, their large accommodation vessel, the former Mersey ferry *Egremont* is moored in the Bag further upriver.

Apart from the ICC clubhouse, here, in this pleasantly salty backwater there lurks all manner of nautical activity, a whole fascinating street of boatyards, engineers, chandleries and other boating businesses, all conveniently close together.

Fuel and water, too, are most convenient; the floating fuel barge *Daniel* is moored off the entrance to Southpool Lake, opposite the town, with diesel and petrol, taps on the short stay visitors' pontoon and a water boat which will come to you in response to a bucket hauled aloft.

However, nowhere is absolutely perfect and there are two things that can detract from a visit to Salcombe — the number of boats at the height of the season, and the fact that in a southerly blow, in spite of the apparently landlocked nature of the harbour, a swell, particularly on the ebb, will be experienced as far up as Scoble Point, rendering the anchorage and moorings surprisingly rough and uncomfortable. The solution to both these problems is to seek out one of the quieter, more sheltered spots further up the estuary.

Southpool Lake dries almost to its mouth, but boats able to take the ground might find a spot just upstream of the moorings, grounding at LW. Ideally, this is a creek to explore with the dinghy, slipping away from the bustle of Salcombe between the steep wooded shores, following the rising tide as it creeps along the muddy shores. At Gullet Point the creek divides, the starboard arm becoming **Waterhead Lake** where you will find the small, forgotten hamlet of Goodshelter and Stone's boatyard; Southpool Lake is very shallow beyond Gullet but the quiet village of Southpool, where there are no facilities, can be reached a couple of hours either side of HW.

Opposite the entrance to Southpool Lake, Middle Ground, a bank with a least depth of 1.5m extends south and east from Snapes Point, and the deep water will be found on the Scoble side of the channel. The ebb funnels through this gap, up to two knots at springs, and opening before you is the traditional upper anchorage of the **Bag,** although now most of it

is given over to permanent moorings. A handy anchorage can be found tucked in just north of wooded Snapes Point close to the edge of the drying mud where you will be sheltered from most weather. Alternatively, for the more convivial, just a short distance upstream, there is the long visitors' pontoon.

The oldest objection to the Bag used to be the long row to town; the outboard has done away with the worst of that although in a fresh southerly breeze and an inflatable it can be a long, wet ride. Far more convenient is the taxi service run by the Harbour authority which can be summoned on VHF Channel 14 — charges within the harbour from Blackstone Rock to Scoble Point are 60p a head; from the Bag you'll pay 80p.

Mabel Shoal inconveniently lies right in the middle of the Bag, with a depth of only 1.2m LAT, and care should also be taken to avoid the rocks extending from Tosnos Point at the northern end of this stretch, the best course to avoid both hazards being to follow the line of moorings along the eastern shore, past the wooded outcrop of Halwell Point where an anchorage can be found close to the shore. Opposite, nestling in the small inlet at **Lincombe** you will see the buildings and slipways of Winters Boatyard which is approached by a narrow winding channel marked by small buoys.

Ahead, the Saltstone Beacon, a striped pole with black triangular topmark, marks a large drying rock, once used by 17th century Non-Conformists for illegal religious meetings, as the stone belonged to none of the local parishes, and was out of legal jurisdiction. Between it and Halwell Point, **Frogmore Lake** is entered. This, too, dries extensively but a very peaceful anchorge can be found just inside the mouth, with 2m at LW, and with a bit of luck, as evening descends you will find some welcome solitude.

After supper, dinghy over for a leg stretch on the lonely pebbly foreshore of Wareham Point, then drift back as dusk descends over the silent wooded shore, the ebb rippling quietly out of the creek, and the peace broken only by the sudden startled cries of the birds settling for the night.

Hopefully, when morning comes, it will be warm and calm, the distant wooded shores indistinct in a gentle, but rising mist as the early sun tries to burn through; it does sometimes happen. If the tide permits, it's time for another trip in the dinghy, following the twisting creek further inland between the rolling fields and grazing cattle to the village of **Frogmore**. The

Away from it all — a quiet anchorage can often be found just inside the entrance to Frogmore Creek

channel is well marked along its port side by red and white striped poles with square topmarks, and shoal draught boats can get right up to Frogmore on a rising tide, but the final half mile is very shallow. Although not a particularly attractive village, a grocery, Post Office and pub cater for most immediate needs . . .

After the grandeur of the entrance, above Frogmore Lake, character of the estuary changes completely, becoming wide and flat, meandering gently into the peaceful South Hams, and on a rising tide for an average draught boat it is a pleasant run up to **Kingsbridge.**

Approaches

Leave the Saltstone well to starboard, and off the wide entrance to Collapit and Blanks Lake you will find the first of the striped red and white poles with red topmarks that clearly mark the western side of the channel, and these should all be left to port.

On the western bank at the north side of **Collapit Lake** there is a conspicuous house with a mooring off it; here the channel divides, the line of red can buoys marking a subsidiary that leads away to the distant group of moorings by the bridge across **Balcombe Lake.** These buoys should all be left well on the starboard hand, and following the poles, the main channel takes you north towards High House Point, where the outskirts of Kingsbridge can be seen, a rather unsightly development of modern houses sprawling across a low rounded hill. Beneath this point the channel turns sharply back to the western shore, there are a number of local moorings along its edges, and upstream Kingsbridge begins to appear. The bank on the eastern shore is large and shallow, and the corner should not be cut. In contrast to the development opposite, on the western shore trees and fields run down close to the channel, which swings northwards again past a private pontoon with a number of local boats alongside. Just upstream is New Quay, formerly the site of Date's shipyard, and the boatyard and private pontoons all belong to the Kingsbridge ferry which lands here.

Mooring and berthing

No public berthing is allowed anywhere along the length of this quay, but keep close, and continue past the ugly modern buildings at its northern end before

The Salcombe visitors' pontoon in the Bag provides a peaceful and sheltered alternative to the facilities off the town

Port guide — Salcombe Estuary

Harbourmaster: Captain J J Blazeby. Harbour Office, Whitestrand, Salcome TQ8 8BU (Tel: 0548 84 3791). Open 0900-1300, 1330-1645 daily during season, otherwise Mon-Fri only. Four Harbour Patrol launches, marked *Harbour Master* operate in season, 0700-2000, 0600-2200 in peak. 0900-1700 at other times

VHF: Harbour Office, Call Sign *Salcombe Harbour* monitors Channels 16, 14 during office hours. Harbour patrols, call signs *Salcombe Harbour One, Saltstone, Blackstone and Poundstone* all monitor Channel 14

Mail drop: Harbour Office will hold mail, also Salcombe Yacht Club

Emergency services: Lifeboat stationed at Salcombe. Local Coastguard, Chivelstone (Tel: 0548 84 259), also Brixham (Tel: 080 45 58292)

Customs: Custom House, Custom Quay, Salcombe (Tel: 0548 84 2835). Harbour patrol

Anchorages: Very restricted space off Salcombe. Off Smalls Cove, E Portlemouth beach, SW and N end of Bag, entrance to Frogmore Lake, W of Saltstone and shoal draught/drying anchorages in many other parts of estuary. Anchoring prohibited in area off Mill Bay

Moorings: 21 visitors' swinging moorings off Salcombe for up to 15m, larger moorings available up to 17m, and three for up to 100 tons TM. Deep water visitors' pontoon in the Bag. Drying visitors' pontoon and alongside wall berth at Kingsbridge

Dinghy landings: Whitestrand pontoon. Salcombe Yacht Club steps. Ferry steps, E Portlemouth beach

Water taxi: Harbour launches double as taxi service. Call *Harbour Taxi* on Channel 14, 0900-2315 during season, shorter hours at other times. Charges vary between 60p and £1 per person depending on location, landing/departing Whitestrand pontoon. Regular ferries from Salcombe to E Portlemouth, South Sands and Kingsbridge when tide permits

Marinas: None

Charges: Harbour dues payable throughout estuary to Kingsbridge, 10p per foot per day, plus VAT on overall length, excluding bowsprits. Deep water visitors' moorings, 19.5p per foot per day plus VAT, inclusive of Harbour dues. Cheaper rates on a weekly basis

Phones: Whitestrand Quay

Doctor: (Tel: 054 884 2284)

Hospital: South Hams Hospital, Kingsbridge (Tel: 0548 2349)

Churches: C of E, RC

Local Weather Forecast: At Harbour Office window

Fuel: Diesel and petrol alongside fuel barge *Daniel*. Monitors VHF Ch 6

Water: On short stay visitors' pontoon. Water boat in response to bucket flown aloft. Tap on Whitestrand Quay

Gas: Calor and Camping Gaz from water boat

Tourist information office: Information Bureau, Mayflower Garage, Main Road, Salcombe (Tel: 0548 84 2736), The Quay, Kingsbridge (Tel: 0548 3195)

Banks/cashpoints: Lloyds and Midland only, Fore Street, Salcombe. Cashpoint Lloyds. All main banks in Kingsbridge, cashpoints Lloyds and Midland only.

Post Office: Fore Street, Salcombe. Kingsbridge

Rubbish: Floating skip off Whitestrand

Showers/toilets: Salcombe Yacht Club. Public toilets at Whitestrand

Launderette: Fore Street, Salcombe (7 days), also in Kingsbridge

Provisions: All normal requirements in Salcombe. EC Thursday but most shops open during season. Ellis's grocery just behind Whitestrand open 0830-1000 seven days a week in season. All requirements at Kingsbridge

Chandlers: Salcombe Chandlers (Admiralty Chart agents), Fore Street (Tel: 054 884 2620). Salcombe Boatstore, Island Street (Tel: 054 884 3708). J Stone & Son, Island Street (Tel: 054 884 3655), also at Goodshelter, E Portlemouth (Tel: 05485 242). Tideway Boat Construction (Tel: 054 884 2987). Winters Marine, Island Street (Tel: 054 884 3838)

Clear water and sandy beaches attract every type of pleasure craft

Repairs: Victory Yard (Tel: 054 884 3838). Tideway Boat Construction, Island Street (Tel: 054 884 2987). J. Stone & Son, see chandlery. Winters Boatyard (Tel: 054 884 3838). Drying out by arrangement with Harbourmaster. Salcombe Boatstore (Tel: 054 884 3708)

Marine Engineers: J. Stone & Son, see chandlery. Victory Yard, Island Street (Tel: 054 884 3838). Sailing, Island Street (Tel: 054 884 2094). Winters Marine, Island Street (Tel: 054 884 3838). Salcombe Boat store, Island Street (Tel: 054 884 3708). Wills Bros, The Embankment, Kingsbridge (Tel: 0548 2424)

Electronic engineers: Burwin Marine Electronics, Island Street (Tel: 0548 84 3321)

Sailmakers: J Alsop, The Sail Loft, Croft Road (Tel: 0548 84 3702). J McKillop, The Sail Loft, Ebrington Street, Kingsbridge (Tel: 0548 2343)

Riggers: Dawson Rigging, Island Street (Tel: 0548 84 3195)

Liferaft/inflatable repairs/servicing: Salcombe Marine, Island Street (Tel: 0548 84 2666)

Transport: Regular buses and ferries on tide to Kingsbridge, with connections to main line trains at Plymouth/Totnes via Dartmouth

Car hire: None

Car parking: Large car park at Batson, Salcombe. Large car park on Quay at Kingsbridge

Yacht club: Salcombe Yacht Club, Cliff Road, Salcombe TQ8 8JQ (Tel: 0548 84 2872)

Eating out: Excellent selection of restaurants/bistros, pubs, cafés and fish and chips

Museums/things to do: Salcombe Museum. Sharpitor Gardens and Overbecks Museum. Spectacular walks on both sides of estuary entrance

Regatta/special events: Salcombe Town Regatta, first week in August, Salcombe Yacht Club Regatta second week in August. Harbour is also popular for dinghy championships

Beaches: Many fine sandy and protected beaches within the harbour

turning across the entrance of the inlet on your port hand where there are a number of local boats moored. The channel now heads towards the slipway and quay on the western shore which marks the beginning of the tree lined basin enclosing the head of the creek. The visitors' pontoon, with a bridge to the shore, will be found on the starboard hand; shoal draught boats should berth on the outside, and visitors with deeper draught should use the berth alongside the wall opposite which is clearly marked. Suitable for vessels of up to 12m both berths dry completely to soft mud and are only safely accessible 2½ hours either side of HW, which occurs about 5 mins after HW Salcombe. If intending to stay for a tide, it is advisable to confirm the berthing availability with the Harbour Office before proceeding upriver.

Facilities

Kingsbridge, an unspoiled country town, forms the confluence of four busy roads through South Devon, and although long dead as a seaport, it bustles with activity as an important shopping centre, with a market on Wednesdays. All normal requirements can be found, except fuel; there are many pubs, restaurants and cafés, and after the distinctly nautical atmosphere of Salcombe a taste of the country makes a pleasant contrast, before, once again, returning downstream, towards the sea, and yet another *Crossing of the Bar.*

> *'For though from out our bourne of*
> *Time and Place,*
> *The flood may bear me far,*
> *I hope to see my Pilot face to face,*
> *When I have crost the bar.'*

Bigbury Bay

River Avon: HW Dover −0523.
Charts BA: 1613. **Stanford:** 13. **Imray:** C6.
Hazards Tidal Entrance with bar, dangerous in onshore wind. Strong currents within entrance. River dries. Murray's Rocks in approach (unlit).

River Erme: HW Dover −0523.
Charts BA 1613. **Stanford** 13. **Imray** C6.
Hazards Wells Rock to SE, Edward's Rock, East and West Mary's Rocks in entrance (all unlit). Drying tidal river, dangerous in onshore winds.

THE SEVEN MILE STRETCH of **Bigbury Bay** is, in prevailing south-westerly winds, not a very attractive prospect, and boats heading across it will usually remain a good two to three miles offshore. However, in calm, settled weather, there are several places within it which make an interesting detour from the normal cruising track.

Hope Cove, is a small fishing village tucked away on the north side of Bolt Tail which can sometimes provide a temporary anchorage in easterly winds. There are no off-lying dangers; sound into the centre of the cove between the small pier and the south shore, but beware the Basses Rock closer inshore which dries 1.3m.

The **River Avon** is, however, the real gem of Bigbury Bay, and for owners of shallow draught boats capable of drying out it can be a delightful spot for an overnight stop, providing there is no inkling of a change of weather to the south or west. Although perfectly sheltered within, in an onshore breeze, and any ground swell, the river entrance is inaccessible, and once inside, if the weather does turn, you might

not be able to get out for some time . . .

To find it, steer directly for the flattened pyramid of **Burgh Island,** (pronounced 'Borough') where the beacon marking the drying Murray's Rocks will be seen on the eastern side. Burgh Island itself is tidal, joined by drying sands to the mainland and the trippery resort of Bigbury-on-Sea. At high tide, a remarkable 'sea tractor' with seats on an elevated platform, maintains the link with the shore. In contrast to the mainland resort, privately owned Burgh Island sports an elegant Art Deco hotel, where Agatha Christie wrote several of her books; today, it has become a popular location for films of similar style and period. On the foreshore, by the landing place, there is also a small pub, the 14th century Pilchard Inn.

The entrance to the Avon is bounded to the east by the extensive sand dunes and beach of the Ham, and apart from a narrow channel, the whole of the approach dries. Ideally it is best to enter an hour before HW, (HW Dover −0523) as the current runs strongly in the entrance. If waiting for the tide, a good sandy anchorage can be found just east of Murray's Rocks in about 2m, which is handy for a dinghy visit to Burgh Island if you wish to pass the time, or to reconnoitre the channel.

The entrance to the river is backed by a high cliff, Mount Folly, and the deepest water over the bar is found by lining up the two conspicuous houses just east of the group of trees on the clifftop. Keep close to the beach on the western side, following the steep shoreline, until the white mark painted on the rock is abeam before turning to starboard towards Lower Cellars Point, which is covered in turf and ferns, above which protrudes the top of a solitary pine tree. Here the river narrows considerably, with a shingly bank along the northern shore, so steer close to the point, where the current can run fast through the narrows, up to five knots on the ebb if the river is in flood. However, once through the gap, you have entered a real hideaway. The river widens, with the landing beach and houses ahead, and immediately to starboard, there is a sheltered pool off the quaint thatched boathouse and grassy quay, tucked beneath the dense foliage of the steep protective cliff. At first sight, with 2m at LW, this would seem to be the ideal anchorage, but holding is poor, and the current runs strongly. Instead, follow the southern shore upstream towards the white

River Avon
Soundings in Metres
0   500   1000 Metres

River Avon — Batham at LW

building with a long thatch on the foreshore, and anchor anywhere clear of the few local small boat moorings, where you will ground, and probably dry out at LW.

Peaceful, totally unspoiled, and far removed from the busier anchorages that you have visited so far, this delightful place is a rare find. Disappearing beyond cornfields sloping down to wooded shores, the river winds upstream between drying sandy banks and reedy saltings for another four miles to the village of **Aveton** (pronounced Orton) **Gifford.** It is a sleeping, almost forgotten waterway but fifty years ago barges regularly worked their way inland with cargoes of lime, stone and coal for the South Hams farms, and the tiny quays at Bantham reeked of the pilchard catches as they were landed and cured. On a rising tide it is well worth further exploration in the dinghy.

Bantham itself is little more than a hamlet, a row of well cared for cob and stone cottages, with deep overhanging thatches, and tiny windows. The village is privately owned, belonging to the Evans Estates, which accounts for the admirable lack of development. There is a village store with basic provisions, Post Office, and the Sloop Inn which does very good bar food. A bigger selection of shops can be found at Aveton where petrol is also available from a garage, if you need an excuse for the dinghy trip.

The large thatched building on the foreshore, in spite of its medieval appearance was actually built in 1937 to celebrate the accession of King George VI, and is nothing more than an enormous boathouse, with two fine figureheads at each end. Within, there is a further surprise, for here you will find Hugh Cater, a boatbuilder who produces magnificent traditional varnished clinker dinghies, and the whole of the upper floor is full of them.

Nearly three miles further north-west, the other forgotten river of Bigbury Bay, the **Erme,** though very attractive, and completely unspoiled, is only really feasible as a daytime anchorage in favourable conditions, and not suitable for an overnight stop. Lacking a sheltering natural breakwater like the Ham, the river mouth is wide open to the south-west, and dries completely beyond the entrance. As it is privately owned by the Flete Estate, and designated as a wild life sanctuary, permission is needed to enter the inner reaches. However, in settled weather and an offshore breeze a pleasant daytime anchorage can be found in

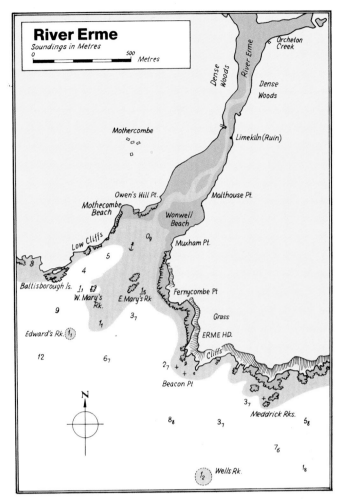

the mouth off the fine sandy beaches at Mothecombe and Wonwell.

Although there are no offshore hazards, care must be taken in the approach to the Erme, as there are several dangerous rocks, in particular Wells Rock, least depth 1.2m just over half a mile south of Erme Head, the eastern flank of the river mouth. Within the entrance there are three more rocks, West and East Mary's Rocks, which dry 1.1m and 1.5m respectively and, further to seaward, three cables south of the low grassy Battisborough Island on the northern shore, Edward's rock, least depth 1.1m LAT. Shallow water extends south west from the Mary's rocks, and the deep channel runs parallel to the sloping slab-like cliffs of the northern shore. Keep to the west of all the hazards, and steer for the southern end of Owen Hill, the prominent isolated cliff topped with a group of conspicuous pines. Mothecombe beach lies just to the west, and sounding in towards it, a good sandy anchorage will be found in about 3m, two cables due south of Owen Hill, and inside the Mary's Rocks.

The River Erme is probably unique in that there are absolutely no facilities within a mile; the clean sandy beaches and clear water are perfect for swimming, and if time permits a dinghy trip should certainly be made some of the way upstream, following the tide up the twisting channel between the sandy banks and steep wooded shores. There are few places on the South Coast that remain quite so unspoiled.

59

River Yealm

Tides

HW Dover −0540. Range: MHWS 5.4m — MHWN 4.3m
MLWN 2.1m — MLWS 0.7m. Attains up to 3 knots in
entrance at spring ebb.

Charts

BA: 30. **Stanford:** 13. **Imray:** C14.

Waypoint

Bar Buoy 50.18.56N. 4.04.05W.

Hazards

West and East Ebb Rocks, Mouthstone Ledge from east;
Outer and Inner Slimer Rocks from west (all unlit). Bar across
northern side of entrance (lit during season only). Under 2m
within entrance at springs. Not recommended in strong S or
SW wind and swell. Newton Creek and large area of upper
reaches dry.

UNDOUBTEDLY ONE OF THE classic havens of the entire South Coast, the small, and beautiful **River Yealm** probably owes much of its unspoilt character to the fact that for many years the narrow twisting entrance was a strong deterrent to visitors by sea, making it very difficult to enter under sail alone. With no beaches or attractions for holidaymakers other than the natural beauty of its wooded shores, it was still very undeveloped well into the 1930s, and it is only since the war that the small cottages have become desirable as holiday and retirement homes. Ironically, although reliable auxiliaries have overcome the problem of the entrance, they have inevitably created another, for the river is now so popular in the height of summer that it is often a tight squeeze to find a berth.

Don't be put off, though. As long as you are not averse to rafting up, and are not determined to have a secluded peaceful anchorage all to yourself, the Yealm is undoubtedly another essential on any West Country cruise; however, ideally, visit it early or late in the season, when it is altogether a different place.

River Yealm, looking up Newton Creek from the Pool, showing the landing pontoon at Yealm Steps. The river mouth lies to the right

Approaches

In spite of the bar, the approach is not as difficult as it might at first seem, although the entrance to the river is totally hidden behind Misery Point. Care must be taken rounding Yealm Head from the east to avoid the Eastern and Western Ebb Rocks, which are just awash LAT three cables south-west of Garra Point. Normally, they can be seen by the seas breaking but are particularly insidious in calm weather. Keep a good half-mile off the shore and do not turn north into Wembury Bay until the conspicuous church tower at Wembury is bearing 010°T.

Approaching from the west, the sloping pyramid of the Great Mewstone provides a fine landmark to locate the river, but keep clear of the Mewstone Ledge, least depth 2m, which extends 1½ cables southwestward, and the Outer and Inner Slimers, 2 cables east of the island, which dry 1.5m and 0.3m respectively. Continue eastwards until you are on the same 010°T bearing on Wembury Church and these will be safely avoided.

The bottom of Wembury Bay is uneven, and rises quickly to around 6m, a factor that can produce very rough seas in strong winds from the south and west,

The visitors' pontoon in the approach to the Pool is a popular berth

when, sensibly, no approach to the river should be attempted, particularly with the easy entrance to Plymouth close by.

Holding 010°T, the first indication of the river mouth is usually the other boats in the vicinity, and if the wind is off the land, vessels anchored in Cellar Bay. As Mouthstone Point draws abeam the leading marks will be seen above and to the left of Cellar Beach, two white triangular beacons with a black line down the centre, giving a transit of 088.5°T which clears rocky Mouthstone Ledge, extending west for one cable from the point. This line passes across the end of the sand bar that extends from Season Point, which dries 0.6m LAT, and between April and October its southern end is marked by a red can (Bar), with radar reflector (F1 R 5 sec) which should be left to port. This is the only light in the river, and without local knowledge, entry at night, except in ideal conditions, with a good moon, is not recommended, certainly never for a first visit.

Almost opposite, perched on a rock, a green beacon with triangular topmark on a white backboard marks the southern side of the channel, which is about 40m wide and between the two there is a least depth of almost 3m LAT. Abeam of the beacon, turn on to 047°T, towards the square white leading mark with red vertical stripe, high in the gorse on the opposite cliff, unless you are intending to stop off Cellar Beach, which is usually a crowded daytime anchorage if the weather is fair. Across this section of the river on the lowest tides there will not be more that 1.2m until Misery Point is rounded, a sharp turn to starboard into the first inner reach. If in doubt about the water, do not attempt the entrance until a good hour after LW.

Anchorages and moorings

Once inside Misery Point you enter a different world as the sea vanishes astern. The channel deepens to well over 2.5m, and runs between steep wooded banks, with little indication that there is any kind of settlement, except the moorings, among them the first

The lovely upper reaches towards Steer Point are often less crowded and perfect for exploration in the dinghy

and largest visitors' buoy, capable of taking up to 25m, just north of Misery Point. The second set of moorings lie on the south side of the channel opposite the red can Spit buoy which marks the sandy spit extending from Warren Point. In spite of the buoy it's a regular grounding spot. These two 25 ton moorings can accommodate up to three visitors at a time, and not much further upstream on the starboard hand is the 150ft visitors' pontoon, which can accommodate up to 25 boats at a time.

You are now in the Pool, a fine, landlocked natural haven, surrounded by high hills, wooded right to the water's edge, the traditional anchorage in the Yealm. Here, overlooked by the prominent Yealm Hotel, the river branches, with the Newton Arm leading off to starboard. This dries almost completely, but two hours either side of HW, the villages of **Newton Ferrers,** half a mile upstream on the northern shore, and the delightfully named **Noss Mayo,** opposite, can be reached with an average draught. Right at the head of the creek, another quarter of a mile or so, there is a public quay at Bridgend and boats drawing up to 2m can reach it at springs, a couple of hours either side of HW, with berths alongside for scrubbing or repairs.

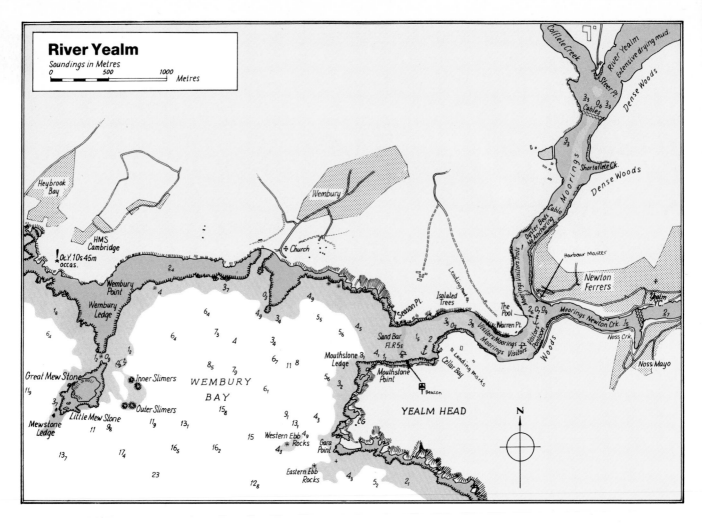

River Yealm
Soundings in Metres

This, and the other drying berths alongside Pope's Quay, Noss Mayo, and the scrubbing posts at Clitters Beach, opposite Madge Point, are all available by arrangement with the Harbourmaster. Bridgend Boat Co have their premises beside the quay, with a slipway and repair facilities.

Off the two villages, bilge keelers can dry out comfortably on the foreshore on reasonably hard ground although the centre of the creek is soft and muddy; take care, however, to avoid the underwater power cables between Newton Ferrers and the eastern side of Noss Creek, which are clearly marked by beacons.

For deep draught boats, the Pool is no longer an easy place to let go during the season as swinging room is so restricted and it is usually necessary to lie to two anchors. Although well protected from any seas, the river can be surprisingly violent in a blow, as the wind eddying round the high shores creates williwaws, and very strong gusts. On several occasions I have seen small craft laid over almost on their beam ends, and great columns of spume and spray whipped off the water in this seemingly perfect shelter. The Harbour is leased from the Crown Estate Commissioners and administered by the River Yealm Harbour Authority, a statutory non-profit-making organisation, and the charges are very reasonable. As a mooring only costs £1 more than anchoring it is probably well worth the convenience and peace of mind to take that option.

Above Warren Point and close to the Wembury side of the river there is a very convenient line of fore and aft trots which can take up to five boats abreast. In addition to these Harbour Authority moorings, there is also an unwritten understanding in the Yealm where space is at such a premium that visitors can pick up any other vacant residents' mooring providing there is no tender or note attached to it. The Harbourmaster is invariably out on the water first thing in the morning, and after 1640 in the afternoon to assist with settling people in. If he is nowhere to be seen afloat, and you have picked up a vacant mooring nip ashore to his office in the driveway of the Yealm Hotel. Conveniently beneath it there is the large dinghy landing pontoon at Yealm Steps, but do not obstruct the outer end as this is kept clear for boats to come alongside and take on water.

Facilities

From the Pool, Newton Ferrers is easily reached by dinghy if the tide permits or a 10 minute walk along the path overlooking the steep sided creek. Alternatively, there are two landing places on the south side of the entrance to Newton Arm, opposite the visitors' pontoon, Wide Slip and Parish Steps, and a delightful footpath leads through the National Trust woodlands to Noss Mayo. Newton was presented to Henri de Ferrieres by William the Conquerer as a reward for his assistance in the Norman invasion, which explains the strange name; Noss derives from the Old English for 'promontory'. Both villages have been very well preserved, although in recent years there has been a regrettable spread of modern bungalows and houses around them. Looking out over

62

the creek, the older cottages are immaculately kept, the whitewash looking almost new and offset with more than a smattering of wisteria and roses over the doorways. Ablaze with flowers their well-tended gardens, neat stone walls and lawns drop away right to the water's edge. There is a Post Office and grocery store in both villages; Newton Ferrers also has a butcher, chemist, Barclay's Bank on Tuesdays and Thursdays, and chandlery and gas and a boatbuilder for repairs are available at the Yealm Boat Co up the hill going out of the village.

As a whole, the Yealm is a quiet, relaxing sort of place. The walks in the surrounding woods, and beside the river are lovely, reflecting the origins of the river's name which is Celtic for 'kind'. The walk over Warren Point out to Season Point, overlooking the river mouth is particularly fine, with good blackberrying in late summer, and a memorable place to watch the sunset over Wembury Bay and the Mewstone. If however, the timing clashes with other pursuits, there are three pubs to choose from in the villages, the Swan and Old Ship at Noss, and the Dolphin and also the bar at the Yealm Yacht Club, on the foreshore at Newton Ferrers. Here, visitors are welcome, and facilities include showers, bar and meals available on Friday and Saturday evenings, with a very good Sunday lunch.

Beyond the Pool, the upper reaches are well worth a trip on the tide, and in a small boat they are navigable for another two miles. Until quite recently the whole of this area was given over to extensive oyster beds but now these only extend for just over 300m upstream of Madge Point. Within this area, marked by notices on posts along the shore, anchoring is strictly prohibited, but upstream the river has been changed considerably by the increase in the number of moorings. The deepest water lies in the centre of the river and depths vary with as little as 0.3m LAT in places and beyond the oyster beds, upstream of the marked underwater power cable, the river is all privately owned by the Kitley Estate. Here, too, anchoring is prohibited throughout as the owner is attempting to maintain it as a nature reserve. At Steer Point the river divides. Cofflete Arm to port and the larger Yealmpton Arm to starboard.

Postscript: Early in 1989 the Yealm Harbour Authority regretfully announced that they will have to restrict the number of visitors in future to a maximum of 90 boats per night at the busiest times of the year, usually during spells of settled weather and particularly on summer Bank Holidays. It is probably best to avoid the river altogether at these times, but they do stress that entry will never be refused to any boat seeking shelter in poor weather.

Port guide — The Yealm

Harbourmaster: Mr M J Simpson, Harbour Office, Yealm Hotel Drive, Newton Ferrers PL8 1BL (Tel: 0752 872533). 1000—1200, 1430–1540, daily in season. Afloat in launch early morning and evenings

VHF: No radio watch

Mail drop: c/o Harbour Office

Emergency services: Nearest lifeboat at Plymouth. Coastguard (Tel: 0752 872301)

Customs: Report arrival. Dial 100 Freephone Customs Yachts. Regular patrols from Plymouth, and letter box

Anchorages: Cellar Bay in offshore winds. In the Pool, but very restricted. Drying out in Newton Arm.

Mooring/berthing: Harbour Authority has several swinging moorings, to accommodate visitors from 25m–7m. Visitors' pontoon for up to 25 boats, and fore and aft trots. Local moorings available to visitors if free. Scrubbing/repair berths available alongside by arrangement with Harbourmaster

Dinghy landings: All tide pontoon at Yealm steps, below Hotel. Parish steps, opposite visitors' pontoon. High water landing at Newton Ferrers slip, Noss Creek, Yealm Yacht Club, Bridgend Quay

Water taxi: None

Marina: None

Charges: Harbour dues, inclusive of VAT, up to 22 ft £3 per night, 23–32 ft £4, 33-38 ft £5, over 38 ft £6. Vessels at anchor £1 per night less; surcharge of £2 per night for multihulls over 30 ft. Cheaper rates for longer periods and boats can be left by arrangement

Phones: Outside Post Offices, Newton Ferrers and Noss Mayo

Doctor: (Tel: 0752 880392)

Hospital: Plymouth nearest, 10 miles

Churches: Two; C of E, Newton Ferrers and Noss Mayo

Local Weather Forecast: None

Fuel: None

Gas: Calor and Camping Gaz from Yealm Boat Co, Parsonage Road, Newton Ferrers (Tel: 0752 872564)

Water: Hose at Yealm steps pontoon at most states of tide.

Tourist information: None

Banks/cashpoints: Barclays open Tuesdays and Thursdays 1000–1400. No cashpoint

Post Office: Newton Ferrers and Noss Mayo

Rubbish: Bins at Yealm Steps

Showers/toilets: Yealm Yacht Club

Launderette: None

Provisions: All basics available, including chemist. EC Thursday. Groceries available in both Newton Ferrers and Noss Mayo, 1000–1200 Sundays

Chandler: Yealm Boat Co, Parsonage Road, Newton Ferrers (Tel: 0752 872564)

Repairs: Yealm Boat Co (above). Bridgend Boat Co, Bridgend Quay

Marine Engineers: Bridgend Boat Co, J Hockaday, Newton Ferrers (Tel: 0752 872369)

Electronic engineers: None

Sailmakers: A. Hooper (Tel: 830411)

Riggers: None

Transport: Buses, six a day, weekdays to Plymouth, for main line train connections. Main roads and airport at Plymouth

Car hire: None. Taxi, C Elliot (Tel: 872682)

Car parking: Very restricted

Yacht Club: Yealm Yacht Club, Riverside, Newton Ferrers, Nr Plymouth (Tel: 0752 872291)

Eating out: Meals at hotels in Newton Ferrers, and pubs at Noss Mayo and Newton Ferrers. Meals at Yacht Club, weekends

Things to do: Extensive walks. Swimming at Cellar Beach

Plymouth

Tides
HW Dover −0540. Standard Port (Devonport).
Range: MHWS 5.5m — MHWN 4.4m MLWN 2.2m — MLWS 0.8m. Ebb streams can attain in excess of 3 knots in Narrows, and 5 knots in upper reaches of Tamar.

Charts
BA: 30, 1967, 1901, 1902, 871. **Stanford:** 13. **Imray:** C14.

Waypoints
Knap Buoy 50.19.52N. 4.09.94W. West Tinker Buoy 50.19.14N. 4.08.62W.

Hazards
Shagstone (unlit). Much commercial and Naval shipping. HMS *Cambridge* gunnery ranges to seaward of Wembury Head. Strong tidal streams in places. Large part of upper reaches dry.

'Plymouth is a Naval and commercial port and has one of the finest natural harbours in the country. It is not frequently used by yachts . . .'

WHEN MY PREDECESSOR, D J Pooley was writing the original *West Country Rivers* in 1957, this paradox held true, and remained so for many years afterwards. Perfect for fleets of warships the sheer physical scale of Plymouth had little to offer smaller craft and, apart from a few rather dirty commercial basins, there was never a really convenient place for visitors to lie. Most of the better anchorages are a long way from the town, and exposed in bad weather. However, today there are three marinas, and facilities for pleasure craft have greatly improved. Although still primarily a Naval Port, with considerable commercial traffic, including regular ferries to Brittany and Spain, and a busy fishing fleet, Plymouth has also come into its own as a yachting centre and focus for a number of major events, including the Single and Double Handed Transatlantic races, the Round Britain and the finishing point for the Fastnet.

Approaches
Certainly, there are no natural problems in the approaches to this vast harbour bounded on the east by the Great Mewstone and Rame Head to the west, with ample deep water for small craft throughout. The hazards are entirely man-made, with shipping the main consideration, and much Naval activity in and around the port. Under the jurisdiction of the Queen's Harbour Master, all movements are controlled by the Longroom, the nerve centre located in a tower just to the west of the entrance to Millbay Docks, VHF Call Sign 'Longroom Port Control', Channel 16, 08, 12, 14. Traffic signals are flown from the Longroom, the most important being a red flag with a white diagonal stripe signifying that shipping traffic is stopped between the Sound and the Hamoaze, the stretch of water running inland to the west of the city where the Naval dockyards are situated. Invariably this will mean that a large vessel is entering or leaving, its manoeuvrability greatly restricted in the narrow channel, and all other vessels must keep clear. Large

Queen Anne's Battery Marina and Sutton Harbour Marina, beyond, are close to the main centre of Plymouth

Although removed from the City centre, Plymouth's Mayflower Marina is completely self contained, providing everything a visiting yacht might require

vessels, and particularly the Naval craft have right of way at all times; in practice, there is no reason why small vessels should get embroiled with big ship movements in Plymouth as for the most part there is no need to follow any of the buoyed channels. Keep well clear, and let common sense and good seamanship prevail.

Hazard number two is the HMS *Cambridge* gunnery range at Wembury which fires to seawards, usually from 0930-1230, 1330-1600 Tuesdays to Fridays, and when active five large red flags are flown at Wembury Point and one on Penlee Point; involving anything from 20mm to 4½ inch shells, the firing is also very audible. The outer limits of the range to the west are just east of the Eddystone light, and to the East Rutts DZ buoy to the east, covering a sector of 130° to 245°T, extending approximately 13 miles to seawards, although the main surface targets, usually large orange floats towed by RAF launches tend to be 6-7 miles offshore; air targets, towed behind light aircraft approach from 7 miles to within 1 mile. Yachts, inevitably, pose a major problem, their presence often delaying firing and their co-operation is greatly appreciated if they can ideally avoid the range altogether or, if on passage, keep close inshore and proceed as fast as possible to clear the area. The range monitors VHF Channel 16, and works on 11, 12 and 14, and it helps them considerably if you can call 'Wembury Range' to identify yourself and advise of your destination. If there seems to be nothing happening although the red flags are up, it means they are hoping to fire and it could just be that it's you that's stopping them. If you wish to phone for firing details, ring Plymouth (0752) 553740, ext Cambridge 412.

The large open roadstead of Plymouth Sound was transformed as a fleet anchorage by the completion of Sir John Rennie's central breakwater in 1841. Just under a mile long, it consumed 4½ million tons of materials, and took 29 years to build. Entry is easy round either end; from the east, after passing the Great Mewstone the Shagstone, a rock marked with a white beacon, is the only hazard on the eastern shore, and it is quite safe to pass between this and the port and starboard buoys to seaward which mark the entrance to the deep water of the eastern channel; further west, the Tinker Shoal, least depth 3.5m is marked by a west

cardinal buoy YBY (Q (9) 15sec) marked 'West Tinker'. Although normally not a problem, seas break on this shoal in southerly weather, when the western entrance is far better. The eastern breakwater end is marked by a pyramid surmounted by beacon with round ball topmark (Occ (2) R 10sec).

From the west, once past Rame Head, keep to seaward of the 'Draystone' red can (Fl (2) R 5sec), south-east of Penlee Point and then steer straight for the lighthouse on the western end of the breakwater (FlWR 10, Iso 4secs over sector 031-039°T). However, in daytime, from well offshore the breakwater ends are not immediately easy to spot; the large round fort in the centre is far more conspicuous.

On the port hand is Cawsand Bay, an excellent anchorage in south-west and westerly weather, off the pleasant twin villages of Cawsand and Kingsand. This is a handy overnight stop on passage along the coast avoiding the detour into Plymouth; anchor anywhere clear of the local moorings where there is about 2.5m LAT and good holding. Ashore there are a couple of pubs, general store, a Post Office and a useful summer ferry service into the centre of Plymouth.

From offshore, the most distinctive features are the large grain silo by Millbay Docks (rather like a huge white cathedral), and Drake's Island to the west, the large square hotel building in the centre, and to the east, two tall power station chimneys on the River Plym, and the high ground of Staddon Heights, topped with radio masts. On either side of the Sound, just inside the breakwater are two prominent forts, Picklecombe on the western shore, now luxury flats, and Bovisand, opposite, the British Sub-Aqua Club diving training centre. Two of 'Palmerston's Follies' they were built as part of a chain along the south coast in the nineteenth century in anticipation of a French invasion that never materialised.

Moorings and anchorages

The thing to decide early is where you intend to berth, as Mayflower International Marina is to the west of the town centre, Sutton Harbour and Queen Anne's Battery Marinas to the east. The other alternatives depend very much on the prevailing weather conditions — either anchoring, or picking up a mooring.

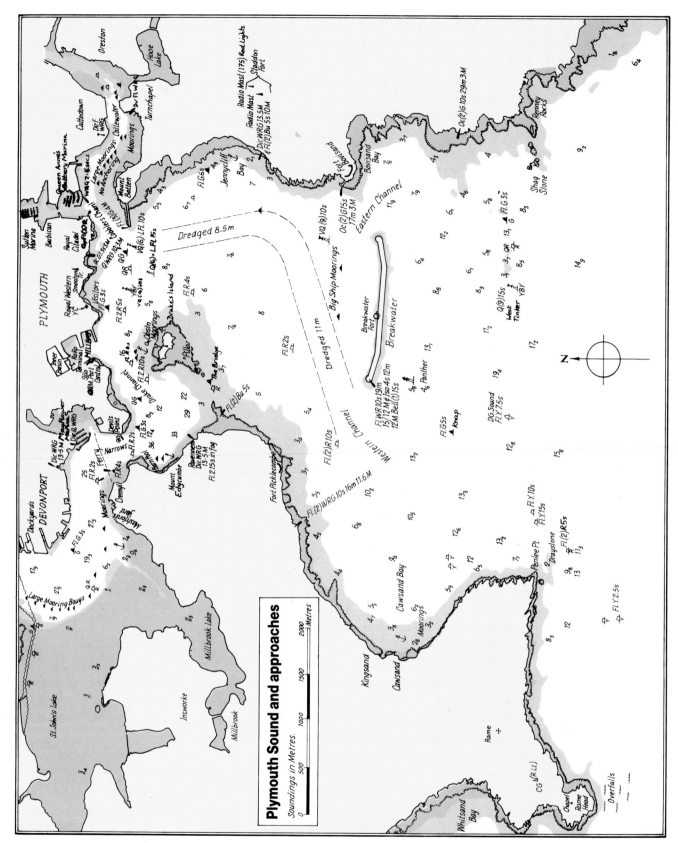

Plymouth Sound and approaches

Soundings in Metres.

0   500   1000   1500   2000   Metres

The approaches to Plymouth are wide and safe but beware of Naval and commercial shipping

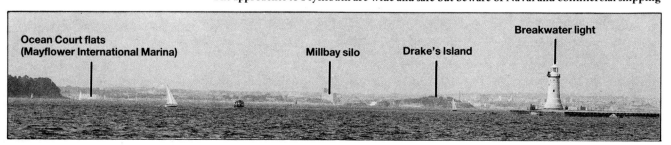

**Ocean Court flats
(Mayflower International Marina)**

Millbay silo

Drake's Island

Breakwater light

The flats at Ocean Court from an unmistakable backdrop to the Mayflower International Marina

The anchorages in the Sound are all free, but suffer from the disadvantage that they are remote from the centre of Plymouth. Jennycliff Bay, protected by Staddon Heights, provides good shelter in easterly weather, sounding in to about 2m at LW. Both Drake's Island and Barn Pool provide shelter in west or south-westerly conditions, and can be approached either by the main deepwater channel round to the east of Drake's Island, or, an hour or so after LW, west of it, using the short cut across the 'Bridge'. Shallows lie on both sides of this narrow passage, and on them dangerous remains of wartime concrete obstructions and dolphins. However, between them there is 1.7m LAT, and the channel is clearly marked to port by a red can, W Bridge and a green conical buoy E. Bridge to starboard. Ahead, the white post just east of Devils Point beacon in line with the west side of the yellow house with three chimneys on the distant shore provides a useful transit of 332°T. At springs, the stream can run through the Bridge at 3 knots, and unless you have a fair wind proceed under power; if at all in doubt use Drake's Channel.

Once through the Bridge, Barn Pool lies to port on the Mount Edgcumbe shore. Sound in to the northern end of the bay, inside the large mooring buoy, where the deep water carries close to the rocky beach, but as there are many underwater obstructions, a trip line is essential. Although eddies extend into the pool at times here you will lie comfortably out of the main tidal stream.

This is a delightfully peaceful spot surrounded by the magnificent woods and grasslands of the 800 acre Mount Edgcumbe Country Park which is open to the public daily, along with Mount Edgcumbe house, a restored Tudor mansion, and there is also a fine coastal footpath to Cawsand.

From here it is possible to walk through the park or, two hours after HW, along the foreshore to Cremyll where there is a good pub and the famous Mashford Boatyard where Chichester and Rose both fitted out for their circumnavigations and many other famous long voyages have begun. A family business run by six brothers this traditional yard has an outstanding reputation for wooden building and repairs. A passenger ferry runs from Cremyll to Stonehouse,

where there are buses into the centre of Plymouth.

The only other feasible anchorage lies north-east of Drake's Island, east of the pier, but clear of the underwater obstruction, least depth 0.9m 400m due north of the pier. Reasonable shelter will be found in south-westerly winds although the proximity to the busy main channel can make it rolly at times. Once known as St Nicholas's Island this is traditionally where Sir Francis Drake lay with his battered *Golden Hinde* on the return from his circumnavigation in 1580 cautiously waiting for news of the political climate that might greet him. Crown Property leased to the City of Plymouth, the island is used today as an adventure training centre for young people.

Swinging moorings for visitors are few and far between in Plymouth. A few lie at the west end of the Hoe off the Sir Francis Drake Pub — formerly the Royal Western Yacht Club. They can be hired from the pub for about £5 a night and landing is convenient at the small boat harbour in front of it. There are also a few moorings in the Cattewater available through the RWYC, the Royal Plymouth Corinthian Yacht Club and Queen Anne's Battery on application.

The Mayflower International Marina

With few moorings or anchorages and a choice of three marinas most visitors to Plymouth tend to opt for the convenience — and expense — of one of the latter! The Mayflower International Marina, the only one in the south-west to be awarded Five Gold Anchors by the National Yacht Harbours Association, lies to the west of Plymouth, and is approached either by the Bridge if conditions permit, or along the deep and well-lit Drake's Channel leaving the W Vanguard (Fl G 3secs) green conical buoy to starboard and through the narrows between Cremyll and the yellow and white beacon on Devils Point (QG). From here the modern buildings of Ocean Court and the forest of masts in the marina are unmistakable — either call ahead on VHF Channel M (foreign yachts 80) for a berth allocation and proceed straight to it or tie up in the reception berth on the outer pontoon which is clearly marked between the striped flags and go to the office for instructions. At night the marina has an approach light (Dir Q WRG) and the south-eastern end of the outer pontoons is marked by (2 FR (vert)).

Much of the Mayflower's success has undoubtedly been due to the fact that it is owned by a consortium of its bertholders. It has a particularly relaxed, quiet and friendly atmosphere, and as a popular stop for long distance cruisers, a genuinely International flavour. Although its position away from the main centre of Plymouth would seem to be a disadvantage it is in fact quite self-contained and the facilities are excellent, with a grocery, chandlery, restaurant, off-license, showers, toilet, and a clubhouse/bar which welcomes visitors. During the season a courtesy bus runs daily into the centre of Plymouth and other services include fuel, water, gas and electricity; weatherfax, marine and electronic engineers, rigging, divers, a crane and 25 ton travelift, and the very good 24 hour security makes it an ideal place to leave a boat for longer periods of time with special rates available.

There are 250 deepwater berths taking up to 34m LOA and 4m draught, with about 30 for visitors although even at the height of the season they always manage to fit you in somehow! Charges for a 26-30 foot boat work out at £9.90 a night (inc. VAT and electricity) 31-40 foot £12.65 with no surcharge for multihulls.

Approaches to Queen Anne's Battery, Sutton Harbour and the Cattewater.

Approaching from seawards and passing to the east of Drake's Island, Plymouth Hoe runs east west, a high grassy slope with the old Eddystone lighthouse, banded horizontally red and white and the tall obelisk of the war memorial both prominent. At its eastern end the large fortress of the Royal Citadel and the Royal Plymouth Corinthian Yacht Club beneath it overlook the western side of the entrance to the Cattewater and Sutton Harbour. The RPCYC has some visitors' moorings in the Cattewater available on application and visitors are made welcome at the club which is open daily 1100-1400, 1900-2230 (except Monday and Sunday evenings) when showers, bar and snacks are available.

Directly opposite, Mount Batten, an isolated hill and home of the RAF base, forms the eastern side of the entrance with a breakwater extending towards an outwardly confusing cluster of buoys marking the deep water channel and a large dolphin on the Mallard Shoal, least depth 3.5m, which has a triangular white topmark surmounted by a sectored light (QWRG). The white sector forms the lower leading mark for the main channel, the upper mark is a light on the Hoe (OccG), giving a transit of 349°T. In practice there is no need for small craft to follow this line; pass between the South Mallard YB south cardinal buoy (VQ (6) + Fl 10secs) and the end of Mount Batten breakwater (2FG(vert)) and into the Cobbler Channel. Ahead, a long wall of vertical piling surrounds Queen Anne's Battery Marina and both this and Sutton Harbour are entered past Fisher's Nose, a granite quay on the western shore with 'Speed Limit 8 knots to the east' painted on it and a light (Fl (3) R). You must proceed

under power beyond Fisher's Nose as it is always a busy corner; most of the large trip boats operate from here, it is the entrance to two marinas and the fishing harbour . . .

The River Plym continues eastwards, and its mouth, known as the Cattewater, is commercial and busy with coaster traffic and administered separately by the Cattewater Harbour Commissioners. Due to the local congestion, anchoring is prohibited within the Cattewater and a road bridge at Laira a mile upstream with 5m clearance effectively closes the river to yachts. Other than a need to visit one of the boatyards at Turnchapel, being mostly industrial it has nothing of interest to visitors and is best avoided.

Queen Anne's Battery Marina

Keep to the starboard side of the channel and follow the marina breakwater to enter, watching out for and giving way to boats emerging as they have priority. At night there are three lights displayed on the breakwater (Occ 7.5secs WRG) on the south side — the white sector giving the approach through the Cobbler channel, (Occ G) on the south-western corner, and (QG) on the breakwater end.

Opened in 1986 this is the newest marina in Plymouth and they can be contacted on VHF Channel M to reserve a berth. Sixty are normally available for visitors most of which lie alongside a continuous pontoon on the inside of the breakwater — the finger piers are reserved for permanent bertholders — and at the height of the season you will probably have to raft up. If you have no VHF berth here and check in at the marina office.

The marina gets its name from the fact that it was formerly the site of a gun emplacement built during the Napoleonic War. Today there are comprehensive facilities, including a grocery, chandler, a good maritime bookshop and many other marine orientated businesses from liferaft repairs to stainless steel fabrication, diving air to sailmakers. There is water and electricity on the pontoons, diesel and petrol are available from the fuel barge at the entrance and there are showers toilets, a launderette, cafe and clubhouse/bar. There is also a large slipway and 18 ton travel hoist for repairs and charges for visitors are 30p per

Approaching Sutton Harbour from the Sound pass between the South Mallard buoy and Mountbatten Breakwater end

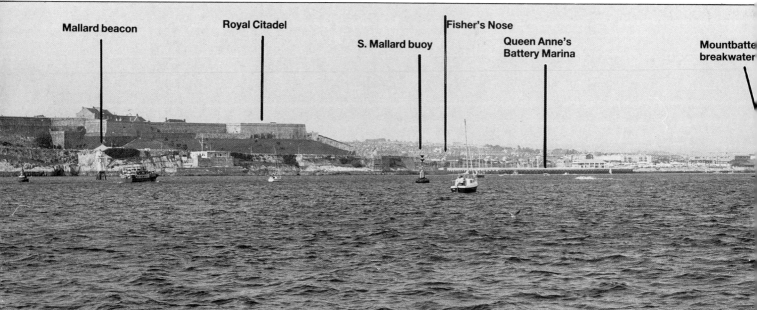

Mallard beacon   Royal Citadel   S. Mallard buoy   Fisher's Nose   Queen Anne's Battery Marina   Mountbatte breakwater

sher's Nose   **Sutton Harbour entrance**   **Fuel Barge**   **Queen Anne's Battery**

Marina entrance

The entrance to Sutton
Harbour is always busy with
ferries and pleasure craft —
yachts must proceed under
power beyond Fishers' Nose

foot per day (plus VAT) with no surcharge for multihulls.

In early 1989 the prestigious Royal Western Yacht Club of England moved to its smart new premises within the marina, after 25 years at its former location at the west end of the Hoe, now the Sir Francis Drake Pub. The enthusiasm of the marina's Managing Director Mark Gatehouse — himself a well-known multihull racer — has established Queen Anne's Battery (QAB) as a major venue for international yachting events, most of which are organised by the RWYC, such as the 'Round Britain and Ireland Race', Fastnet finish, 'Twostar' and, of course, the 'Singlehanded Transatlantic' and this will now make scrutineering and hosting these events much more convenient for all concerned.

The fifth oldest club in England, founded in 1827, the RWYC has a few visitors' moorings in the Cattewater available on application at around £5 a night and visitors are welcome to use the club which is open 0900 — 2300 with showers, bar and restaurant.

During the big race events space at QAB is inevitably at a premium and it is unlikely that you will find a berth without a prior booking. Another slight drawback to the marina is its position opposite the main nautical centre of Plymouth, the Barbican, and the rest of town. The surrounding hinterland is rather run down and industrial, a long and not very prepossessing walk; it is possible to dinghy over and land by the Mayflower Sailing Club which also welcomes visitors with a bar and showers available, but by far the simplest solution is the marina water taxi at 50p a head which lands and picks up near the Mayflower Steps.

The Barbican

Here, you step immediately into the bustling and historic area of the Barbican, the tourist centre of Plymouth, and a particular magnet for the American visitors flocking to see the spot where the Pilgrim Fathers reputedly embarked aboard *Mayflower* and sailed for the New World in 1620. The Naval City of

Plymouth was blitzed more heavily than anywhere else in Britain during the last war, and tragically, large areas were completely destroyed. The Barbican, alone, remains as an outstanding example of what this medieval city was like before 1941, a maze of intricate narrow streets, and fine examples of Tudor buildings, many of them now shops, restaurants and pubs in this interesting and attractive area surrounding Sutton Pool. Several are museums, including the Elizabethan House, in New Street, and nearby, the sixteenth century Merchant's House in St Andrew's Street which houses the Museum of Plymouth History, open weekdays 1000-1300, 1415-1730, 1700 on Saturdays. Another more recent tourist attraction are the two large murals close to Blackfriars Ope, the controversial works of a local artist.

Sutton Marina

Sutton Harbour, is, however, not totally the haunt of the holidaymakers for it is the busy base for the Plymouth fishing fleet, and also a large number of sea-angling boats. Privately owned by the Sutton Harbour Improvement Company, the harbour is entered between the narrow pier heads (FlR) and (FlG), which mark its limits and vessels leaving have priority. To port lie the fishmarket and quays, dead ahead the Sutton Marina. Depths in the harbour, and approach to the marina are dredged to 2m below LAT and the visitors' arrival berth is clearly marked on the outer end, adjacent to the fuel pontoon. At night the eastern end of the outer pontoon displays a (QR) light.

With a total of 310 berths, Sutton Marina was the first in Plymouth and, subject to availability, can accommodate between 25 and 30 visitors, although, generally, these are limited to boats not much larger than 10m LOA. As elsewhere, it is best to call ahead during the season. The new Port Control office is located right at the end of Sutton Pier, overlooking the fuel pontoon and a 24 hour VHF watch is maintained on Channels 16, and M, call sign Sutton Harbour Radio. On site facilities are not quite as comprehensive as the other marinas, but there is a shower, toilet and

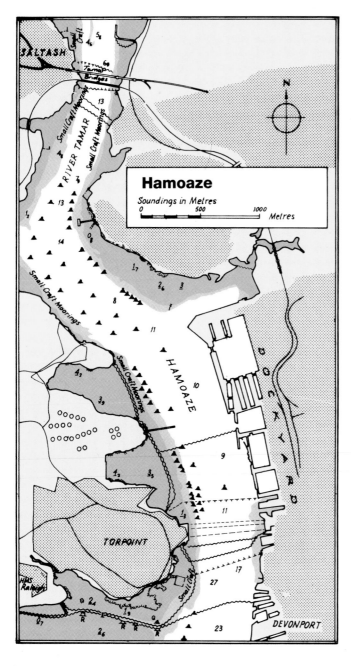

redbrick, and architecturally unimaginative, with wide boulevards, and rather demanding shopping precincts; somehow one feels a lot of opportunity was lost in the rebuilding. The main line railway station to London and the North lies to the north of the main centre, within easy walking distance, and the Bretonside bus and coach station lies between the Barbican and the city centre.

However, in contrast to the mundanity of mid-twentieth century planners, the seafront is a grand spectacle. It is a short walk from the Barbican, following Madeira Road up past the Citadel, and the elevated promenade winds beneath the grassy slopes of the Hoe, overlooking the rocky foreshore and cliffs below, which are dotted with bathing platforms, pathways, and the large open air swimming pool.

Climbing higher on to the open space of the Hoe, the views across the Sound from this natural grandstand are magnificent, and even more so if you pay an extra 25p to climb to the top of Smeaton's former Eddystone lighthouse, built in 1759, dismantled in 1882, and rebuilt on the Hoe in 1884.

The Hoe, bowls and Sir Francis Drake will forever remain synonymous, a seemingly remarkable display of sang-froid, contentedly playing on as the vast Spanish Armada sailed unchallenged into the Channel. Far more a seaman than a bowls player, Drake, of course, knew only too well that his ungainly ships could not leave the Sound against the head wind until the ebb began.

The Hamoaze and beyond

One of the real advantages of Plymouth if the weather turns against you is the great potential for exploring further inland along the Rivers Tamar and Lynher. Heading west past the Hoe, Millbay Docks, with its conspicuous silo is commercial and of no interest to visitors. It is the terminal for the RoRo ferries to Roscoff and Santander, and care should be taken to avoid these large vessels entering and leaving. Beyond the Narrows and the Mayflower International Marina you enter the wide Hamoaze, its eastern shore lined with the extensive Royal Naval dockyards at Devonport established by King William III in 1691. This is always a fascinating stretch of water particularly for the younger crew members as there are invariably a variety of warships and submarines berthed along the quays. For the Skipper, however, it is a more demanding exercise as it is usually busy and a careful eye should be kept on other ship movements; remember, too, that civilian craft are not permitted to pass within 50 metres of military vessels, Crown Property or enter the Dockyard basins. The large figurehead of the founder, King William III, at the southern end of the dockyards is known locally as 'King Billy'. Behind him, the large covered slipway is the oldest in any of the Royal dockyards, and as you pass upstream, the first group of three huge sheds is the undercover frigate repair facility, the next massive building with a very large crane is the complex where Britain's nuclear submarines are refitted.

Large chain ferries link Devonport with Torpoint

launderette, and 24 hour security. A number of marine businesses, including electronic engineers and chandlery are located on Sutton Pier beside the marina; shops and all the facilities of the Barbican are a short walk around the quayside. Water, petrol and diesel are all available daily 0730-2100 in summer; daylight hours, winter. Charges for a 30-footer are £10 per night, inclusive of VAT, with reduced rates for longer stays. Close by on the eastern side of the Harbour is the comprehensive boatyard of Harbour Marine, with a 25-ton crane, slipway and full repair facilities available.

The City of Plymouth

Within ten minutes' easy walk from the Barbican, the city centre of Plymouth, with a population of over 250,000, can obviously provide anything that might be required. The post-war redevelopment of the main shopping area surrounding Royal Parade is mostly

Visitors to Queen Anne's Battery Marina berth alongside the inside of the breakwater.

on the Cornish bank and, until 1962 when the Tamar road bridge was opened at Saltash, a mile further upstream, this was the only road link across the river. The ferries have right of way; if in doubt always pass astern and give them a good berth.

St Germans River

The Lynher, or St Germans River is the first opportunity to get away from the bustle of the Hamoaze, and its wide mouth opens to port, upstream of the dockyards, beyond the large warship moorings. The river dries extensively, but on the tide is navigable for four miles to the private quay at St Germans where it is possible for bilge keelers to dry out and occasionally it is possible to lie alongside by arrangement.

There are a few buoys in the lower part of the river; red cans should all be left to port and conical green buoys to starboard. The channel enters along the northern side, past Wearde Quay, where there are local moorings, and the first two port hand buoys clear Beggar's Island, a gravelly shoal awash at HWS on the southern side of the entrance. Just east of Sand Acre Point and the first green buoy, there is an anchorage, but the proximity of the main line railway tends to disturb the potential peace. The channel trends south to avoid the spit extending from the northern shore marked by another green buoy, passing a number of moorings belonging to the RN School of Seamanship at Jupiter Point, a wooded promontory with a jetty and pontoons. The next red buoy is close to the northern shore, off Anthony Passage, where there is a pub, and it is possible to anchor off the mouth of Forder Lake. West of Forder Lake as far as the next creek, Wivelscombe Lake, an underwater power cable and gas pipeline cross the river and anchoring is not advisable.

Ince Point, the western side of Wivelscombe Lake is surmounted by Ince Castle and south of it there is another anchorage in about 3m LAT. At high tide this is a broad expanse of water, surrounded by lush fields and gently rolling hills, peaceful and unspoiled, with very little evidence of human intrusion. However, from here on depths reduce considerably, with generally less than 1m LAT and drying banks are extensive on both shores. The various salty creeks are ideal for dinghy exploration, but on the flood, with an eye on the sounder, the river should be explored further, for the best is yet to come. Keep close to the next green buoy off Black Rock Point, where the channel narrows considerably, and at the next red can the shores ahead close, becoming steep and wooded

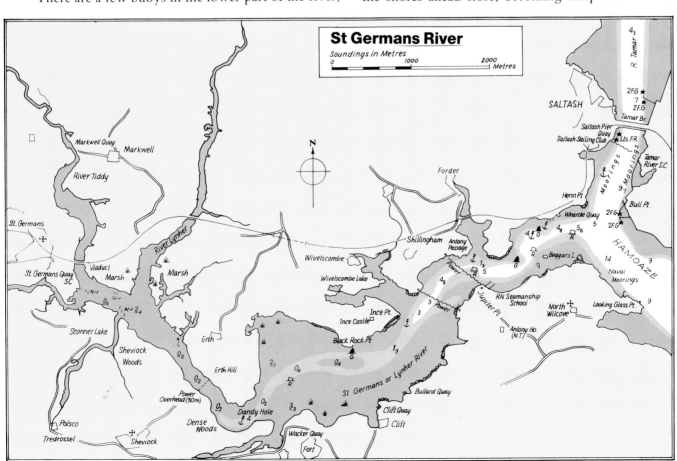

along Warren Point, and the river disappearing as it turns tightly behind the rounded slope of Erth Hill. Here, just on the bend, is a superbly isolated anchorage in Dandy Hole, just west of Warren Point, a fortuitous pool where there is 3m at lowest tides. Surrounded by the high woods, this is as peaceful a spot as you are likely to find, well sheltered and totally away from it all.

From Dandy Hole to St Germans the river effectively dries completely, the wooded shores opening out again and the twisting channel is marked by R/W posts to port, G/W to starboard, swinging from the eastern shore above Erth Hill to the western off Sconner Lake, north, then west again towards St Germans Quay dwarfed beneath the railway viaduct across the river.

There are a number of drying moorings off the private quay, and other local boats berth alongside on the soft mud. Downstream of the old warehouse buildings no berthing is allowed, but upstream, where the St Germans Quay Sailing Club is based, space can sometimes be found for an overnight stay by arrangement with the club. The Club bar is open Wednesday and Saturday evenings, Sunday lunchtime and water is also available. It is a peaceful corner, just a few cottages and the old grassy quayside disturbed only by the rumble of the trains overhead. There is a tap on the Quay; the village is about half-a-mile away where there are basic provisions, pub and a Post Office. Occasional trains run to and from Plymouth.

River Tamar

The Tamar, however, is altogether a far bigger proposition for it is twelve miles to Calstock, and ideally a full flood tide is needed. In the narrow upper reaches the streams run strongly, particularly on the ebb, in excess of 5 knots when the river is in spate. Due to the current, and the amount of debris, trees, branches, etc., in these circumstances such a trip is not recommended.

Today, the river is a tranquil place, a quiet rural waterway that betrays little indication of its former importance as one of the busiest industrial areas in the West Country. Extensive granite quarries, and rich tin, copper, silver and arsenic mines in the upper reaches were all serviced from the sea, with large sailing schooners, ketches and barges plying far inland. Apart from a few overgrown and derelict quays, it is now difficult to imagine such a hive of maritime activity; fortunately, the heritage has not been totally lost; at Cothele, far upstream, there is a restored Tamar barge and a museum, and Morwellham, almost at the head of navigation is a former Victorian port that has been restored as a tourist attraction.

Above the Lynher, the channel is broad and deep past Saltash on the western shore, beneath the twin road and rail bridges. The latter, yet another of Isambard Kingdom Brunel's remarkable achievements, took seven years to build and was opened in 1859 to carry the Great Western Railway from London into Cornwall.

There are many local moorings off Saltash, and a small quay where it is possible to land, although there is little really to interest the visitor. Continuing upstream beyond the bridges on the eastern shore is Ernesettle Pier, an MOD munitions depot, and the two long lines of Admiralty trot moorings running upstream with barges upon them lie on either side of the main channel.

A line of four green conical buoys marks the eastern bank, and the northernmost, marked 'Neil Point' in orange letters, lies off the entrance to the River Tavy. Sadly this attractive tributary is closed to sailing boats by the railway bridge across its mouth with 7.6m clearance; the river dries almost completely at LW, but power boats or dinghies can explore it on the tide, as

Well away from it all, Dandy Hole is a tranquil anchorage in the unspoiled St German's River

Space is very limited at St German's Quay; best to anchor downstream at Dandy Hole and explore by dinghy to check the channel and see if a berth is available

far as Bere Ferrers, where there is a pub and limited provisions.

Between the buoy and Neil Point, on the western shore, is a drying bank. Keep close to the starboard side of the channel, before steering north to Weir Point, a wooded promontory where a large overhead power line crosses the river. Almost directly beneath it, the channel is marked by a post with a square red topmark to port, and a yellow conical buoy to starboard. Ahead lies the small village of Cargreen, with a number of local moorings which indicate the deeper water.

Cargreen

Before the first world war Cargreen was still a major crossing point for the Tamar but the growth of motor traffic resulted in the enlargement of the Torpoint ferries, and the decline of Cargreen. Today it is another peaceful village, not much more than a single street running down to the quay. There is a Post Office, closed on Tuesday afternoons, and a general store which closes on Friday afternoons. Anchor clear of the local moorings where there is about 2m LAT, and no charges. Land just up river of the Spaniards Inn by the Cargreen Yacht Club which has no facilities for visitors, and no fuel or water is available.

Beyond the moorings the channel is marked on the starboard side by a green beacon with a triangular topmark, and it is a straight run northwards to the distant moorings off Weir Quay, which lie on both sides of the deeper water. Here, there is a boatyard, with visitors moorings, fuel and showers.

Keep close to the wooded shore beyond Holes Hole, where there is an old quay and several hulks. Follow the low cliffs right round the outside of this bend as the bank extending from the south shore is very shallow, and the moorings lie along its edge. From here onwards, between March and September, salmon netsmen will be encountered and care should be taken to pass slowly, keeping a lookout for the nets extending from the banks. As the extensive reed beds come abeam to starboard head across to the southern shore, and again hold close to the steep woods.

Continuing upstream, with the exception of a few deeper pools, there is less than 1.5m LAT, the river narrows considerably, and winds almost back on itself. The channel is not marked, but generally the deepest water lies along the outside of the bends.

Large excursion boats run regular day cruises from Plymouth to Calstock depending on the tides and if encountered in these upper reaches there is not a great deal of water to spare. Less manoeuvrable, too, their skippers appreciate it greatly if you can pull over to let them pass.

The channel continues to follow the western bank with Pentillie Castle looking down from the hillside and past Halton Quay with a curious building rather like a railway signal box that is, in fact, one of the smallest chapels in England. Bearing across the eastern shore past extensive reedbeds, upstream, there is a prominent house with two gables, and on the bank a post with triangular white topmark which should be kept in line with the left hand gable to hold the channel. Beyond the post, the deeper water swings back to the western bank, then midstream as Cothele Quay appears.

Cothele Quay

With sufficient water it is possible to berth temporarily alongside the quay which has been preserved by the National Trust as part of the Cothele estate, and is home for the restored Tamar barge *Shamrock*. A 57ft ketch this vessel was built in 1899 and is co-owned by the National Maritime Museum, the only surviving example of the barges that were once an essential element in the life of the waterway, and during the summer she is occasionally sailed by enthusiasts. There is a small museum on the quay devoted to the maritime history of the river, and about ten minutes walk from the quay Cothele House, a splendid Tudor mansion and gardens are open daily April–October, 1100–1800.

Calstock

Past the moorings off the Quay, the prominent building of the Danescombe Hotel with its elegant veranda stands on the hillside above the final sharp bend into the Calstock reach, and as the reed beds open to starboard, beyond them the viaduct will come into view. A line of moorings lies in the centre of the channel off Calstock Boatyard on the port hand bank; some of these are sometimes available for visitors drawing up to 1m but it is best to phone ahead to enquire. Deeper draught boats may be able to dry out alongside their small quay, where diesel is available.

Because of the moorings, the poor holding, and the narrow channel used by the pleasure boats, anchoring is not recommended downstream of the viaduct, and the only feasible place for a visitor to stop is beyond it, just upstream of the pleasure boat landing pontoon, where there is a pool with just over 2m LAT.

Once the busiest port in the upper Tamar, looking at Calstock today it all seems inconceivable; the quays where ships lay two or three abreast have mostly crumbled into disrepair, and the attractive cluster of cottages and small Georgian houses clinging to the steep roads up the hillside betray little evidence of their busy past. On the opposite shore, now lost in the reeds and sedge, the famous shipyard of James Goss was building large wooden vessels as late as 1909 when the last, the ketch *Garlandstone* was launched, and she is still afloat today. If you need proof, or an excuse for a pint, go and take a look at the photographs in the pub.

Most normal facilities are available, including two pubs and a restaurant; petrol at the garage, and a branch of Lloyds bank open Mondays only, 1000-1230. There are also trains to Plymouth.

Beyond Calstock the river becomes much narrower, very shallow and tortuous, and is best explored further only by dinghy, or small, shallow draught boats. Morwellham, just over two miles upstream, is a monument to the industrial past of the Tamar, a former copper port restored by the Dartington Amenity Trust. Open daily during the season as a tourist attraction, it is even possible to take a train ride deep into one of the old copper mines.

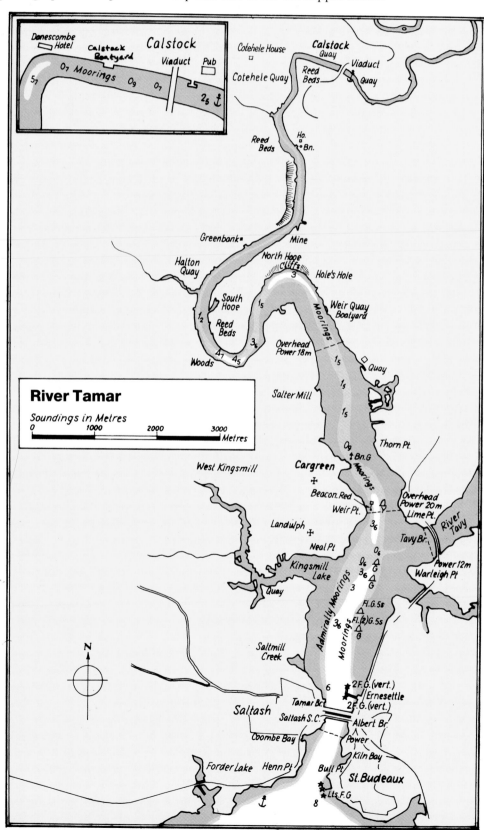

Boatyard

Fairway

In the peaceful upper Tamar visitors' moorings and showers are available at Weir Quay

Port guide — Plymouth

Harbourmaster: Captain J D Lock, RN, Queen's Harbourmaster, HM Naval Base, Plymouth (553005). Assistant QHM, Longroom, Stonehouse, Plymouth PL1 3RT (663225). Cattewater Harbour Master, Commander Anthony Dyer, 2 The Barbican, Plymouth PL1 2LR (665934)

Sutton Harbourmaster, Mr Pat Marshall, Harbour Office, Guy's Quay, Sutton Harbour, Plymouth (Tel: 0752 664186

VHF: Longroom Port Control, Ch 16, 08, 12, 14. Cattewater Harbour Office, 16, 12, 14, M (Mon — Fri 0900 — 1700). Sutton Harbour Radio, 16, 12, 14, M. See marinas

Mail drop: All marinas will hold mail. Royal Western YC. Royal Plymouth Corinthian YC.

Emergency services: Lifeboat at Plymouth. Coastguard (Tel: 0752 822239).

Customs: Custom House, The Parade, Plymouth PL1 2JP (Tel: 0752 662091)

Anchorages: Cawsand Bay. Off Jennycliff. Barn Pool. Drake's Island. St Germans and Tamar Rivers

Moorings: RWYC/RPCYC visitors' moorings, Weir Quay

Dinghy landings: RPCYC

Water taxi: Queen Anne's Battery Marina — Mayflower Steps

Marinas: Queen Anne's Battery Marina, Coxside (Tel: 0752 671142). Visitors' berths available. VHF Channel M. Sutton Harbour Marina, Sutton Harbour (Tel: 0752 664186). Visitors' berths available. VHF continuous Channel M. Mayflower International Marina, Ocean Quay, Richmond Walk PL1 4LS (Tel: 0752 556633). Visitors' berths available. VHF continuous Channel M

Charges: None for anchoring. RWYC mooring £5 per night. Weir Quay £2/night plus VAT. Average charge per night for 30 footer, inc. VAT: Queen Anne's Battery £10.30; Sutton Harbour £10; Mayflower Marina £9.90

Phones: At all marinas; Barbican, Yacht Clubs

Doctor: (Tel: 0752 53533)

Hospital: Freedom Fields (Tel: 0752 668080)

Churches: All denominations

Local weather forecast: At all marinas. Weather fax at Mayflower International Marina

Fuel: Diesel and petrol at Queen Anne's Battery, Mayflower Marina, Sutton Harbour Marina, Mashfords Boatyard, Cremyll. Diesel only at Calstock Boatyard and Weir Quay

Paraffin: Mayflower Marina. Queen Anne's Battery

Gas: Calor/Camping Gaz, Mayflower Marina, Queen Anne Marine, Queen Anne's Battery

Water: At all marinas and Yacht Clubs. Calstock Boatyard and Weir Quay

Tourist information office: The Barbican, opposite fishmarket

Banks/cashpoints: All main banks in City centre have cashpoint facilities

Post Office: The Barbican. Main PO in City centre, St Andrew's Cross

Rubbish: All marinas have disposal facilities

Showers/toilets: At all marinas for visitors, and also at RWYC, RPCYC, MSC. Public toilets on Barbican, Weir Quay

Launderettes: At all marinas

Provisions/half day closing: Everything obtainable. EC Wednesday but most shops open in season. Many shops open on Sundays

Chandler: Cloads, 13 Barbican (Tel: 0752 663722). Yacht Parts Plymouth, 7 Stokes Lane, Barbican (Tel: 0752 663352). Queen Anne Marine, Queen Anne's Battery (Tel: 0752 670870). AE Monson, Vauxhall Quay, Sutton Harbour, Admiralty Chart Agents and bonded stores (Tel: 0752 665384). Sutton Marine, Sutton Pier (Tel: 0752 662129). Ocean Marine Services, 43 Bretonside (Tel: 0752 23922) and also at Mayflower Marina (Tel: 0752 500977). Vosper Marine, Sutton Road, Sutton Harbour (Tel: 0752 228569)

Repairs: Mashford Bros, Cremyll (Tel: 0752 822232). Harbour Marine, Sutton Road (Tel: 0752 666330). Mobile Marine Services, Queen Anne's Battery (Tel: 0752 268677). K R Skentelberry & Son, Laira Bridge Boatyard, Plymstock (Tel: 0752 42385). Island Marine, The Quay, Turnchapel (Tel: 0752 42863). A Blagdon, Richmond Walk (Tel: 0752 561830). A S Blagdon & Sons, Embankment Road (Tel: 0752 228155). Ron Greet Yacht Services, Turnchapel Marine (Tel: 0752 42969). Eddystone Marine Services, Richmond Walk (Tel: 0752 568223). Weir Quay Boatyard, Weir Quay, (Tel: 0822 840474). Calstock Boatyard (Tel: 0822 832502)

Marine engineers: Mobile Marine Services (Tel: 0752 2686677). Queen Anne Marine (Tel: 0752 670870). Chacewood Engine Services (Tel: 0752 265143). All at Queen Anne's Battery. Marine engineer at Mayflower Marina, Mashfords, Cremyll

Electronic engineers: Greenham Marine (Tel: 0752 228114). Marconi Marine (Tel: 0752 665759). Commercial Marine and Electrical (Tel: 0752 673387). Oreston Electrical (Tel: 0752 44929). All at Queen Anne's Battery. Sutton Marine, Sutton Jetty (Tel: 0752 662129). Ocean Marine Services, Mayflower Marina (Tel: 0752 500977). Electronics Afloat, mobile service (Tel: 0752 335727)

Sailmakers/repairs: The Sail Locker, Queen Anne's Battery (Tel: 0752 670156). Clements, Richmond Walk (Tel: 0752 562465)

Riggers: Sutton Rigging, Sutton Road (Tel: 0752 269756). Peter Lucas, Mayflower International Marina (Tel: 0752 551099)

Communications: Regular main line trains and bus services to London and the North. Good road connections to M5 motorway at Exeter. Plymouth airport, regular flights to London and Continent. Ferries to Roscoff and Santander

Car hire: All main agencies

Car parking: Large amount of car parks. All marinas have customer car parking

Yacht clubs: Royal Western Yacht Club of England, Queen Anne's Battery, Plymouth (Tel: 0752 660077). Royal Plymouth Corinthian Yacht Club, Madeira Road, The Hoe, Plymouth PL1 2NY (Tel: 0752 664327). Mayflower Sailing Club, Phoenix Wharf (Tel: 0752 662526)

Eating out: Vast selection from Indian to Greek, Spanish to Chinese. Many pubs with food; cafés, fish and chips. Several night clubs till 0100

Museums/things to do: City steeped in maritime history. Elizabethan House, Plymouth Museum in the Merchant's House, Royal Citadel, Barbican, Priest's House, Smeeton's Tower, The Hoe. Large shopping centre. Walks from Mount Edgecumbe Country Park at Cremyll. Cothele Quay, Morwellham Quay, River Tamar

Regattas/special events: Port of Plymouth Regatta, end of July. Popular venue for many national dinghy championships. Single/two handed transatlantic start. Fastnet finish. Round Britain and Ireland Race.

Passages

Rame Head to the Manacles

Favourable tidal streams

RAME HEAD	Bound West: 2 hours before HW Dover
	Bound East: 4 hours after HW Dover
DODMAN POINT	Bound West: 3 hours before HW Dover
	Bound East: 3 hours after HW Dover

WEST OF PLYMOUTH and the Yealm, **Fowey** is the next probable destination on a coast-hopping cruise and at over 20 miles away, it is one of the longest legs. Although no great distance in itself, yet again the odds are very much in favour of winds forward of the beam and, once past Rame Head, the tidal streams are weak inshore and of no great assistance. Three miles south of Looe the streams rotate in a clockwise direction, attaining a maximum at springs of about one knot, east by north HW Dover −0520, but no more than ½ knot west by south HW Dover +0035. Somehow, this passage always seems to take longer than anticipated.

In the far distance, given reasonable visibility, twenty-three miles west-south-west of Rame Head is the long, flat topped headland of the Dodman, with its distinctively rounded end. However, immediately to the north-west of Rame Head, Whitesand Bay falls back, a succession of sandy beaches and rocky outcrops, backed by a continuous line of steep and broken grassy cliffs, between 30m and 76m high. The direct course to Fowey keeps you a good couple of miles offshore, which is no great disadvantage as this is one of the less inspiring stretches of coast. Rocks extend a cable immediately to the west of Rame Head, and north-west of the point is a dangerous wreck awash at LWS marked by a red can. Following the sweep of the bay inshore there are rifle ranges by the old fort at Tregantle, where there are a number of flagstaffs along the cliffs, and if the red flags are flying you should keep well clear.

Sounding like a perfect setting for an Enid Blyton children's adventure, **Portwrinkle,** almost two miles west of Tregantle, is a very tiny boat harbour, which dries completely and is fringed by extensive rocky ledges. There are a few houses nearby, and the village of Crafthole can be seen on the skyline. From here onwards, the coast continues in a long, high sweep with extensive rocky ledges and hazards extending up to two cables offshore, including the Longstone, a prominent rock 18m high. At **Downderry,** which straggles along the cliffs, precipitous paths lead down to a beach, and to the south there are the Sherbeterry Rocks, a large area of shallows extending just over two miles offshore, with least depths of 4.9m, which can produce an area of rough water particularly in onshore winds when this whole stretch of coast should be avoided, and a good offing maintained.

Looe Island, a rounded hump, 44m high, lies close to the shore, almost linked to the mainland at LW, a perfect natural daymark for the drying fishing port of **Looe** just to the east, which is mostly commercial with limited facilities for yachts, and is dangerous to approach in south or south-easterly winds of any strength and ebb tide as it has a long and very narrow entrance. In offshore winds, however, there is a good anchorage just off the harbour. Rounding Looe Island, the Rennies, a group of drying rocks extend three cables south-east from the island, and at times, in fresh wind against tide a small race will be found up to one mile from the shore. From offshore, a very tall TV mast, 586m high, can be seen inland, 10 miles due north of Looe Island, displaying a number of fixed red lights at night.

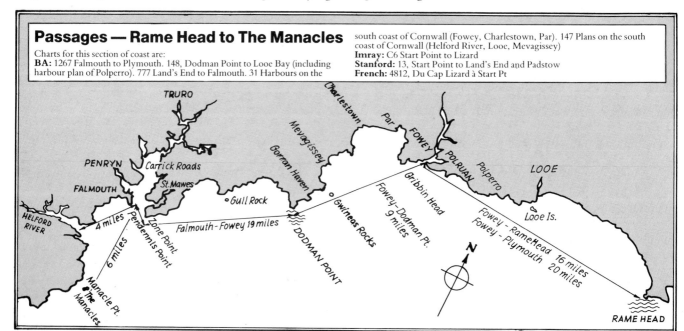

Passages — Rame Head to The Manacles

Charts for this section of coast are:
BA: 1267 Falmouth to Plymouth. 148, Dodman Point to Looe Bay (including harbour plan of Polperro). 777 Land's End to Falmouth. 31 Harbours on the south coast of Cornwall (Fowey, Charlestown, Par). 147 Plans on the south coast of Cornwall (Helford River, Looe, Mevagissey)
Imray: C6 Start Point to Lizard
Stanford: 13, Start Point to Land's End and Padstow
French: 4812, Du Cap Lizard à Start Pt

Approximate distances — nautical miles

'Gribbin Head and the flat top of the Dodman are features of the passage west'

RAME — MANACLES

Marine beacons

Penlee Point	50	298.8	PE
Lizard	70	298.8	LZ

Aero beacons

Plymouth	20	396.5	PY

Coastal Radio

Pendennis Radio, working channel 62.

Beyond Looe the coast becomes more interesting again. There is a measured mile (1852.9m to be precise) beginning just west of the island, the transits formed by two white beacons with a vertical black stripe at each end, running as far as the approach to Talland Bay. This is an attractive sandy beach backed by trees and fields popular with holidaymakers and its end is formed by the 100m high headland of Downend Point, which has a large granite war memorial near the summit. Downend Shoals, ½ mile due south, have a least depth of 2.6m and should be passed well to seaward if there is any sea running. If bound for **Polperro,** the small fishing village harbour just over ½ mile west, it is best not to turn inshore until the white beacon and Coastguard lookout on Spy Glass Point just east of the harbour are bearing north. Approaching from the west, a prominent TV mast will be seen high on the cliffs just before the village opens. Like Looe, Polperro is not a place much frequented by yachts, and although space is very restricted, there is usually room for a couple of visitors to dry alongside the quay, or anchor just south of the harbour. In bad weather a storm gate closes the harbour completely.

From **Polperro** to **Fowey,** in good weather, the coast is very attractive with impressive cliffs up to 91m in height occasionally broken by steep green and grassy coombes and gullies running down to small coves. The water is deep to within two cables of the shore and there are no hazards beyond that, except the insidious Udder Rock, which dries 0.6m, two miles west of Polperro and ½ mile offshore, which is marked by an unlit south cardinal buoy, YB. A white beacon on the cliffs, and a white mark on a rock on the shore also provide a transit for this hazard, bearing 020°T, and a prominent white mark on the western side of Lantic Bay just open of steep Pencarrow Head,

135m high, provides a cross bearing of 283°T. At night, if you are in the red sector of Fowey light you will pass Udder Rock to the south but, better still, keep further to seaward and open the white sector. Generally, if making the passage from Plymouth to Fowey at night, the dominant feature is the Eddystone to the south-east, (F1(2) 10 sec 24M) but you will be on the 13M limit of the fixed red sector visible through 112–129°T. Rame Head is unlit, and beyond it the few shore lights are the harbour entrance at Looe (Occ WR 3 sec 8M), and Fowey (L Fl WR 5 sec, W11M, R9M).

In daylight, although completely hidden from the east, the entrance to **Fowey** harbour is not difficult to find, thanks to the huge red and white horizontally striped daymark, a square pillar 104m high built by Trinity House in 1832 on Gribbin Head which extends as a long promontory to the south-west of the river mouth. Lantic Bay, immediately west of Pencarrow Head, is a mile east of the entrance, backed by National Trust land, and the beach, though mostly covered at HW, is a beautiful stretch of clean sand when the tide is lower, with a good anchorage off it in northerly winds.

Beyond it there is a conspicuous white house high on the cliffs, and a ruined round tower. As the headland draws abeam, Punch Cross, a white cross on a large rock, will come into view to starboard, with a Coastguard lookout and houses along the cliff above, and the river mouth and town of Fowey, will emerge, with high ground on either side. Deep, and free from hazards it can be approached in any weather, although obviously strong southerly winds and ebb tide will produce very rough conditions and breaking seas in the entrance. As well as being a popular yacht harbour, this is also a very busy commercial port, exporting large quantities of china clay, so be ready for surprise encounters with sizeable ships in the entrance which is only a cable wide at its narrowest point. They, of course, have priority, so keep well clear.

The passage from **Fowey** to **Falmouth** is about 20 miles, and the tide is once again a definite factor to consider for rounding the Dodman. The Lizard and Start Point both instantly evoke races, but somehow the Dodman seems to elude such an association, which is strange, as there can often be quite an unpleasant amount of disturbance in its vicinity. Close to the point streams run at nearly two knots at springs, and with wind against tide, the uneven depths and shoals of the Bellows and Field can produce a small but very unpleasant race extending a good mile offshore. If a westerly wind of any strength is prevailing ideally try to round the Point at slack water just before the main ebb begins to the south-west, about three hours before HW Dover, which means leaving Fowey two hours after local HW (Dover −0600). The whole promontory of the Dodman provides a considerable lee in westerly weather, and it should be remembered that a fresher wind and larger seas are likely to be encountered once past the point, particularly in a south-westerly when it can be a long ten mile beat to windward to reach Falmouth, along an exposed stretch of coast that provides no shelter in between.

The only hazards between Fowey and the Dodman are both well marked; Cannis Rock, drying 4.3m, inshore of the Cannis Rock south cardinal buoy YB (Q6 + L Fl 15 sec) positioned ½ mile south-east of Gribbin Head, and also covered by the western red sector of Fowey lighthouse, and the Gwineas Rocks, the largest of which dries 8m just over two miles north-east of Dodman Point, with Gwineas an east cardinal buoy BYB (Q (3) 10 sec) two cables to the south-east.

Clearing Gribbin Head, St Austell Bay opens to the north-west, and the coast running away towards the Dodman, nine miles south-west of Fowey provides a good sheltered area of water in westerly winds, an attractive miniature cruising ground in its own right. Beyond it, the land rises, the distant sprawl of houses around **St Austell** culminating in the high, jagged skyline of the 'Cornish Alps' — the huge spoil heaps surrounding the extensive china clay workings of this important local industry. From offshore, when they catch the sun, the similarity to a range of snow covered mountains is an undeniably remarkable, and possibly confusing, sight.

The china clay port of **Par** is commercial and of no interest to visitors, but does provide another very distinctive landmark on the northern shore of the bay, four large chimneys that are even more conspicuous when belching out white smoke.

Your course will take you well away from the land, closing it east of the Gwineas Buoy, but the town and white lighthouse of **Mevagissey** are easy to spot on the western shore, a V-shaped gap in the cliffs, surmounted by houses on both sides. **Gorran Haven,** a drying small boat harbour lies due west of Gwineas rocks. As always, particularly near the rocks, keep a good lookout for pot buoys.

Close to, the Dodman is impressive, a rounded bluff, 111m high, flat topped with steep cliffs along the eastern side but with a more sloping western side, a lovely stretch of National Trust property covered in gorse, ferns and grass. High on the south-western tip there is a large white cross erected in 1896 by a local vicar.

On a fine calm day, it is quite feasible to pass within a cable of the foot of the cliffs, as the water is deep and unimpeded; in any sort of sea or weather, stand well out, up to two miles in fresh conditions. A notorious headland for shipwrecks, particularly in fog, it is strange that no light or fog signal was ever established there, particularly as both St Anthony light (OcWR 15 sec 22M), and the Lizard light (Fl 3 sec 29M) are obscured from the Dodman. Apart from the lights of villages ashore there are no aids to navigation at night until St Anthony light appears on a north-westerly bearing, although sometimes its loom will be seen sooner. There is also a noticeable set into the bays between the Dodman and Falmouth; in poor visibility or at night give the coast a good berth.

Once past the Dodman, Veryan Bay opens to the north, an attractive but uncompromising cliff-lined stretch of coast, broken at intervals by small sandy coves.

The western extremity of Veryan Bay, Nare Head, five miles distant, looks similar to the Dodman, but has the distinctive triangle of Gull Rock, an island 38m high ½ mile to the east. Although Veryan Bay is almost free from offshore dangers, with no rocks more than two cables from the shore, there is one notable exception, Lath Rock, least depth 2.1m LAT, almost midway across the bay, fortunately just inside the direct line from the Dodman to Gull Rock.

Gull Rock is a jagged pyramid, with sparse grass around its whitened summit, clear evidence of the many seabirds that nest there and give it its name. In fair weather it is possible to pass between the rock and the steep cliffs at Nare Head, 80m high, but the Whelps, a reef with a number of drying rocks, mostly 4.6m, extends ½ mile to the south-west of Gull Rock.

Gerrans Bay, much of which is surrounded by National Trust land, is of a similar aspect to Veryan, although the cliffs along its western side become less precipitous. Probably the best of all the anchorages along this section of coast is off **Porthscatho** which does give shelter from the west, a small fishing village now popular with holidaymakers. There is a small pier on its southern side which gives protection to the drying foreshore, with a reasonable anchorage just to the north-east. Basic provisions, Post Office and several pubs ashore make this a popular day sail from Falmouth.

Gerrans Bay has seen many shipwrecks in its time, with vessels mistaking it for the entrance to Falmouth, but the most spectacular in recent years was the capsize of Simon Le Bon's maxi, *Drum England* in gale force conditions during the 1985 Fastnet.

The Bizzies lie almost on the line from Gull Rock to Porthmellin Head, and should be avoided in fresh winds and ground swell which can create quite an area of overfalls around them.

Beyond Gerrans Bay the rounded profile of Zone Point continues to hide the elusive St Anthony light, and a certain nagging doubt can tend to creep in at this stage of the passage. There used to be a conveniently conspicuous row of coastguard cottages high on Zone Point which have since been demolished by the National Trust. It is surprising that no daymark was ever established here as the entrance is not easy to locate from the east until at last the white lantern peeps into view from behind the headland. Just over a mile south of the light, Old Wall, a rocky shoal with least depth of 7m rises steeply from the sea bed and can produce an area of rough water in strong southerly winds. In fine weather it is a popular fishing area and easy to spot from the number of angling boats in its vicinity.

The entrance to the **River Fal** is a mile wide and safe to enter in any conditions, the only hazard being Black Rock right in the middle, marked by a conspicuous but unlit beacon which can be passed either side. In strong southerly winds, with an ebb tide out of the estuary, rough seas will, however, be encountered in the approach and entrance. The ebb, which can attain up to two knots at springs, if fresh water is running down the river, begins at HW Dover −0605.

It is just over five miles from St Anthony Head to Manacle Point, away to the south-west, and between them Falmouth Bay is a fine natural roadstead, well sheltered from the north to south-west, but open to the east and south, much used by large vessels as an anchorage, and increasingly so for offshore bunkering.

From Pendennis Head, neatly crowned with a castle, the hotels and beaches of the Falmouth seafront form a broad sweep to the west, and the large cream coloured Falmouth Hotel at the eastern end is particularly prominent. Depths reduce gradually towards the shore, which is fringed with rocky ledges, but there are no dangers further than a cable from it, except large numbers of poorly marked pot buoys. In offshore winds it is possible to anchor off Swanpool Beach just north of the prominent and wooded Pennance Point; a mile to the south Maenporth is another popular cove, and during the summer a large inflatable racing mark is usually anchored to seaward.

From Falmouth, the entrance to the **Helford River** is not easy to distinguish; the various headlands of similar shape blending together. Low cliffs run between Maenporth and Rosemullion Head, which is flat topped and rounded, covered in gorse and thick bushes, with isolated houses along it. Between it and Mawnan Shear, there are steep grassy cliffs, with a dense clump of woods, and a conspicuous white house at its eastern edge. The Gedges and August Rock which dry 1.4m lie three cables east-south-east marked to seaward by August Rock, a green conical buoy, during the summer months only. This is the only real hazard in the approach to the Helford River, and once past the Gedges the entrance opens clearly. It is exposed to the east, when the shallowing water produces particularly steep short seas, and being unlit should not be attempted at night without local knowledge.

Gillan Creek, due south of the Gedges, is an opening in the southern approach to the Helford, an attractive, but mostly drying inlet between Dennis Head, which is grassy and 43m high, and the much lower promontory of Nare Point with a square Coastguard lookout on the end. Beware Car Croc, a rock just awash at LW in the entrance of Gillan Creek, marked with an east cardinal buoy BYB which should be left to starboard when entering. There are also rocky ledges extending a cable to seaward of Nare Point.

Proceeding south from Falmouth or the Helford, the extensive rocky nightmare of the Manacles involves a detour to the east. Just over a mile south-east of Nare Point there are two large unlit Admiralty black and yellow mooring buoys, and to seaward, the 2D buoy, Y (Fl Y 2.5 sec), known locally as the three mile buoy, lies just over three miles south of St Anthony, and almost the same distance east of the entrance to the Helford River. This part of the bay is much used for search and rescue exercises from RNAS Culdrose, and if you see Admiralty vessels and helicopters hovering in the vicinity keep well clear.

Manacle Point is a rather untidy looking headland, badly scarred by extensive old quarry workings, and just to the north, by the small cove of Porthoustock, are the unsightly remains of the huge stone loading chutes on either side of the bay. Jagged pinnacles of rock extend from the point, which continue to form the reefs offshore, marked by the Manacle buoy, east cardinal (Q (3) 10 sec), 1½ miles to the east, which always tends to appear further out to sea than you anticipate, particularly when approaching from the south. The Manacles are undoubtedly one of the most treacherous hazards along the Cornish coast. Right in the approach to a busy port it was inevitable that this area of half-tide rocks and strong currents should claim so many ships over the years. Their sinister name actually derives from the Cornish 'maen eglos', meaning Church stones, for the spire of St Keverne Church is prominent inland.

Close to the Manacles the tidal streams run at up to two knots at springs and, bound round the Lizard, aim to leave Falmouth or the Helford about three hours after local HW to gain the best advantage. There is an inshore passage through the Manacles regularly used by local fishing boats but do not be tempted to follow them as it is very narrow in places with unpredictable eddies and currents exceeding three knots. Do not be too amazed, either, if you see a reasonable sized coaster seemingly emerging from among the rocks. Incredible though it seems, they regularly load stone at Dean Quarry alongside the cliffs just south of the Manacles.

At night, approaching from the south, the Manacles lie within the red sector of St Anthony light, 004–022°T.

Before radar a very large percentage of the wrecks along this section of coast occurred in calms and fog rather than extremes of weather, and in poor visibility it can be very difficult, as a number of the headlands and bays have a similar appearance and audible aids are few and far between; Eddystone Light, (Horn (3) 60 sec), Nailzee Point, Looe, (Siren (2) 30 sec occasnl), Cannis Rock buoy, (Bell) — note there is no other fog signal at Fowey — Mevagissey, (Dia 30 sec), Gwineas buoy (Bell), St Anthony Head (Horn 30 sec), Manacles Buoy (Bell). Remember that there is generally a northerly set into the bays, and although the 10m sounding line provides a good indication of relative position clearing most of the hazards close to the shore, such as the Dodman, this is little more than two cables off. If in doubt, err to seawards, and do not follow local fishing boats, particularly close to the Manacles — there is no telling where they might go.

Looe and Polperro

Tides

HW Dover −0545. Range: MHWS 5.4m — MHWN 4.2m
MLWN 2.0m — MLWS 0.6m. Strong streams within Looe
harbour at springs.

Charts   BA: 147, 148. **Stanford:** 13. **Imray:** C6.

Waypoint

Looe Banjo Pier Head 50.21.02N. 4.27.00W. Polperro West
Pier Head 50.19.84N. 4.30.92W.

Hazards

Looe: Looe Island and Rennies rocks to south (all unlit).
Polperro: The Rannys and Polca Rock in approaches (both
unlit).

Both harbours dry to entrance, and are dangerous to
approach in onshore wind and sea. Polperro harbour mouth
closed in bad weather. Busy fishing harbours, keep clear of
local boats. Beware pot and net buoys in approaches.

MIDWAY BETWEEN Plymouth and the next popular cruising haunt of Fowey lie the small harbours of Looe and Polperro, both of which dry almost completely at LW, and are, therefore, only of interest to vessels able to take the ground comfortably or lie alongside. In addition, both are primarily fishing ports, with restricted space, where commercial activity takes precedence. With narrow entrances, neither harbour should be approached in onshore winds of any strength.

Approaches

The largest of the two, **Looe,** lies nine miles west of Rame Head at the mouth of the River Looe, which divides the town into East and West Looe, linked by a bridge with 3m clearance across the upper end of the harbour. From offshore, the entrance is easily located, lying to the east of the large rounded lump of Looe Island, 44m at its highest point, half a mile offshore. This is privately owned, the residence of two remarkable sisters, Evelyn and Babs Atkins who threw up a civilised existence in suburban Epsom and moved on to the island in 1965, a tale related in the book *We Bought an Island*. Tales of contraband and smuggling inevitably abound but the most bizarre episode in the island's history had to be during the last war when it was bombed by an over zealous German pilot who mistook it for a large warship. Today it is open to the public, and a small landing fee is charged, the proceeds going towards its upkeep. It is also known locally as St George's Island and, if approaching from the west, keep a good half mile to the south to avoid the drying Rennies Rocks (4.5m). South of them, in certain combinations of wind and tide quite a brisk area of overfalls can form. Do not attempt to pass between the island and the mainland, which is rock strewn and shallow and, ideally, approach Looe from the south-east, leaving the island a good two to three cables on the port hand as you close the land and head directly for the end of the Banjo Pier — its shape gives it the name — which forms the eastern side of the harbour mouth. Midmain is an isolated rock south-west of the entrance marked by a lighted beacon with east cardinal topmark, (Q (3) 10 sec), and on the rocks to the north there are two red beacons closer to the harbour.

If waiting for the tide a good anchorage lies just east of the pier head, 2m LAT. The entrance is long and little more than 50m at the narrowest point, drying right to the mouth at springs, and accessible after half flood for boats of average draught. It is flanked by high cliffs along the western side, with rocky ledges at their foot. Only enter under power, keeping close to the Banjo Pier. The tide runs strongly, up to 5kts on

A busy fishing port, facilities for visiting boats are very limited in the narrow drying harbour at Looe

West Looe
Visitors' berth

Local moorings

Fish quay

Harbour office

East Looe

To sea

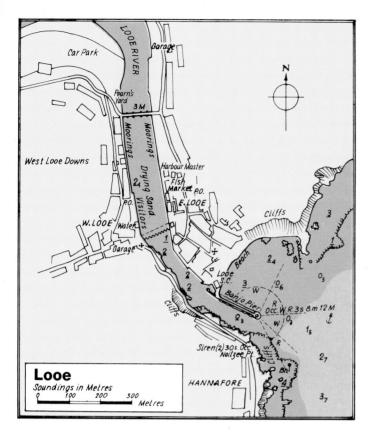

Looe
Soundings in Metres
0   100   200   300
                    Metres

the ebb at springs, and careful allowance should be made for this when manoeuvring. Beware, too, of the numerous self drive motorboats — always an unpredictable hazard — the fishing boats entering and leaving, and the small passenger ferry at the southern end of the harbour. Although the pier head is lit, (sectored Occ WR 3 sec) — the white light covering the safe approach — entry at night is not recommended due to the narrow entrance and absence of lights within. It is far safer to anchor off and enter in daylight; because of the fishing boat movements, a riding light is essential.

Moorings

The quays on the east side of the harbour are reserved for the fishing fleet, and further upstream stands the new fishmarket where the Harbourmaster's office is also located. Below the bridge a number of local boats lie on trot moorings, all of which dry, and the only berth available is clearly marked with a yellow sign 'Visitors Berth Only' at the southern end of the West Looe quay, just above the ferry steps, and you should report to the Harbourmaster on arrival. The quay is lined with wooden piles and a fender board will be very handy; you will ground about four hours after HW, drying out on a firm sand and gravel bottom. Anchoring is prohibited throughout the harbour because of the moorings and underwater pipes and power cables.

Facilities

A picturesquely situated little town Looe clings to the steep hills overlooking the river and during the season it pays the inevitable price and is absolutely inundated with visitors, the crowds thronging through narrow streets that were never designed for such an influx. In East Looe gift shops abound, but West Looe retains more of the original feel of this old fishing community with thick-walled pastel painted cottages amidst a network of narrow alleyways and cobbled yards.

Overall, facilities are good, with plenty of shops, numerous restaurants, cafés and pubs. Fresh water is available from taps on both quays, and petrol from the local garage. There is no longer a permanent fuel berth, and diesel for the fishing fleet is provided by a daily lorry. There are branches of Lloyds, Midland and Barclays banks, a chandlery, and two boatyards upstream of the bridge both with slipping facilities. Looe Sailing Club, in Buller Street, East Looe has a licensed bar and showers are available.

Now the second busiest fishing port in Cornwall, Looe has expanded again in recent years, suffering like so many others some very lean times after the collapse of the pilchard industry in the 1930s, and more recently the mackerel fishery in the 1970s. The holiday industry has in many ways helped to sustain the commercial fishermen through some of the harder times as this has long been a popular sea angling port and home of the Shark Fishing Club of Great Britain and, though nowhere in the league of *Jaws,* a surprising number of Porbeagle and Blue sharks are caught in the warm waters off Cornwall during the summer. Definitely not man-eaters, they are rarely found close to the shore. Potting, longlining, trawling and most recently scalloping are the main other fishing activities, supporting a local fleet of 35 trawlers.

Even busier at the turn of the century a fleet of over 50 large luggers still worked from Looe, decked boats up to fifty feet, their transom sterns distinguishing them from the double ended luggers of the west Cornish ports. The pilchards, small fish similar to the herring, were traditionally caught in long seine nets during the summer months, with open boats working from coves and beaches, but as the shoals moved further offshore, the larger boats were built and long drift nets began to replace the seine.

However, of all the Looe luggers, probably the best known — certainly the most travelled — has to be *Lily,* built by Ferris in 1896. Her fishing days over, sometime in the 1930s, a young enthusiastic couple

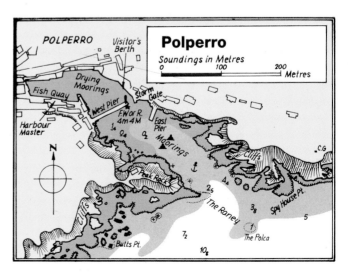

Polperro
Soundings in Metres
0   100   200
                           Metres

spotted her in nearby **Polperro**.

'Anne stood by the helm. 'I think,' she said, 'we've found our ship.' We scrambled aboard and went below. The fishwell took up the whole of the middle of the ship. We pulled up the floorboards and looked into the bilge. There were firebars, cannonballs, cogwheels and shingle. She was dry as a bone but smelt to heaven of fish and tar. In the fo'c'sle was a bogie stove eaten with rust, and a single locker on the starboard side. Aft was a single-cylinder Kelvin. Anne's face was flushed with excitement. 'If she only costs us twenty-five pounds, we can afford to have her converted into just what we want. It'll be like buying a new boat.' 'I hadn't the heart to tell her that a surveyor might find she was rotten.'

She turned out to be very sound indeed, and thus a humble Looe lugger was revived to become Peter and Anne Pye's famous gaff cutter *Moonraker of Fowey*. While her sister ships were towed to a final, rotting resting place up the Looe River, for it was considered unlucky to break them up, *Moonraker* suffered no such ignomony, proving to be a very seaworthy cruising boat, and ranging far and wide from the Baltic to Tahiti, and Alaska to Brazil, her voyages delightfully described in *Red Mains'l, The Sea is for Sailing,* and *A Sail in a Forest*.

There are no such bargains to be found in Polperro today, and the people who throng there are not searching for boats to buy, merely postcards, cream teas and souvenirs. It is not, however, a particularly recent phenomenon, as a guide book written in the 1920s reveals, describing it as . . .

'a human bees' nest stowed away in a cranny of rocks. Its industries are four: the catching of fish, the painting of pictures, handicrafts and — latterly — the entertainment of visitors, for it is probably the most charmingly unexpected village in all England . . .'

The pressure of visitors in recent years has resulted in the welcome banning of all cars from **Polperro** during the day with a large car park on the outskirts. The ten minute walk down the hill comes as a considerable shock to many of today's car-bound explorers unused to such inconvenience and exertion; with great relief, they soon spot the horse drawn bus.

Approaches

Arriving from the sea, therefore, you have the definite edge on the rest of the masses, for if the tide and weather permit, you can enter freely into the centre of this exceptionally attractive harbour set in a narrow cleft among the cliffs. Just under three miles west of Looe Island, and five miles east of Fowey, it is not, at first, the easiest place to find. No attempt should be made to approach it in any southerly wind and seas, particularly south-east; not only are the approaches dangerous in these conditions, it is quite likely that the protective gate across the entrance will be closed.

Approaching from the east, once past Looe Island, a pair of transit beacons will be seen on the mainland marking the beginning of a measured mile; the second set of beacons marking its end lie just east of Talland Bay, its western side formed by Downend Point. From south of the point a V-shaped cleft in the high cliffs will begin to open, and houses of Polperro will be seen. Steer to within two cables of the inlet, and Peak Rock will be seen on the western side, pyramid shaped, topped with jagged boulders, and on the eastern side the lookout building on Spyglass Point. The main hazard is Polca Rock, (1.2m) about 200m south-west of the point. The Rannys, two rocks drying 0.8m, will usually be seen awash just off Peak Rock; proceed with caution, passing between these and the hidden Polca, before turning into the inlet and heading for the outer harbour wall. There are several fishing boat moorings in the approach and it is possible to anchor either above or below them in between 2m and 4m if conditions permit or waiting for the tide.

Moorings

The inner harbour dries to just beyond its mouth at springs, and can be entered after half flood. Fishing boats use the inside of the western pier, and the rest of the harbour has many fore and aft small boat moorings. Berthing for visitors is very limited, with space for a couple of boats alongside the east quay wall immediately inside the entrance. There is a small charge, and Chris Curtis, the Harbourmaster, will appear at sometime to collect it; alternatively, seek him out at his office in the small fish market on the western side of the harbour.

Only 10m wide, the entrance is closed by a steel storm gate in heavy weather when the harbour can often take a severe pounding.

'In the time of a storm Polperro is a striking scene of bustle and excitement. The noise of the wind as it roars up the coombe, the hoarse rumbling of the angry sea, the shouts of the fishermen engaged in securing their boats, and the screams of the women and children carrying the tidings of the latest disaster are a peculiarly meloncholy assemblage of sounds, especially when heard at midnight . . . When the first streak of morning light comes, bringing no cessation of the storm, but only serving to show the devastation it has made, the effect is still more dismal. The wild fury of the waves is a sight of no mean grandeur as it dashes over the Peak, and falls on its jagged summit, from whence it streams down the sides in a thousand waterfalls and foams at the base. The infuriated sea sweeps over the piers and striking against the rocks and houses on the Warren side, rebounds towards the Strand, and washes fragments of houses and boats into the streets where the receding tide leaves them in sad confusion.'

This was written in 1871, in the remarkable *History of Polperro* by Jonathan Couch, grandfather of Sir Arthur Quiller-Couch, and the description makes it easy to imagine the mayhem in November 1824, when three houses, the inner and outer piers and fifty boats were destroyed in the worst south-easterly storm ever experienced. But on a balmy summer's evening, fortunately, Polperro can be a very different place, the harbour ablaze with colour, the cheerful red, green and yellow of the boats contrasting with the subtle backdrop of white, pink and slate hung cottages, their reflections shimmering at the height of the tide. Quite oblivious to the infuriated seas that sometimes sweep their vantage point, the holidaymakers bask contentedly on the warm, weathered stone of the

'The most charmingly unexpected village in all England', Polperro lies hidden in a narrow cleft between the cliffs

harbour wall, grasping the very last of the sun's fading glow as the valley sinks into shadow.

Facilities

In spite of its popularity the village has, fortunately not been over developed, and is carefully administered by the Polperro Harbour Trustees, with the declared intention of maintaining its unique character. The tiny narrow streets, and houses, overhanging the harbour and the diminutive River Pol, apart from the smart paint and good state of repair, have probably outwardly changed little since John Wesley was forced to change his lodgings in 1762 because the room beneath him was 'filled with pilchards and conger eels, the perfume being too potent . . .' Prior to the advent of the tourist industry, fishing, and smuggling were the main activities, the rabbit warren of alleyways ideal for evading the Excise men. Special boats were built for the trade, and one, *Unity* was reputed to have made 500 successful trips, crossing to France in just over eight hours with a fair wind.

In spite of the crowds, it is still an intriguing place to explore, particularly in the evening when the coaches and day trippers have all gone on their way.

Facilities are limited to provisions, Post Office and branches of Barclays and Midland banks, open 1000–1430, May-September. There are several restaurants, and four pubs, and even a Smugglers' Museum. Petrol is available from a garage in the village, and water from a tap on the west quay.

Port guide — Looe and Polperro

Harbourmaster: Mr H Butters, Harbour Office, The Quay, East Looe (Tel: 050 36 2839). Mr C Curtis, Harbour Office, West Quay, Polperro

VHF: None

Emergency services: Lifeboats at Plymouth and Fowey. Coastguard (Tel: 050 36 2138)

Customs: None. Clear at Plymouth or Fowey

Anchorages: Looe; east of Banjo Pier. Polperro; clear of moorings in harbour approach

Berthing: One visitor's berth in Looe, on west quay. Space for two visitors on east quay, Polperro

Charges: Looe; 22p per foot per night plus VAT. Polperro; 20p per foot/night Inc VAT

Phones: East and West Quays, Looe. Fish market, Polperro

Doctor: (Tel: 050 36 3195)

Churches: C of E, Methodist, and RC at Looe. C of E, and Methodist at Polperro

Fuel: Diesel from lorry at Looe. Petrol from garages

Paraffin: Looe Harbour Chandlers, East Quay

Gas: Looe Harbour Chandlers

Water: Taps on east and west quays, Looe. Tap on west quay, Polperro

Tourist information: Guildhall, East Looe

Banks/cashpoints: Looe; All main banks, no cashpoints. Polperro; Barclays and Midland, 1030–1430

Post Office: East and West Looe. Polperro

Rubbish: Bins on quayside, Looe and Polperro

Showers/toilets: Showers at Looe Sailing Club. Public toilets, East and West Looe. Toilet overlooking east quay, Polperro

Launderette: East Looe

Provisions: Everything available, East Looe. EC Thursdays, but most places open in season. Food available Sunday AM. All basics in Polperro, EC Saturdays, but open in season

Chandler: Looe Harbour Chandlers, East Quay, Looe (Tel: 050 36 4760). Norman Pearn & Co, Millpool Boatyard, West Looe (Tel: 050 36 4355)

Repairs: Norman Pearn & Co, above. Curtis Frank & Pape Bros, West Looe (Tel: 050 36 2332)

Marine Engineers: Marine Engineering (Looe) Ltd, The Quay, East Looe (Tel: 050 36 2887). J B Marine Engineers, The Quay, East Looe (Tel: 050 36 3998), and also at boatyards

Transport: Trains and buses to main line at Liskeard from Looe. Infrequent buses to Polperro

Yacht clubs: Looe Sailing Club, Buller Street, East Looe (Tel: 050 36 2559)

Eating out: Good selection of restaurants and pubs

Museums/things to do: Museum and aquarium at Looe. Pleasant walks to seaward and also up river. Boat trips to Looe Island, good swimming from safe beaches. Smugglers' Museum at Polperro and spectacular walks along cliffs

Regattas/special events: Looe Regatta and Polperro Rowing Regatta in August

Fowey

Tides
HW Dover −0550. Range: MHWS 5.4m — MHWN 4.3m.
MLWN 2.0m — MLWS 0.6m.

Charts
BA: 31. Stanford: 13. Imray: Y52.

Waypoint
Cannis Rock buoy 50.18.35N. 4.39.88W.
Hazards
Udder Rock 3M to east, Punch Cross (both unlit). Cannis Rock (lit). Busy commercial port, beware shipping in narrow entrance. Upper reaches dry; main harbour dredged to 7m. Fluky winds within harbour.

'Fowey is the harbour of harbours, the last port town left without any admixture of modern evil. It ought to be a kingdom all of its own. In Fowey all is courtesy and good reason for the chance sailing man . . . and I have never sailed into Fowey or out of Fowey without good luck attending me.'

HILAIRE BELLOC obviously rather liked Fowey, but he was not alone among literary men and women to succumb to the romantic charm of this delightful town and deep narrow river. Daphne du Maurier lived here for many years, Sir Arthur Quiller-Couch, 'Q' immortalised it in his famous sagas as *Troy Town*, and his friend Kenneth Grahame, also used it in *Wind in the Willows*.

Approaches

The entrance, although only a cable wide at its narrowest, is deep and easy except in strong onshore winds and ebb tide. Keep to the middle of the channel, leaving the white cross on Punch Cross rock and the triangular white beacon on Lamp Rock to starboard, and high St Catherine's Point, with its small fortress, and narrow Readymoney Cove to port, where anchoring is prohibited because of underwater cables. At night, the inner lighthouse on Whitehouse point, midway up the western shore, gives a sectored light (Iso WRG 3 sec) and the white sector leads straight in. Just upstream, the only other navigation lights are two vertical fixed red lights at the end of the Polruan ferry landing which should be left to port. The only possible problems, day or night, are likely to be a large ship emerging, or fluky winds.

Moorings

Once past Polruan fort, the river widens, and the moorings, then the village of Polruan itself, will come into view along the eastern side of the harbour, with the mouth of Pont Pill, a wide creek at their upper end. The main river runs northwards, with Fowey stretching along its western side in neat terraces climbing the steep hillside overlooking the harbour. Whitehouse Quay is a small pier on the Fowey shore where a small passenger ferry runs across to Polruan, and a little further upstream the low black and white twin gabled building with a veranda and large flagstaff is the Royal Fowey Yacht Club. There is an average of 7m at LWS dredged right through the centre of the harbour, and plenty of water to within half a cable of the shore as far as Town Quay, which dries at LW, and is used by local fishing and trip boats, easily located by the tower of St Fimbarrus Church behind it, and the prominent King of Prussia hotel. Albert Quay, a short distance beyond, has a large landing pontoon with a bridge to the shore, which is dredged and accessible at any state of the tide, although further inshore it dries at LW. Short term mooring, up to two hours, is allowed alongside this pontoon free of charge, which is very handy for shopping, landing crew or taking on fresh water as there is a hose provided. Be warned, though, boats abusing this excellent facility, using it for an overnight stop, for instance, will be charged five times the normal mooring rate in the harbour.

Opposite, there are usually a number of large ships moored fore and aft in the centre of the stream, waiting to berth at the china clay wharves upriver, and although this narrow waterway seems at first

Fowey is deep and of easy access in most conditions; the bulk of the moorings lie off Polruan and Pont Pill

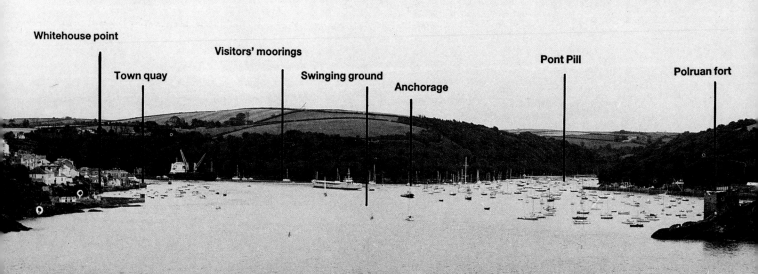

Whitehouse point · Town quay · Visitors' moorings · Swinging ground · Anchorage · Pont Pill · Polruan fort

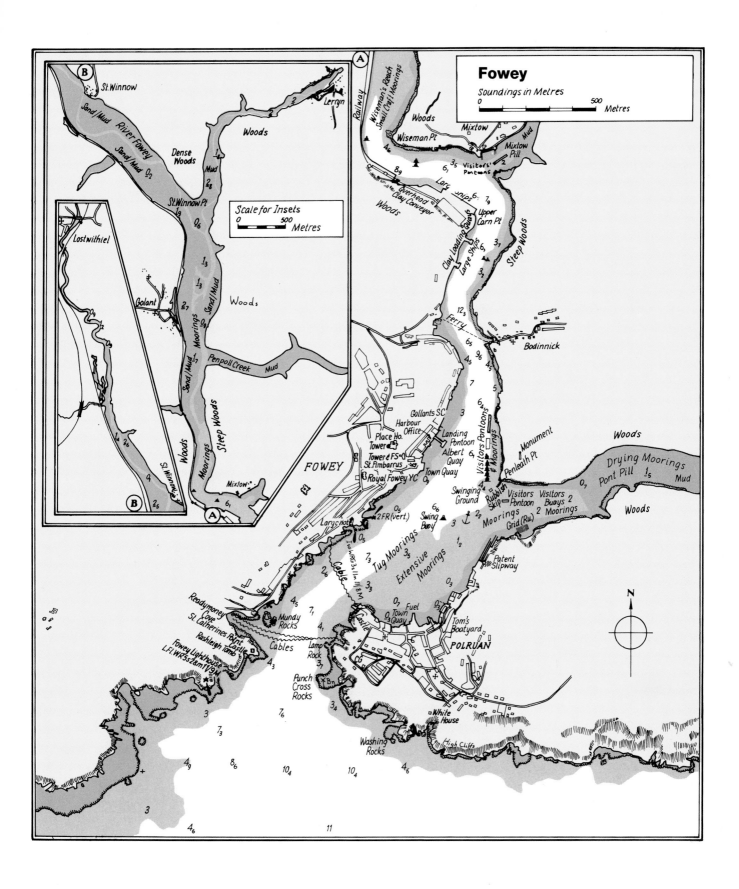

appearance an improbable place for much commercial activity, you have now entered the ninth largest exporting port in England, shipping over 1.5 million tons of china clay a year, and handling nearly 850 ships. Most average between 7 and 8,000 tonnes, but the largest to date, the Finnish vessels *Astrea* and *Pollux,* were nearly 17,000 tons, and 540 ft in length. It is fascinating to watch the apparent ease with which these vessels are manoeuvred to their berths, in

particular the technique of 'drudging' them backwards up the river, towing from the stern, with their anchors dragging on a short scope to hold the bows in position.

Considering that in addition over 4,000 yachts now visit the port annually, somehow, the commendable Harbour Authority has managed to achieve a remarkable balance between running their intensive commercial activity, and at the same time catering admirably for the large numbers of pleasure craft that pour in during the summer. Facilities have been improved considerably in recent years, a continuing policy, and the main area for visitors to head for is the 'swinging ground' just opposite the Royal Fowey YC. During the season the Harbour launch, affectionately known to all as *Zebedee* is on the water seven days a week from 0830 until dark, and in the afternoon keeps a particular lookout to assist new arrivals. Although the Harbour Office and launch both monitor VHF Channel 16, and should be called on their working Channel 12, either Fowey Harbour Radio or Fowey Harbour Patrol, the landlocked nature of the harbour tends to make reception poor from outside, and you will probably not make contact until you are in the entrance when you will have been spotted anyway.

There are 16 swinging visitors' moorings for up to 16m LOA along the east side of the river just upstream of Pont Pill and a 30m pontoon. Another identical pontoon is in the mouth of Pont Pill, and within the creek, which is dredged to 2m for some distance, there are also fore and aft moorings, very handy if you want a bit peace away from the mainstream and ideal for leaving a boat if stuck for time or weather. All the visitors' moorings are either yellow or white, clearly marked 'FHC Visitor' and there is also a floating rubbish skip close by which should be used in preference to taking it ashore. Finally, half a mile upriver, there is another visitors' pontoon in the entrance to Mixtow Pill which is particularly useful in bad weather (see page 88).

Anchoring is not allowed in the fairway, near underwater cables or close to landing places, and only permitted to the east of the swinging ground, off the entrance to Pont Pill, but this sometimes entails having to move when larger vessels are being manoeuvred. As in the River Yealm, the difference between dues for anchoring, and dues for lying to an FHC facility for example, only amounts to £1 for a 30 ft boat, which is an obvious incentive to use them, and well worth it for the peace of mind.

Facilities

Landing is easy at the Albert Quay pontoon where dinghies can be left on the inside and also at the Royal Fowey YC, pulling them clear of the steps, remembering that the foreshore here dries at LW. Members of other clubs are welcome to use their facilities, where there are excellent showers, meals by arrangement, and a good bar. Here, among the various burgees, is one that, for me, a dyed in the wool romantic, always induces a certain nostalgic twinge, as

it belonged to *Moonraker of Fowey* and was presented to their club by Peter and Anne Pye.

The Fowey Gallants Sailing Club just upstream from Albert Quay also extends a friendly welcome to visiting yachts, although facilities here are limited to a bar, and food at weekends.

The alternative to rowing, and one of the most popular facilities in Fowey in recent years is the very efficient and convenient water taxi service which runs from Albert Quay pontoon, and can be called on VHF Channel 16. Operating seven days a week in season from about 0800 until 2330, for a mere 70p a head this does away with the problem of worrying about the dinghy, and with a sheltered cuddy, is a particularly enticing prospect when it is pouring with rain and blowing.

The town is essentially just one main shopping street, very narrow in places, with houses rising up from it and still very much as Sea Rat described it in *Wind in the Willows*

'. . . the little grey sea town I know so well, that clings along one steep side of the harbour. There, through dark doorways you look down flights of stone steps, overhung by great pink tufts of valerian and ending in a patch of sparkling blue water. The little boats that lie tethered to the rings and stanchions of the old sea-wall are gaily painted as those I clambered in and out of in my own childhood; the salmon leap on the flood tide, schools of mackerel flash and play past the quay-sides and foreshores and by the windows the great vessels glide, night and day, up to their moorings or forth to the sea. There, sooner or later the ships of all seafaring nations arrive; and there, at its destined hour, the ship of my choice will let go its anchor . . .'

Not quite as grey today, as most of the buildings are

There is no charge for a temporary stay on the Fowey Harbour Commission landing pontoon at Albert Quay — the visitors moorings lie beyond along the far shore

Approaching Fowey from the south-east both Punch Cross and Lamp rocks are clearly marked and lie close to the shore

Fuel is only available in Fowey alongside Polruan Quay around high water, and care must be taken to check the depths at neaps

Dust rises in the distance from the china clay conveyors, but upstream, Wiseman's Pool is quiet and sheltered in all weathers

brightly painted and very well preserved, it is also undoubtedly a lot busier than when Kenneth Grahame was writing, with cars and people squeezing through the narrower bottlenecks. Nevertheless, it is still a delightful place, and spared the over-commercialism of so many of the other Cornish harbours, perhaps a reflection on the fact that such a large proportion of its visitors come in by sea, for the atmosphere certainly reflects this.

Belloc's eulogy continues, '. . . *whatever you may need in gear is to be had at once*' — which is certainly true except perhaps on Sundays, with everything that a cruising crew might require from basics like food, drink, launderette and banks, to sailmakers, boatyards and chandler, and a Spar Foodstore open 0800-2100 daily, 0900-2100 Sundays. There are a variety of options for eating ashore from cafés and fish and chips to far more up-market bistros and restaurants, catering for just about every possible gastronomic need. Obtaining fuel is the only real problem in Fowey, as the only diesel and petrol available alongside is at Polruan Quay which is tidal — there's only 1.5m at HW neaps so check the depth carefully. Fuel can also be obtained in cans from the garage in Fowey, but hopefully during 1989, plans to provide an all-tide fuel barge in the harbour will materialise, which will be a major improvement.

Polruan, clinging to an even steeper hillside than Fowey, can provide all the basics. It is an attractive, far quieter little village, where, sensibly, visitors' cars are prohibited in season, and left parked at the top of the hill. Groceries are available at the Cottage Stores seven days a week, there is a butcher, another chandler, a couple of pubs, and a waterside bistro/bar. C Toms & Sons Boatyard is still very much involved with traditional boatbuilding, and often a peep into their large shed reveals a big wooden fishing boat under construction. Their slipway, one of the largest in the area, can take vessels up to 28m, and 100 tons; the Harbour Authority also has a large slipway further up along the Polruan shore in their own repair yard which is used to maintain their tugs, dredger and barges, but private vessels up to 150 ft can be hauled by arrangement, and it is also possible to dry out alongside the wall here for repairs.

The major sailing event of the year, Fowey Regatta Week, takes place during the third week in August, when the harbour is packed to absolute capacity, with feeder races from Plymouth and Falmouth, including a large contingent of their gaff-rigged working boats. Racing takes place every day both outside and inside the harbour, and two particular attractions are the very close competition among the local one design class, the Troy's — a colourful fleet of 18 ft three-quarter decked bermudian sloops, which sport a distinctive 4 ft bowsprit. These were first built in 1929 and 18 survive today — and also the spectacular finale of the week, the Harbour Race for the Falmouth Working Boats. However, if you are seeking peace and quiet, be warned that this is the one week to avoid Fowey altogether.

Historically, Fowey has a wild and romantic past, which started when the port began to develop in the 12th century after the previous harbour at Lostwithiel, six miles inland, began to silt up. By virtue of its deep water and easy access trade soon flourished with a large fleet of its own. By 1346 it was able to supply 47 ships and nearly 800 men for the siege of Calais, more than any other port in England, and it seemed to give the Fowey men a particular taste for adventure. Little more than pirates, they continued to wage their own private war against the French long after hostilities had officially ceased; daring raids across the Channel and bloodthirsty skirmishes not only earned them a lot of plunder but also the nickname of 'Fowey Gallants'.

The French hit back in 1457, raiding and setting fire to the town, forcing its inhabitants to take refuge in Place House, the seat of the Treffry family. Rebuilt and much altered in later years, it remains today the prominent large house with tall towers just behind the Church. However, this attack only stimulated the activities of the Gallants, one of whom, John Wilcock seized no less than fifteen French ships in as many days, becoming a source of great embarrassment to King Edward IV, who sent a message to Fowey, 'I am at peace with my brother of France'. Not impressed the Gallants cut off the unfortunate messenger's ears and nose, an act of defiance that resulted in considerable punishment for the town. The ringleaders were hanged, goods seized, ships distributed to other ports and the huge protective chain slung from the forts at the harbour mouth removed and, duly chastened, the wild men of Fowey returned to more peaceful pursuits, fishing, shipbuilding, trading and, of course, smuggling . . .

Although the river is still navigable on a good tide as far as **Lostwithiel,** there is only deep water for a mile as far as Wisemans Reach, beyond which the river dries almost completely, a mixture of sand and mudbanks. There is no marked channel, but shoal draught boats and dinghies can explore on a flood tide, and, bilge keelers can anchor and dry out off **Golant,** where there are a large number of small boat moorings and a pleasant little village with basic provisions and a pub. Beyond, Lerryn Creek bears away, steep-to and wooded, and the rest of the upper reaches of the river are similarly attractive and ideal for a sailing dinghy. Deeper draught boats, however, normally remain in the lower part of the harbour except, perhaps, when it begins to blow from the south-west when, in spite of its landlocked nature, conditions can sometimes become very uncomfortable. Perfect in so many other ways, this has to be the one major drawback to Fowey, for a very annoying swell sets in, even off Polruan, and with a gale of wind against tide in the harbour it can get surprisingly rough and, at the mercy of both elements, very rolly at times.

Traditionally, boats used to run upriver and anchor in **Wisemans Pool,** but this is now so full of moorings that it is impossible. Sometimes a few are available, so it is worth contacting the Harbourmaster for his advice but the best option is now Mixtow Pill. This is dredged to 2m LAT and there is a 30m pontoon available for visitors, with space for at least six 30 foot boats, and excellent shelter in all weathers. Note, however, that shores on either side are private and landing is not allowed. Owners of bilge keelers can, of course, always sneak off to dry out comfortably right out of the way in the upper reaches!

Proceeding upstream, the river narrows above the town, steep and wooded on the eastern bank past the pretty hamlet of **Bodinnick,** and *Ferryside,* the prominent house by the water where the du Maurier family were brought up, still lived in by Daphne's sister Angela, but keep a lookout to avoid the ferry itself which carries cars across to Fowey. Beyond, the large clay loading wharves and dolphins appear along the west bank, always a fascinating stretch of river with ships of many nationalities berthed alongside, but everything, including the surrounding trees is wreathed in fine white dust, like a gentle fall of snow. The deep channel turns sharply to port at Upper Carn Point opposite the entrance to Mixtow Pill, and particular care should be taken to look out for large ships rounding this bend. At the end of this short reach, overlooked by high woods, the docks finish, and the channel turns back to the north round Wiseman Point, a wooded rocky promontory, and, thick with moorings, Wiseman's Pool appears.

If however, the weather does turn and you are stuck in Fowey for a few days, apart from the museum and aquarium, the real thing to take advantage of is the number of fine walks the area can provide, particularly the Hall Walk which skirts a large part of the harbour. Ideally, leave the dinghy in Fowey, catch the ferry to Bodinnick and the walk is signposted on the right

Although the River Fowey narrows above Bodinnick ferry it is deep and always busy with vessels loading china clay

halfway up the steep hill leading out of the village. Far from arduous, the grassy track gently follows the contour line right round Penleath Point to the large stone memorial to Sir Arthur Quiller-Couch, where there are magnificent views of the harbour, then on through the woods and wild flowers above Pont Pill, and down to the hamlet of Pont with its old quay and water mill. From here the track climbs again following another wooded hillside with more lovely views all the way back to Polruan were you can catch the ferry back to Fowey and, perhaps, a cream tea.

Another favourite is the walk to seaward of Fowey along the road to Readymoney Cove where a track leads up on to St Catherine's Head, pausing, perhaps, to look at the old fortress, built by Henry VIII in 1540, with fine views into the harbour, and above it, a curious structure that can just be seen when entering from sea, two granite arches surmounted by a Maltese cross, that looks like the top of a huge crown. It is, in fact, the tomb of William Rashleigh, his wife and daughter, descendents of Charles Rashleigh who not only built the port of Charlestown, but also *Menabilly* on Gribbin Head. For many years this was the home of Daphne du Maurier, and supposedly the house she immortalised in her novel *Rebecca*. Following the coast path out towards Gribbin Head you skirt the private grounds and woods surrounding *Menabilly* where there are spectacular views of the harbour mouth, coast, and particularly lovely scenery around Polridmouth Cove just before you reach the huge beckoning daymark, silent witness to so many departures and arrivals, such as *Moonraker*'s at the end of her voyage to the Pacific, forty days out from Bermuda . . .

'The sun soaked up the haze, and the town of Fowey was just out of sight. In an hour or two, or three or four, a breeze would come and we should sail in through the Heads into the harbour from which we had set out three years ago. What changes should we find, I wondered, and how should we take to living on the land? Would Christopher pad about the city in bare feet and bowler hat, and should we be content with creeks?

My thoughts were disturbed by the sound of a vessel's engine and a boat came up that was familiar. She stopped, her sails casting their shadows upon the water. Her people welcomed us.

'Come aboard,' I said, 'and have some coffee.'

And I hurried down to start the Primus.

Presently Anne looked out.

'Hullo,' she said, 'where have they gone to?'

'They wanted to get in,' said Christopher. 'They've already been two nights at sea.'

Port guide — Fowey

Harbourmaster: Captain Mike Sutherland, Harbourmaster's Office, Albert Quay, Fowey (Tel: 0726 83 2471/2472). Harbour patrol in season

VHF: Fowey Harbour Radio or Fowey Harbour Patrol, VHF Channel 16, working 12, 0830–2100 in season
Mail drop: Harbour Office or RFYC

Emergency services: Lifeboat at Fowey. Coastguard, MRSC Brixham (Tel: 0804 58292)

Customs: Custom House Fowey, (Tel: 0726 83 3777). Patrol launch

Anchorage: Off entrance to Pont Pill, clear of moorings and coaster swinging ground

Moorings/berthing: All Harbour Commission. Temporary berthing pontoon, up to two hours off Albert Quay. 16 deep water moorings, two visitors' pontoons near Pont Pill and additional moorings within Pont Pill. Pontoon in Mixtow Pill

Charges: For 30 ft boat per night inc VAT, at anchor, £3.50. On FHC facility, £4.50

Dinghy landings: Albert Quay pontoon. RFYC. Inside quay at Polruan

Water taxi: From Albert Quay pontoon, 0800–2330, seven days, VHF Channel 16 or hail

Marina: None

Phones: Near Town Quay, RFYC, outside Post Office

Doctor: (Tel: 0726 83 2541)

Hospital: (Tel: 0726 83 2241)

Churches: All denominations

Local Weather Forecast: F.H.C. Noticeboard on Albert Quay

Fuel: Diesel and petrol alongside quay at Polruan, but tidal restrictions. In cans from Fowey Garage & Marine, Lostwithiel Street in Fowey

Paraffin: Troy Chandlers, Fowey. The Winkle Picker, Polruan

Gas: Calor/Gaz, Troy Chandlers. Upper Deck Marine, in Fowey. Gaz at Winkle Picker in Polruan

Water: Albert Quay pontoon

Tourist information: In Post Office (Tel: 0726 83 2398)

Banks/cashpoints: Barclays, Lloyds, Midland. No cashpoints

Post Office: In main street, turn right at Albert Quay

Rubbish: Floating skip off Pont Pill

Showers/toilets: At RFYC. Public toilets on Town Quay

Launderette: The Dhobey Room, 0800–2000, 1200 Sundays, by Fowey Boatyard, with own dinghy landing

Provisions: All requirements including delicatessen, EC Weds or Sat. Shops usually open in season. Spar Foodstore open late and Sunday, Fowey. Cottage Stores open seven days, Polruan

Chandler: Troy Chandlers, Lostwithiel Street, (Tel: 0726 83 3265), open 0800 to 2000 in season. Admiralty Chart Agents, Upper Deck Marine, Albert Quay (Tel: 0726 83 2287). Fowey Marine Services, Station Road (Tel: 0726 83 3236). The Winkle Picker, The Quay, Polruan (Tel: 0726 87 296)

Repairs/hauling: C Toms & Sons, Polruan (Tel: 0726 87 232). Fowey Boatyard, Passage Street, Fowey (Tel: 0726 83 2194). W C Hunkin & Son, Bodinnick (Tel: 0726 87 221)

Drying out: By arrangement with Harbourmaster

Marine Engineers: C Toms & Sons (Tel: 0726 87 232)

Electronic engineers: Marine Electronics of Fowey (Tel: 0726 833101).

Sailmaker/repairs: Mitchell Sails, North Street, Fowey (Tel: 0726 83 3731)

Transport: Buses to main line railway at Par

Yacht clubs: Royal Fowey Yacht Club, Whitford Yard, Fowey PL23 1BH (Tel: 0726 83 2245). Fowey Gallants Sailing Club, Amity Court, Fowey (Tel: 0726 83 2335)

Eating out: Very good selection for size of town. Fish and chips to bistro/restaurants

Museums/things to do: Fowey Museum, Aquarium, both in middle of town. Good walking, Fowey and Polruan

Special events: Fowey Regatta/Carnival, third week in August

Mevagissey and St Austell Bays

Charlestown: HW Dover −0555.
Charts: BA 31. **Stanford** 13. **Imray** C6.
Hazards: Inner floating basin entered by narrow entrance and tidal lock, and narrow entrance. Dangerous in onshore winds. Drying rocks to south and east.

Mevagissey: HW Dover −0600
Charts: BA 147, 148. **Stanford** 13. **Imray** C6.
Hazards: Inner harbour dries. Black rock off North Quay

(unlit). Busy fishing harbour. Dangerous to approach in onshore wind, and outer harbour very exposed in easterly gales.

Gorran Haven: HW Dover −0600.
Charts: BA 148. **Stanford** 13. **Imray** C6.
Hazards: Shallows extend well to seaward. Cadycrowse rock east of pier (unlit). Fine weather anchorage only and dangerous in onshore wind.

ST AUSTELL AND MEVAGISSEY Bays are well sheltered from the west. The depths reduce gradually and the tidal streams are weak with high water throughout this section at HW Dover −0555. Tywardreath Bay is the area in the extreme north of St Austell Bay, and **Polkerris,** a small fishing cove on the eastern side, has a good anchorage off it in easterly winds. To reach it from Fowey, there are no hazards more than two cables from the shore, once the south cardinal Cannis Rock buoy has been passed, south-east of Gribbin Head, and you can safely follow the coast this distance offshore around the western side of the Gribbin for a couple of miles until the houses and small harbour wall come into sight. Anchor about three cables to the south-west of the pier where there is about 1.5m at LW. The whole bay dries out completely, but boats able to dry out can anchor inside the harbour or lie alongside the pier. It is an unspoiled little hamlet tucked snugly beneath the cliffs and trees with a high wall along the sandy foreshore protecting it from the seas which roll in unchecked in southerly gales. Once a busy fishing harbour, but now little more than a cluster of houses, there is a pub, and a café in the old lifeboat house which was closed down in 1922 when the station was transferred to Fowey.

Par, with its four conspicuous chimneys, further to the north-west, is approached over a large area of drying sands. However not only is it tidal but the harbour is also privately owned. It is a busy china clay

port swathed in white dust, of no interest to visitors and entry is only permitted in an absolute emergency. Mid-way across the bay on the outer edge of Par Sands is Killyvarder Rock, which dries 2.4m and is marked by a red beacon, south of which there are often quite a cluster of coasters at anchor in the clay-tinged turquoise water waiting to berth at Par.

Charlestown, another china clay port two miles south-west of Par is, however, of more interest, as this is now much less used commercially. Also privately owned, the inner floating basin is entered through a very narrow entrance and tidal lock, yet another masterful bit of engineering by John Smeaton, who built the third Eddystone lighthouse. Now only occasional ships use the ingenious overhead chutes, but more recently this unspoiled 19th century harbour has been used by several film companies for location filming and also for episodes of the BBC's *Onedin Line.* Late in 1987 the whole harbour was sold, and at the time of writing future plans for its development had not been revealed. A few pleasure craft are based here, and it is possible to lock into the basin on the tide by arrangement with the Harbourmaster 24 hours in advance (Tel: 0726 73 331), although it's hardly worth the effort and expense for an overnight stay. However, in offshore winds it is possible to anchor off just east of the piers and dinghy ashore for a visit. The harbour mouth dries completely, well beyond the outer breakwaters at springs; on the tide land inside at the

Visitors to Mevagissey normally raft alongside fishing boats on the south pier

slip to the left of the lock gate. Apart from the harbour, there is now also a large Visitor's Centre, a well conceived concept devoted to the maritime history of the port and surrounding area, and the wrecks along the Cornish coast, with much inside to keep children amused, and some life-like animated reconstructions. There is a café in the centre, Post Office/store and a pub.

Depths reduce gradually around St Austell Bay, tidal streams are very weak, and there are no dangers more than a cable from the shore. There are many fine sandy coves and beaches, and in favourable weather it is possible to sound in and anchor off most of them. Robins Rock, just south of Porthpean dries, and there is an isolated drying rock 0.1m ½ cable off Ropehaven beach.

Black Head, a bold rocky point with a grassy summit 46m high forms the division between St Austell and Mevagissey Bays, and the fishing port of Mevagissey is two miles further to the south-west. Midway between them is the lost harbour of **Pentewan,** at the northern end of the long stretch of Pentewan sands, another tidal basin once approached by an artificial channel that has now completely silted up.

Mevagissey, the best known harbour in the bay is a classic Cornish fishing town with good shelter in the prevailing winds, but exposed in easterlies, when it can be dangerous to enter and very uncomfortable inside. It comprises an outer harbour and an inner harbour which dries completely and the latter is restricted to local boats only. Fishing boat moorings take up most of the available space afloat in the outer harbour which results in very limited space for visitors. It is predictably a popular place with holidaymakers, and becomes very busy in season but in spite of a certain amount of commercialism it retains much of its character; pastel cottages, slate hung, with cement washed roofs creep up narrow alleyways to overlook the harbour, rather like a small version of Brixham. It is well worth a visit providing there is no inkling of the wind turning to the east but remember, however, that fishing is still a very important part of the town's life, with quite a large trawling and potting fleet, and also a number of pleasure and angling boats. At all times, commercial activity takes precedence and although every effort is made to accommodate short stay visitors, be prepared to move when asked, and do not impede the fish landing and other boat movements.

The approach is easy, with no off-lying dangers except the Gwineas rocks if arriving from the south. Steer for the white lighthouse (Fl(2) 10 sec 12M) on the South Pier, keeping close to it, as a shallow sandy bank, drying 0.3m LAT extends east from the end of the north pier. The outer harbour is available even at LWS, with depths alongside the inside of the outer end of the South Pier to just over 2m. Visitors normally berth here, rafting alongside fishing boats between the steps. Mr Rafferty, the Harbourmaster listens on VHF Ch16 0900-2100; his office (Tel: 0726 843305) is a clearly marked white building on the north pier, but do not leave your boat completely unattended in case

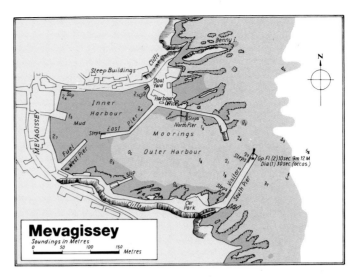

you have to move. Because of the restricted space and also mooring chains anchoring is not allowed, but there is sometimes a possibility of a mooring being available in the outer harbour; wherever you lie, charges for a 30 ft boat are very reasonable; £2.50 per night, inclusive of VAT.

Renowned for smuggling activity and one of the largest centres on the south coast of Cornwall for the 18th and 19th century pilchard fishery, Mevagissey was a rough, unruly place in its heyday, reeking with the stench of fish, with huge landings, sometimes in excess of 30 or 40 thousand fish per boat, all of which were counted by hand.

There is an excellent small museum close to the Harbour Office, a fine old wooden building dating from 1745, that was once part of a boatyard, and right next to it, another 'real' boatyard remains where John Moore still builds beautiful traditional wooden fishing boats.

Although swarming with people in summer, a wander around the town is pleasant, and most requirements can be found, including branches of Lloyds, Midland and Barclays banks open 1000–1430, June-Sept, and even an aquarium. There are plenty of cafés, fish and chips and a few restaurants, and some good pubs. A small amount of chandlery is available, Calor and Camping Gaz, and fresh water alongside the south pier. Visitors are allowed to enter the inner harbour only to reach the fuel berth on the inside of the west quay where diesel and water can be obtained after half flood. Petrol is only available in cans from a nearby garage, and there is also a marine engineer if needed.

South of Mevagissey, **Gorran Haven** is an attractive fine weather anchorage, sheltered in westerly winds, with a drying small boat harbour and a gently shelving clean sandy beach. Approaching from the north keep midway between Gwineas Rocks and the low promontory of Chapel Point, sound in and anchor two cables east of the sea wall; in settled weather bilge keelers can dry out comfortably closer inshore. A narrow street of old fishermen's cottages, there is a Post Office, general store (open Sundays), several cafes, a pub, and the start of a lovely coast path up to Dodman Point.

River Fal

Tides

HW Dover +0600. Range: MHWS 5.3m — MHWN 4.2m.
MLWN 1.9m — MLWS 0.6m. HW Truro approx 8 mins after
HW Falmouth. Streams attain over 2kts in upper reaches at
springs.

Charts

BA: 32, 154, 18. **Stanford:** 13. **Imray:** Y58.

Waypoints

Eastern dock breakwater end 50.09.31N 5.02.90W.
Black Rock E. Cardinal buoy 50.08.66N. 5.01.77W.

Hazards

Black Rock (unlit, but outside lit buoyed channel). St Mawes
Buoy/Lugo Rock (unlit). Governor Buoy (unlit). Busy
commercial port, beware shipping movements in vicinity of
Docks, Penryn River, and upper reaches of Fal. Large areas
of upper reaches dry. Beware pot and net buoys.

'FALMOUTH FOR ORDERS' — just a few words that evoke so much, and although lofty spars, square yards and billowing spreads of canvas no longer grace the Western Approaches and deep laden rust-streaked hulls waiting on the whims of commerce have long ceased to swing at anchor in Carrick Roads, **Falmouth,** by virtue of its far westerly position is still a major port of landfall and departure for many of the smaller sailing vessels that now cross the lonely oceans of the world and the ensigns of many nations are a familiar and romantic sight around the harbour during the summer months.

For the majority with less exotic cruising ambitions, apart from a bit of wishful thinking, the River Fal and its tributaries offer everything that a yachtsman might require. As my own adopted home port, in spite of an inevitable degree of bias, most visitors would probably agree with me that it has to be one of the finest sailing areas in England, and certainly, it ranks as one of the great natural harbours of the world.

Approaches

Flanked by St Anthony Head to the east, grass topped with low cliffs and a handsome lighthouse (Occ WR 15 sec 22M, Red Sector 004°-022°) built in 1835, and Pendennis Point nearly a mile to the west, the entrance is easy and can sensibly be made in any weather, although a gentle ride is hardly likely to be encountered in a southerly gale with an ebb tide. There is, however, no such thing as total perfection, and although deep the entrance does have one notable hazard, Black Rock, perversely right in the middle,

which uncovers at half tide, and is marked by a distinctive but unlit black conical beacon with a pole and two spheres on top. You can enter either side of Black Rock, the buoyed deepwater channel for commercial shipping to the east, the western channel, quite safe for small craft has a least depth of 6m; do not, however, be tempted to pass too close to Black Rock as shallows extend nearly 200m north and south. At night, first time, it is wisest to keep to the deepwater channel which is well lit, with Black Rock east cardinal buoy, BYB (Q (3) 10 sec) to port, and Castle conical green (Fl G 10 sec) to starboard. From here, steer up towards West Narrows, red can, (Fl(2)R 10 sec), but midway between them you can bear away towards the eastern breakwater end (Fl R 2 sec). This will ensure that you safely pass north of the unlit Governor, BYB east cardinal buoy.

Pendennis Castle, initially completed in 1543, was part of Henry VIII's massive chain of coastal defences from Milford Haven to Hull, built in response to fears of religious inspired invasion from Europe. However, it was his daughter Elizabeth who instigated the building of the large outer walls and bastions during the war with Spain, particularly after Penzance, Newlyn and Mousehole were raided and burnt in 1595. But the awaited attack never came, and Pendennis never fired its guns in anger. Preserved today by English Heritage, this, and its counterpart at St Mawes are open daily during the summer, and the walk up to the headland along Castle Drive, with a grandstand view of the docks, estuary, and Falmouth Bay is definitely recommended.

From Falmouth Harbour, the Penryn River runs upstream between Greenbank and Flushing Quays towards Falmouth Marina, and the FHC visitors' moorings lie along the edge of the fairway

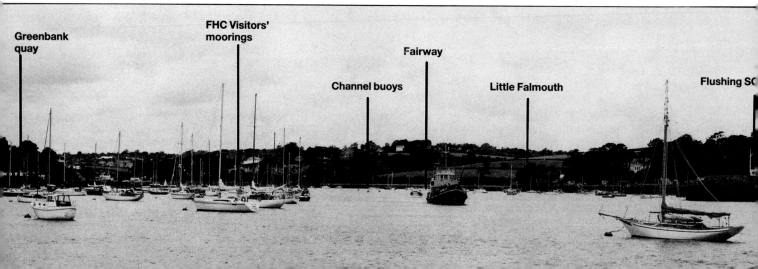

Greenbank quay · FHC Visitors' moorings · Fairway · Channel buoys · Little Falmouth · Flushing SC

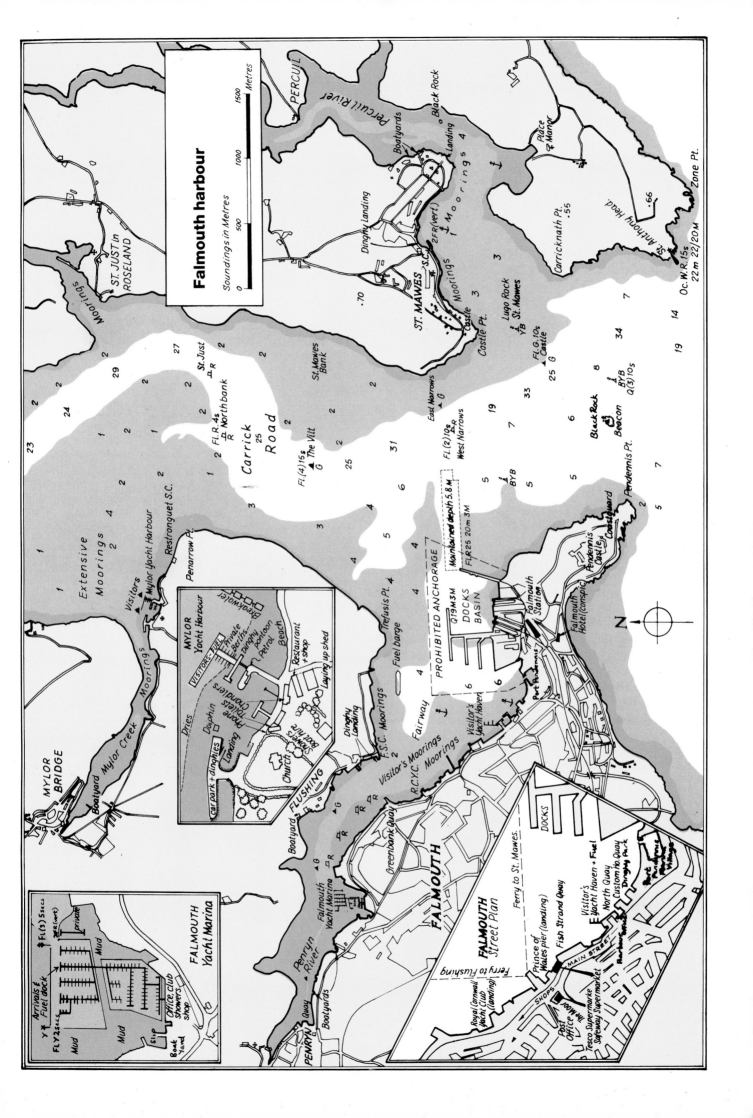

Just below the castle ramparts, the squat modern building on the hillside is the Falmouth Maritime Rescue Co-ordination Centre, the Coastguard base that has even been involved in rescues as far away as the Ascension Islands, thanks to satellite technology. Monitoring channel 16, the local working channels are 67, 10, 73, call sign Falmouth Coastguard. It should not be confused with Pendennis Radio, VHF coastal station, which should be called direct for link calls on channel 62.

Moorings

With anchorages, moorings, alongside berthing and a marina, the Fal has a wide if somewhat bewildering variety of options for visiting boats, but Falmouth itself does tend to be the first stop, and with ample deep water well into the inner harbour there are no problems entering. Follow the northern arm of the docks but not too closely, and keep a wary eye on shipping movements in and around them, particularly when rounding the western end which should be given a wide berth — tugs, ferries and fishing boats, and sizeable ships have a nasty habit of emerging, often at speed.

Dating from around 1860, Falmouth Docks are privately owned by a company headed by yachtsman Peter de Savary, with dry docks capable of taking ships up to 100,000 tons. Although chiefly concerned with ship repair they are again emerging as an important bunkering facility and are the base for his America's Cup Challenge.

Opening ahead and to port the town of Falmouth spreads along the hillside overlooking a large area of moorings. Bear round past the western side of the docks, and steer for Custom House Quay dead ahead, leaving the lifeboat to starboard, where you will find the main anchorage and also the Falmouth Harbour Commissioners Visitors' Yacht Haven. Here, May–September, there is alongside pontoon berthing for 40 boats, up to a maximum 12m LOA, 1.8m draught. For berthing information, the Harbour Office, call sign *Falmouth Harbour Radio,* monitors VHF channel 16, and works on 14, 13, 12, as does their patrol launch *Killigrew* which is usually on hand during working hours, when there is also a Supervisor on the Yacht Haven.

Facilities comprise water, fuel barge, with diesel,

petrol and water for customers. Basic showers, washroom and toilet facilities are provided for Yacht Haven visitors close by on Custom House Quay, just behind the Licensed Boatman's Hut, in the south-eastern corner. There is also a rubbish skip on North Quay by the haven. An alternative for fuel, particularly for larger vessels is *Ulster Industry,* the long red barge moored just south of Trefusis Point on the far side of the harbour. This is open 0900–1700, Mon-Fri, and can be contacted on VHF channel 16, otherwise berth alongside.

The old quays are over three hundred years old, surrounding a drying inner basin which makes an attractive focal point on the Falmouth waterfront. It is used by local fishing, working, and pleasure boats, all providing obvious entertainment for the holidaymakers. Two pubs overlook it, the Chain Locker and the Globe, with tables and seats on the quay, the former the more nautical of the two, and there are some other fine old buildings, including the Harbour Office, and Custom House built in 1815 with its adjoining large brick chimney, The King's Pipe, still used for burning contraband.

A regular ferry to St Mawes runs from Custom House Quay, and alongside in the basin is the former Falmouth harbour steam tug *St Denys,* built in 1929, now part of the Falmouth Maritime Museum which is open daily, and a great favourite with children — the Museum itself is situated in the centre of town. The Yacht Haven is by far the most convenient alongside berth in town as it is close to a number of bistros and restaurants and not far from the main shops.

If you decide to anchor instead — more privacy, and less to pay — let go east of the Yacht Haven, clear of the quay and local moorings, but also well away from the Docks, as anchoring is prohibited within a cable of the jetties, an area of water regularly used for swinging large vessels into their berths. Depths vary between 1.5m and 2.5m, and the holding ground and shelter is good in anything except northerlies, but the wash from the ferries and pleasure boats can make it fairly lively at times, and in the season it can get crowded. The best place to land is on the inner end of the Yacht Haven, where dinghies can be left afloat. An alternative anchorage will be found north of Prince of Wales Pier, outside the local moorings in 2–3m, but inside the fairway leading up to the Penryn River.

Away from the main tourist centres, pretty St Mawes is a popular anchorage, but let go clear of the ferries and the local moorings

There are visitors' berths, fuel and water available on the outer end of the pontoon at Mylor Yacht Harbour although the depth alongside is restricted at LW. Visitors are welcome at Mylor Yacht Club right on the end of the Quay. (P.100)

Falmouth Visitors Yacht Haven is very convenient for the town

Shelter is normally good throughout the inner harbour except in strong east or south-easterly winds when a surprising amount of sea can build up across the fetch from the St Mawes shore. Fortunately, easterly gales are rare, particularly in summer. Keep well clear of the Prince of Wales Pier as it is constantly busy with large tripper boats, and ferries to Flushing and St Mawes; there is, however, a good dinghy landing in the boat harbour on the inner end of the pier which is particularly handy for the main supermarkets.

Finally, between Prince of Wales Pier and Greenbank Quay there are 20 swinging visitors' moorings; the Harbour commissioners, K1 to K6, and T1 to T6, marked FHC, and nine marked RCYC Visitor belonging to the Royal Cornwall Yacht Club. Their fine clubhouse stands on its own quay, below the elegant row of tall Regency houses along Greenbank, just upriver of the new, extensive Packet Quays waterfront development. Their moorings can be reserved in advance through the Club Secretary, and visitors from other recognised clubs are made very welcome. Established in 1871, the club is open every day except Monday and, among its many activities, organises the Azores and Back Race every four years, the last in 1987. Facilities include showers, bar and dining room; there is a good dinghy landing and boatman/launch which operates between 1000 and

1900, daily (Tuesday 1400-2300) — contact through the club on VHF Channel 37. Fresh water and scrubbing alongside the club quay is also possible by arrangement.

Packets, Quay Punts and Working Boats

On his way home from El Dorado in 1596 Sir Walter Raleigh put into the Fal and found little more than a small fishing village, known as Smithick, and the nearby manor house at Arwenack, home of the Killigrew family. His advice that it might make a good harbour was not instantly taken up, but by 1670, the Killigrews had got round to building Custom House Quay, which turned out to be a stroke of luck rather than foresight, ultimately transforming Falmouth into a thriving seaport of major importance. Impressed by the new Quays, the Post Office decided to establish its Packet Service here in 1688. This fleet of fast, armed sailing ships, generally brigantines of around 200 tons, with appropriate names like *Speedy* and *Express,* were all privately owned and chartered to the Crown, carrying mail, bullion, and passengers, not only to Europe but as far afield as the West Indies, and the Americas, a round trip averaging 15 to 18 weeks. It was a tough, dangerous business, the valuable cargoes resulting in frequent attacks by privateers and pirates, but many owners and captains made fortunes, and around Falmouth, particularly along Greenbank and opposite, in the small village of Flushing, large elegant houses rose along the waterfront, graphic evidence of the new-found wealth, and by 1800, over 40 packet ships were based in the port.

As the first port of call for most inbound shipping Falmouth, before the days of wireless, often received the first news of dramatic events abroad, such as the death of Nelson, and the tradition of calling at the port to notify arrival and find the final destination for cargoes — 'orders' — resulted in much trade for Falmouth and the development of the famous Quay Punts. These deep, sturdy and for the most part, open boats, were between 25 and 32 ft long, and ranged the approaches to the Lizard 'seeking' for ships when they arrived off the port. The particular rigours of the job produced a remarkably seaworthy craft; yawl rigged

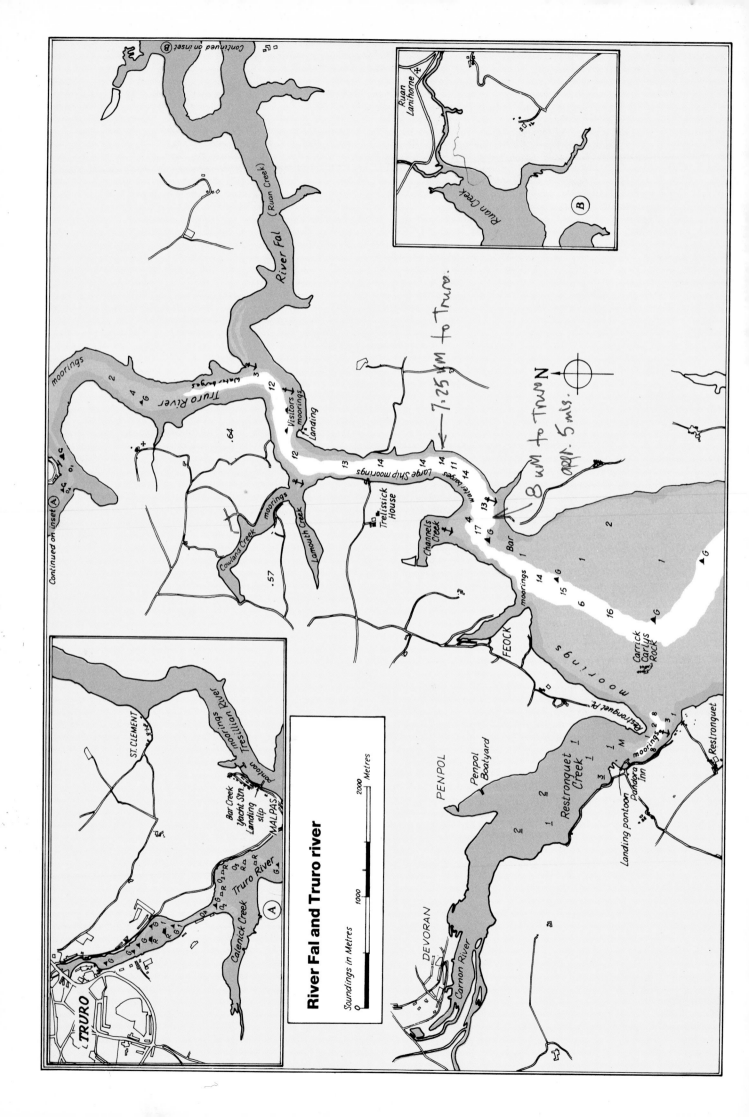

River Fal and Truro river

Soundings in Metres

0   1000   2000
Metres

Fuel Berth

The fuel and arrivals berth at Falmouth Marina is easy to find on the outer pontoons which are accessible at all states of the tide

with a stumpy mainmast to enable them to sail in under the lower yards of the big sailing ships. Only one was ever lost performing her job, *Fat Boat* that specialised in collecting the accumulated cooking fat from the incoming ships to sell it ashore. Swamped off Black Head in 1904 she sank in seconds, but many of her more fortunate contemporaries were later decked in and converted to yachts which are still sailing, and a number of yachts were built along their lines. The Quay Punting still continues in Falmouth today with a small fleet of sturdy motor launches operated by the Falmouth Licensed Watermen.

The other traditional craft that originated in the estuary of the Fal are the Working Boats, the sailing oyster boats that are now unique in Europe, their freak survival resulting from the local bye-laws prohibiting the dredging with anything other than sail or oar. Gaff cutters varying between 20 and 32 ft in length, although mostly around 28 ft, a number of these three-quarter decked boats still work the natural oyster fishery during the winter season, drifting down tide across the banks in the upper part of Carrick Roads, and hauling their dredges by hand. During the summer, however, they race, a tradition continued by the Falmouth Working Boat Association, formed in 1979 to preserve the unique character of the class. With wooden boats some of them well into their 80s, and several much younger, fibreglass hulls that have been in production since the 1970s, and even one in ferro, this impressive fleet of up to 20 boats at times, with huge gaff rigs, lofty coloured topsails and long, lethal bowsprits is one of the most spectacular sights in Falmouth, and one that you cannot possibly miss, certainly if you are around at the weekend. The boats, with their large open cockpits have room for plenty of crew, and if you feel like trying it, just ask, as someone will invariably take you along.

In marked contrast, the other distinctive Falmouth racing fleet, the Sunbeams, epitomises the elegance of the 20s and 30s, and the far off days when the mighty J

class regularly raced in Falmouth Bay. They are classic three-quarter decked bermudian sloops with long overhangs, just under 27 ft overall and this immaculately maintained, colourful small fleet is one of two in the country, the other based in the Solent where the first boats were built in 1923. Local racing in Falmouth is very active all round, and Falmouth Regatta Week, during the second week of August, organised by the Port of Falmouth Sailing Association, is the major event.

The advent of the steam ships finally removed the good fortune that Falmouth had enjoyed for over 150 years, and in 1852 the Post Office transferred the mail service to Southampton. Wireless did away with the need to call for orders but the decline in the port was brief for it was not long before the new docks were commenced in 1858; building ships, repairing them and cashing in on the new needs of the steamers for bunkers.

With the arrival of the railway in 1863 another new industry began to emerge — tourism. In 1865 the Falmouth Hotel was the first to rise from the fields along the seafront, and the holidaymakers had begun to arrive; today, more than ever, they are the mainstay of the town's prosperity.

Falmouth is a pleasant and popular port of call and the facilities are excellent, with fuel, water, provisions, chandlery, and sailmakers, all convenient to the waterfront. There is a comprehensive variety of restaurants, bistros and pubs, and two night clubs for the adventurous.

Falmouth Marina

However, the biggest yachting facility in Falmouth, the Marina, is about ½ mile further upstream, on the Penryn River, beyond Greenbank Quay, which is not difficult to miss as it has Greenbank Hotel in huge letters along it. From here on the river becomes shallower, but the main channel always has over 2m and is buoyed, red cans to port, and conical green buoys to starboard, the first red can being the only one lit (QR). The southern shore is particularly shallow; drying banks extend well out and are covered with oyster beds where anchoring is prohibited and you run aground at your peril.

Opposite, **Flushing** is an attractive small village, with limited provisions, two pubs and a restaurant on the quay, where a small fleet of local fishing boats land their catches. The building on the lower 'New' quay is Flushing Sailing Club, which is generally only open at weekends or when evening racing is taking place; there is a bar but no other facilities. A very pleasant walk can be had from Flushing out to Trefusis Point and right round to Mylor if you are feeling energetic with lovely views of the Fal and there is a pleasant sandy beach at Kiln quay, popular with locals and a regular site for barbeques.

From downstream the Marina is hidden behind Boyars Cellars, or Coastlines as it is otherwise known, a jetty with warehouses on the port hand where quite large coastal petrol tankers regularly discharge, usually arriving and leaving near HW. In the channel they

Falmouth's spectacular gaff-rigged working boats are a dramatic sight when they race

have complete priority and you should keep well clear. Opposite, at Little Falmouth, are the slipways and large sheds of Falmouth Boat Construction where there has been a boatyard since the early 1880s, and site of the first dry-dock in Falmouth.

The proposal to dredge out and build a marina in the muddy creek at Ponsharden was greeted with great local scepticism when it was first proposed in 1979, but the success of the Falmouth Marina has proved itself beyond all doubt, with a further major expansion completed in 1987 which has increased the total number of berths to 330, with nearly 70 usually available for visitors.

The new expansion has meant that the old narrow approach channel has been eliminated and there is access for boats drawing up to 1.8m at LW, although a certain amount of care is recommended at LWS. The isolated pontoon just beyond Boyars Cellars is private berthing for local boats with 2FR vert lights on its northern end; beyond this, visitors should keep to port of the BY pole with E Cardinal topmark (Fl(3) 5 sec) and proceed to the reception berth by the fuelling pontoon which is clearly marked on the outer end of the marina, where the berthing master will allocate a berth. Alternatively, call ahead on VHF channel M, particularly if you are over 13m LOA. The BY Pole with St Andrew's Cross topmark (Fl 2 sec) beyond the fuel berth marks the northern and western edges of the dredged channel. At night this light should be kept open to port of the E Cardinal light in the final approach.

Facilities are good, and the marina has a friendly atmosphere. Charges are reasonable, from £7.30 per night (inc. VAT), which includes use of the new (1989) clubhouse/bistro, showers and launderette. Chandlery, diesel, Calor and Camping Gaz, water at the berth, and electricity can be provided if required. Berthing masters are on duty from 0700 to 2300 during the season, and there is also a night watchman

With over 300 berths, the Falmouth Yacht Marina on the Penryn River provides excellent facilities

providing 24 hour security. In addition, there is a 30 ton mobile hoist and full repair facilities. Petrol can be obtained from a nearby garage, there are shops on site and five minutes away a large superstore, which is particularly convenient for big provisioning jobs. The only real drawback to the Marina is its distance from the centre of Falmouth, which is about 15 minutes walk away; there are, however, regular buses every 20 minutes.

Between the marina and **Penryn,** ½ mile further upstream, the river dries completely. During the Middle Ages Penryn was a port of considerable importance, until its trade was wrested away by the development of Falmouth and the gradual silting of the river. It is possible to reach Penryn Quay after half flood, but it is much used by local fishing boats and surrounded by very sticky deep mud at LW. Scenically the river does not really have a lot to recommend it, although the town is architecturally very interesting. However, if you have problems, Penryn is where you're likely to end up as most of the main marine businesses are located in the area, and if you wish to avoid going upriver by boat regular buses run from the centre of Falmouth.

On the opposite side of the creek to the marina is Port Falmouth Boatyard, which has a 120 ton slipway and 18 ton mobile hoist, Williams Boatyard is upstream and K Cruisers and Fox's yards are in Penryn itself, although access to them is restricted by a road bridge. Further upstream right at the head of the creek is Islington Wharf, a new development where a number of marine orientated businesses are located, and it is possible to dry out alongside, although again, very muddy. Overall, there are several chandlers in the area, including a large second hand one, marine and electronic engineers, three sailmakers, and also liferaft repair and servicing. In fact, just about everything you might possibly need.

But the real beauty of the Fal is that it also provides all the other ingredients of a successful cruise; magnificent scenery, safe clear water for sailing, and some delightful anchorages where you can escape from the crowds ashore, and find some welcome peace and quiet.

Stretching nearly three miles inland and almost a mile wide **Carrick Roads** is a broad stretch of water, surrounded by rounded hills, fields and low rocky shores. At the south-eastern end, opposite Falmouth, is the entrance to the Percuil River and **St Mawes,** which has only one hazard in the approach, Lugo rock, two cables south of the prominent castle, least depth 0.8m, marked by St Mawes, a south cardinal buoy YB, which should be left to port when entering. The houses of the small village of St Mawes run along the northern shore and off them there are a number of local moorings, and a small boat harbour lies beyond them. There is a fairway up to the jetty end which is used constantly by the ferries and pleasure boats, so anchor well clear between it and the moorings. Going ashore land on the large slipway or beach and not on the pier where you will be charged a landing fee.

Away from the main holiday track, St Mawes has remained somewhat aloof, a former fishing village with a particularly mild climate that resulted in its early popularity for retirement and more recently,

holiday homes, a combination that has resulted in a welcome resistance to over-development and commercialism. Built at the same time as Pendennis, St Mawes Castle is a particularly well preserved example of its type, a clover leaf formation of three immense bastions, now open to the public and surrounded by gardens with fine views across to Falmouth.

The village provides all the necessary basics: food, banks, Post Office and there is a small chandler, a delicatessen, cafés, restaurants and several pubs, including the popular Victory Inn tucked away up an alleyway. Fresh water is available from a tap on the quay near Lloyds Bank, but diesel is only available in cans from the Freshwater and Percuil boatyards further upriver. Calor Gas and some chandlery is also available from Percuil Boatyard.

St Mawes Sailing Club overlooks the quay, and visitors are welcome to use their bar and showers; they also have three red and white chequered visitors' moorings up the Percuil off the Old Stone Works Quay, which belongs to the club and is used as a dinghy store and is a handy place to land, just a short walk from the village. Ask at the clubhouse or phone ahead (Tel: 0326 270686) for availability. Visitors' moorings can also sometimes be arranged through the St Mawes Harbourmaster, Mr Tatum, whose office is on the Town Quay (Tel: 0326 270553), or the Freshwater Boatyard (Tel: 0326 270443).

Perfect in easterly winds, the anchorage off St Mawes is exposed to the south-west, and shelter then can only be found up the **Percuil River,** around the bend past Amsterdam Point, but anchoring is difficult because of the large number of local moorings. Shoal draught boats, however can creep close inshore to anchor, and ground at LW off the beach at Place Manor, a peaceful spot overlooked by silent woods. The Percuil River winds away inland, drying to a large extent, but shallow draught boats can follow it with a rising tide as far as Percuil with the local moorings all lying in the line of the deeper water. Here it is possible

The peaceful beauty of the Percuil River can provide a welcome escape from the crowds at the height of the season

to anchor clear of the local moorings in mid-stream, just grounding at LWS but do not wander anywhere close inshore above Polvarth Point as oyster beds, marked by withies, lie on both sides of the river. Ideally, this is one of those places best explored by dinghy, the deserted creeks are alive with herons and other wildlife and there is excellent berrying late in the summer.

Leaving the narrow Percuil, do not be lulled into a false sense of security by the broad waters of Carrick Roads for large areas are shallow at LW, as many have discovered to their surprise. The main channel is very deep, however, averaging 25m LAT, and trends towards Penarrow Point, a low promontory with a prominent pillar on the western shore, then over to the eastern bank towards St Just Creek, where there are a number of moorings. At half flood there is ample water everywhere, but upstream of St Mawes Castle St Mawes Bank extends from the shore, least depth 1.2m in places. **Mylor Creek,** west of Penarrow Point is a very popular base for a large number of local boats which lie on extensive moorings in Mylor Pool, but the surrounding shallows in the approaches have as little as 1.2m in places at LAT, and with springs, or a draught over 1.5m, it is always best to wait until a couple of hours after LW, passing close to the red can North Bank buoy off Penarrow Point, and maintaining this sort of distance from the shore as you bear round towards the moorings.

Restronguet Sailing Club, a very active dinghy racing centre, is the modern building on the foreshore, and beyond it are the houses, quays and pontoons of **Mylor Yacht Harbour.** Formerly the Royal Navy's smallest Dockyard and base for the old wooden waller HMS *Ganges* it was not until the late 1960s that this picturesque corner began to develop into the busy yard that it has since become.

The yard has some visitors' moorings off the pontoons, marked 'C', and these can be booked in advance, otherwise call on VHF channel M 'Mylor Yacht Harbour' during working hours, or berth alongside the northern side of the outermost pontoon clear of the fuel berth and enquire at the office ashore. Approaching the pontoons beware the low floating breakwater to the east, and remember that alongside the outer pontoon there is only 1m at MLWS.

There is no public transport to Mylor Yacht Harbour but it is very self-contained, with water and diesel at the fuel berth, petrol at the end of the main quay, showers, toilets, a small launderette, and licenced cafe/restaurant. The chandler/foodstore is open seven days a week, and as well as boating clothing and an electronics engineer/supplier, the comprehensive yard facilities include a 25 ton travelift, and engine spares and service for Volvo, Perkins, Lister, Vetus, Bukh and Petter. Last but not least, the very friendly Mylor Yacht Club is on the quay and visitors are welcome to use the clubhouse and bar. The old quays of the dockyard form a sheltered and attractive setting overlooked by the lovely church of St Mylor, and some of the gravestones surrounding it are a fascinating reflection of the local maritime heritage,

the peaceful resting place of Packet Commanders, and many sailors and dredgermen.

Overhung with trees, the narrow entrance into Mylor Creek is very full of moorings but widens further in, continuing for nearly a mile to the village of Mylor Bridge, where there is a Post Office, shops and occasional buses to Falmouth. All of the upper part of the creek dries, and at **Tregatreath** is Gaffers and Luggers boatyard, where traditional shipwright work blends harmoniously with modern technology for it is here that the gaff-rigged fibreglass working boats are produced by Martin Heard.

From Mylor Pool, it is tempting to head directly for **Restronguet Creek** just upstream, certain disaster if the tide is near LW as beyond the outer moorings the extensive banks almost dry at LW.

Instead, return to the main channel, heading for the moorings off **St Just,** a particularly pleasant spot in an east wind, when Mylor inevitably suffers the most, and although there are many local moorings a reasonable anchorage can be found just clear of them, south of Messack Point or off the southern shore. Shoal draught boats able to dry out can work their way right into the creek and anchor there if space permits. Land on the shingle beach at the head of the inlet that encloses a drying tidal pool, where you will find Pascoe's Boatyard nearby. Small quantities of diesel are available here, in cans, and also Calor refills, but the undoubted pride of the creek is the 13th century church. Often described as having one of the most beautiful settings in England, it nestles against the wooded hillside overlooking the peaceful creek, surrounded by a breathtaking blaze of camelias and rhododendron bushes in summer.

Near low water continue to keep close to the main channel, which bears north-west from St Just towards **Restronguet.** It is shallow between the mouth of the creek and the main channel, south of the two beacons, north and south cardinal marks, on Carrick Carlys Rock, but with a couple of hours of flood you should be able to get up to the Pandora Inn, the most likely reason for a visit to the creek. There are concentrated moorings in the deep pool at the narrow mouth of the creek off Restronguet Point, a low promontory with some very expensive looking properties along it, and the stream runs fast through the narrows. Deep draught boats can anchor east of the entrance off Weir Point before you reach the moorings. Either land on the beach and walk along the path to the pub, or take the dinghy, an easy row with the tide, and make sure you return on the ebb. Boats able to dry out, however, can go right up to the large pontoon off the pub. With its huge thatch, and attractive waterside location the Pandora is inevitably a very popular local watering hole which takes its name from HMS *Pandora* the ship that captured the *Bounty* mutineers — on his return in 1790 her Commander bought this 13th century inn, and today, not only can you find food and drink at the pub, but also a very handy shower and toilet block, a small launderette, and fresh water.

The food at the Pandora is considerably better than average 'pub grub' and there is a good selection of real

ales. It does, however, tend to become crowded in the main holiday season.

The rest of Restronguet Creek widens considerably above the Pandora, fringed by woods and fields down to the water's edge. It is very shallow and dries extensively, but can be explored by dinghy for over a mile as far as **Devoran,** a small village on the northern shore where there is a Post Office and general store. Once a busy port and a site of considerable industrial importance in the 1880s, exporting copper and tin, the alluvial deposits from the mining eventually resulted in Devoran's demise, silting the river to such an extent that it is now only accessible a couple of hours either side of HW. Penpol Boatyard lies about ½ mile downstream, but here there are no real facilities for visitors; the yard specialises in high quality yacht hull finishing and building.

Beyond Restronguet, leave Carrick Carlys Rock to port, and on a falling tide keep to the deepwater channel which is marked by conical green starboard hand buoys. The bank to the east is particularly shallow, as little as 0.2m in places at LW, and this is the main area of the oyster fishery in winter. Opposite, there are a number of moorings off **Loe Beach,** shingle and sand, and popular for swimming. A few visitors' moorings are sometimes available if you enquire at the café, otherwise anchor off. Just above the beach, Pill Creek is a narrow wooded inlet, completely taken up by local moorings.

The real upper reaches of the Fal and Truro Rivers begin at Turnaware Point, wooded, with a low shingle foreshore on the eastern bank. The change is dramatic as the wide expanse of Carrick Roads narrows into a deep waterway and the most attractive part of the river begins. Keep close to the western shore, covered in trees, and fringed with cliffs, as a notorious grounding spot, Turnaware Bar, extends north-west from the Point. It is clearly marked by a green conical buoy which must be left to starboard. Here the streams begin to run strongly, 2–3 knots at springs. Immediately north of the buoy is **Channals Creek,** a popular local anchorage, well sheltered in anything except southerlies, and out of the main tidal stream. Sound in off the edge of the deep channel to about 2m at LW. Shoal draught boats can get much closer inshore where they will ground. A fine sweep of grassland leads up from the water's edge to the impressive facade of Trelissick House built in 1750, and now owned by the National Trust. The house is not open to the public but the gardens are from March to October; a particular delight for lovers of hydrangeas as there are over 130 varieties. Land at the rocky point on the east side of the bay and follow the footpath along the shore, a very pleasant walk through extensive woods.

The inside of Turnaware Point is another popular spot at weekends, particularly for picnics and barbeques and there is another good anchorage off it and little **Tolcarne Creek,** which is overlooked by steep woods, where you can anchor just clear of the deep water. The only thing that can detract from this otherwise delightful spot is the increasing use of it by water skiers, but mid-week it is usually peaceful.

Rounding the corner, past a line of concrete emergency water barges, the biggest surprise of the Fal comes into sight. Here, in the narrow river, surrounded by high wooded shores lie a line of large merchant ships on fore and aft moorings, out of all proportion to their surroundings. Their numbers vary depending on the fortunes of world shipping trade, but at times there are over 20 vessels laid up in the river as this is one of the cheapest places in the world, with deep water, between 13m and 15m, and excellent shelter. Although somewhat incongruous these silent, waiting leviathans have a certain mournful fascination but do not be too distracted by them; the tide runs strongly, and the high shores and ships make the breeze very fluky and it is easy to get set on to the large moorings. In addition, midway along this reach is the King Harry Ferry, which runs on chains, providing a short cut for cars between Falmouth and St Mawes. Identical at both ends, ascertain which way it is running and always pass astern, and not too close.

Lamouth and **Cowlands Creeks** open to port, both attractive and wooded, and both drying almost as far as the moorings at their mouth, where an anchorage can be found, between them and the deep water. Small craft can explore further on the tide, as far as the peaceful hamlets of **Coombe** and **Cowlands** where bilge keelers could dry out on the foreshore. Roundwood Quay, where the creeks meet is all National Trust property, a finely preserved granite quay with more pleasant walks leading from it.

Opposite, the river turns sharply to the east off

Falmouth Yacht Haven is particularly busy at weekends

Tolverne Point with more large ships sometimes in midstream, and on the shore you will see the thatched Smugglers Cottage, a popular local spot, with a landing pontoon and a number of mooring buoys for customers. This corner has an interesting history as during the last war it was used as an assembly point for part of the American fleet of D-Day landing craft, and was even visited by General Eisenhower. For nearly a hundred years trip boats have run here from Falmouth for cream teas, and although not a pub it has a licensed restaurant where lunches, suppers and barbeques, weather permitting, are a regular feature. The fascinating collection of photos and momentoes in the cottage are well worth seeing, in particular the *Uganda* room, devoted to the famous cruise ship and Falklands veteran that was laid up in the Fal between 1985 and '86.

At the next junction, just above Tolverne, the rivers divide, the Fal fading away rather insignificantly into Ruan Creek which continues to the east, and the Truro River, heading northwards. One of my favourite anchorages is at the entrance to **Ruan Creek,** just off the old ruined boathouse on the edge of the bank where there is about 2m at LW. Small coasters still run up to Truro on the tide, occasionally at night, and an anchor light is recommended. Shoal draught boats can push further into the creek letting go just beneath the northern shore where you will ground at LWS. It is overlooked by dense woods along the edge of Lord Falmouth's estate and although the river is often busy with trip and ferry boats during the day, at night this becomes a remote and peaceful retreat. The banks dry extensively along the south shore and the whole creek not far beyond the mouth. However, on the tide it can be followed deep into the rural depths of Cornwall, the wooded shore enclosing an extensive and completely isolated area of small creeks, perfect for a sailing dinghy.

A former naval base, Mylor Yacht harbour is now a self contained base for many local yachts where visitors are welcome

The deep water ends as you reach the **Truro River,** and just upstream of tiny Church Creek with the ruined spire of Old Kea Church rising above the trees on the port bank, lies the Maggotty Bank. This extends across the river from the eastern shore, least depth 0.7m, and the channel is very narrow between the west shore and the green conical buoy at the outer edge of the bank. Following the bend round to starboard, past Woodbury Point where there is an isolated cottage, there is a deeper pool, but in Malpas Reach, where there are many moorings, there is as little as 0.3m at LWS in places. The tide runs strongly, a good 2 knots at springs, and anchoring is not easy. At **Malpas,** pronounced 'Mopus', the elevated houses overlook the river, and below them is the yard of Malpas Boats with a private landing pontoon. They can usually provide visitors' moorings at £5 a day; either phone ahead (Tel: 0872 71260) or to enquire berth temporarily on the end of their pontoon, but do not leave your boat unattended as this is also used by

Trefusis Point darkens beyond the moorings in Falmouth harbour as the last light begins to fade

the ferries to Falmouth. Customers can leave their dinghies on the pontoon, and a shower/toilet, water and diesel in cans are also available. Close by there is a very small shop/Post Office, phone and the Heron Inn which does good pub food.

Tresillian River branches to starboard, where the Bar Creek Yacht Station can be seen with a long landing jetty. Most of this creek dries, but some visitors' moorings for bilge keelers are available from the yard, with diesel and water in cans.

Truro River continues past Malpas, broader and shallower from here onwards, and not many boats proceed much further. However, a few coasters do still use it so do not anchor in the channel which is well buoyed. Do not leave Malpas any earlier than three hours before HW Truro, and keep in midstream, leaving the green conical buoy and private landing pontoon off the new quayside development at Victoria Point to starboard. A large bank extends west of this point so keep well towards the western shore before turning north past the first of two more green conical buoys which must be left to starboard. After the second, the channel swings back to the eastern bank, high and wooded, past three port hand red cans, and west again off Sunny Corner where there are always a number of boats laid-up on the beach. At the next red

In the upper reaches of the Fal below Malpas steep wooded shores rise high above the river, and many secluded anchorages can be found

can, aim for the end of the Lighterage Quay, where the coasters berth, and keep close to it after the next green buoy as the river narrows to less than 100m. Once past the quay it widens again; ahead, the Cathedral and houses of Truro can now be seen but the channel winds back to starboard past another green buoy off the playing fields. It holds close to the eastern bank with alternate red and green buoys to port and starboard, then swings back towards another long quay on the western bank. There are three more starboard hand buoys, and at the last one steer north-east towards the yellow building and quay and then into the narrows, with a large modern Tesco superstore to port, and the deepest water closest to the old warehouses to starboard. Around the bend at Town Quay the river divides into three cul-de-sacs — berth on the starboard side of the central one between the steps and the bridge, and report to the Harbour Office in the western arm by the dredger berth.

There is water here for about two hours either side of HW with a handy tide gauge by the steps, and if you wish to remain longer you will dry out in soft mud, not a particularly wonderful spot but well compensated for by the attractive Cathedral City of Truro, a major shopping centre which is able to provide all requirements. There is a chandler and fresh water right on the quay, many good pubs and restaurants within a few minutes walk and a main line railway station should you need to land or pick up crew.

Falmouth — postscript

Between the Docks and Custom House Quay the extensive new development is the marina village of Port Pendennis, another of Peter de Savary's Cornish interests, due for completion in 1991. It is likely that further berthing for visitors will eventually be incorporated along this new waterfront.

Harbourmasters: Falmouth: Captain David Banks, Harbour Office, 44 Arwenack Street, Falmouth TR11 3JQ (Tel: 0326 312285 or 314379). Blue harbour patrol launch *Killigrew*. **Truro/Penryn:** Captain R Bigwood, Town Quay, Truro (Tel: 0872 72130 or 73352 for Penryn). **St Mawes,** Mr D Tatum, The Quay, St Mawes (Tel: 0326 270553)

VHF: Falmouth Harbour Radio VHF channel 16, working 14, 13, 12. 0800-1700 daily

Mail drop: Harbour Office will hold mail, also RCYC, Falmouth Yacht Marina and Mylor Yacht Harbour

Emergency services: Lifeboat at Falmouth. Falmouth Coastguard, MRCC, VHF channel 16, working 67 and 73 (Tel: 0326 317575)

Customs: Custom House, Arwenack Street, Falmouth (Tel: 0326 314156). Patrol launch *Curlew* VHF channel 16, working 10, 14

Anchorages: Off Custom House Quay; in harbour clear of moorings. Off St Mawes, St Just, off Restronguet, Loe Beach, and in upper reaches of river. Charges within Falmouth harbour

Moorings/berthings: FHC Visitors' Yacht Haven, North Quay, Falmouth (Tel: 0326 312285) summer only up to 1.8m draught, and 20 deep water visitors' moorings. RCYC nine visitors' moorings off Club. Falmouth Yacht Marina, North Parade, Falmouth (Tel: 0326 316620). Mylor Yacht Harbour Ltd, Mylor, Nr Falmouth (Tel: 0326 72121). (Tel: 0326 270686). Malpas Boats, Malpas, Nr Truro (Tel: 0872 71260)

Charges: (For 30ft boat per night inc VAT) FHC Yacht Haven £7; moorings £4.50; at anchor £2. Special rates for over a week. RCYC moorings £4.50. Falmouth Marina £9.30. Mylor Yacht Harbour, alongside £5.75; moorings £3.45. Malpas Boats £5. Town Quay, Truro, £4

Dinghy landings: Yacht Haven, North Quay. Fish Strand Steps, Prince of Wales Pier, RCYC. Mylor Yacht harbour pontoon. St Mawes, slipway

Water taxi: None, but RCYC has boatman and launch, 1000-1900 daily in season, Tuesday 1400-2300. VHF Channel 37

Phones: Nearest to Yacht Haven in entrance to Chain Locker pub. RCYC. Falmouth Marina. By church at Mylor. Malpas

Doctor: (Tel: 0326 312033)

Dentist: (Tel: 0326 313310)

Hospital: Nearest casualty Truro City Hospital (Tel: 0872 74242)

Churches: All denominations

Local weather forecast: Board on flagstaff by Visitors' Yacht Haven. Falmouth Yacht Marina office

Fuel: Barge on Visitors' Yacht Haven, summer only, petrol and diesel, 0900-1800. *Ulster Industry* fuel barge in harbour, diesel only Mon-Fri 0900-1700. Falmouth Marina, diesel daily 0700-2230. Mylor Yacht Harbour diesel and petrol during season 0830-1730, 1700 Sat

Paraffin: West Country Chandlers, High Street, Falmouth. Cox and Co, The Moor, Falmouth

Gas: Calor/Gaz, West Country Chandlers. Falmouth Marina. Falmouth Chandlers, Commercial Road, Penryn. Mylor Chandlery, Mylor Yacht Harbour

Water: Yacht Haven, Falmouth Marina, Mylor Yacht Harbour, St Mawes, Malpas, Town Quay, Truro

Tourist information: The Moor, Falmouth (Tel: 0326 312300)

Banks/cashpoints: All main banks have cashpoints

Post Office: The Moor. Sub Post Office in newsagents close to Custom House Quay

Rubbish: Skip on North Quay. Skips at Falmouth Marina and Mylor Yacht Harbour

Showers/toilets: Custom House Quay. RCYC. Falmouth Marina. Mylor Yacht Harbour. St Mawes SC. Malpas Boats

Launderettes: Centre of town, Falmouth. Falmouth Marina. Mylor Yacht Harbour

Provisions: All requirements in Falmouth, EC Weds but many shops open in season. Number of shops open on Sundays, inc Spar at Albany Road, ten minutes walk from harbour and North Parade Stores opposite Falmouth Marina entrance. Most provisions also at St Mawes, basics at Mylor Yacht harbour, seven days a week in season

Chandlers: West Country Chandlers, High Street, Falmouth (Tel: 0326 312611). Bosun's Locker, Upton Slip, Falmouth (Tel: 0326 312414). Mainbrace Chandlers, Falmouth Yacht Marina (Tel: 0326 318314). Nautibits Used Boat Gear, Port Falmouth Boatyard. (Tel: 0326 317474). The Boathouse, Commercial Road, Penryn (Tel: 0326 74177). Falmouth Chandlers/Merthen Marine, Commercial Road, Penryn (Tel: 0326 73988) closed Sat. Monsons, Commercial Road, Penryn (Tel: 0326 73581) bonded stores. Mylor Chandlery Ltd, Mylor Yacht Harbour, Nr Falmouth (Tel: 0326 75482) seven days in season. Reg Langdon, New Bridge Street, Truro (Tel: 0872 72668). Penrose Outdoors, Town Quay, Truro (Tel: 0872 70213)

Admiralty chart agents/compass adjusters: Marine Instruments at Bosun's Locker, Upton Slip, Falmouth (Tel: 0326 312414)

Liferaft service/repair: Penryn Marine, Penryn (Tel: 0326 76200). Inflatable Boat Services, Penryn (Tel: 0326 77600)

Repairs/hauling: Falmouth Boat Construction Ltd, Little Falmouth Yacht Yard, Flushing, Nr Falmouth (Tel: 0326 74309) slipways. Port Falmouth Boat Yard, North Parade, Falmouth (Tel: 0326 313248) slip/hoist (18 ton). Falmouth Yacht Marina hoist (30 ton). William's Boatyard, Penryn (Tel: 0326 73819). Penryn Bridge Boatyard (Tel: 0326 73322). Fox's Boatyard, Penryn (Tel: 0326 76041). Mylor Yacht Harbour (Tel: 0326 72121) (25 ton). Travelift. Heard's Boatyard, Tregatreath, Nr Mylor, Falmouth (Tel: 0326 74441). Freshwater Boatyard, St Mawes (Tel: 0326 270443). Percuil Boatyard (Tel: 0872 58 564). Pascoe's Boatyard, St Just in Roseland (Tel: 0326 270269). Malpas Boats, Malpas (Tel: 0872 71260). Bar Creek Yacht Station, Malpas (Tel: 0872 73919)

Marine engineers: Marine-Trak (Tel: 0326 76588 or 314610). SF Marine and Motor Services (Tel: 0326 76146). Falmouth Yacht Marina (Tel: 0326 316620). Penryn Marine at Mylor Yacht Harbour (Tel: 0326 76202). Falmouth Boat Construction (Tel: 0326 74309). Mylor Yacht Harbour (Tel: 0326 72121). Robin Curnow, outboards/Seagull agents, Penryn (Tel: 0326 73438). Nautibits (Tel: 0326 317474)

Electronic engineers: Mylor Marine Electronics, Mylor Yacht Harbour (Tel: 0326 74001). Sea-Com, Falmouth (Tel: 0326 76565)

Yacht refrigeration: Arctic Refrigeration, Church Road, Penryn (Tel: 0326 76016)

Sailmakers/repairs: Penrose, Upton Slip, Falmouth (Tel: 0326 312705). Spargo, King & Bennett, The Boathouse, Commercial Road, Penryn (Tel: 0326 72107). H & D Daniels, Bohill Wharf, Penryn (Tel: 0326 73261). South-West Sails, Islington Wharf, Penryn (Tel: 0326 75291)

Riggers: The Boathouse, Commercial Road, Penryn (Tel: 0326 74177). Falmouth Boat Construction, Flushing (Tel: 0326 74309). Mylor Yacht Harbour (Tel: 0326 72121). Nautibits (Tel: 0326 317474)

Transport: Branch line to main line connections to London and north at Truro. Daily coach connections with rest of country. Road connections to M5 via Plymouth. Newquay Airport, 45 mins

Car hire: Godfrey Davis (Tel: 0326 312192)

Car parking: Several large car parks in Falmouth. Parking at Falmouth Yacht Marina and Mylor Yacht Harbour

Yacht Clubs: Royal Cornwall Yacht Club, Greenbank, Falmouth (Tel: 0326 311105/312126). Flushing Sailing Club, New Quay, Flushing, Nr Falmouth (Tel: 0326 74043). Mylor Yacht Club, Mylor Yacht Harbour, Nr Falmouth (Tel: 0326 74391). Restronguet Sailing Club, Mylor Yacht Harbour, Nr Falmouth (Tel: 0326 74536). St Mawes Sailing Club, 1 The Quay, St Mawes (Tel: 0326 270686)

Eating out: Many options, from Chinese/Indian, fish and chips to good *à la carte*. Many bistros

Museums/things to do: Falmouth Maritime Museum, off Market Street, Falmouth. Pendennis and St Mawes Castles. Good safe beaches/walks

Special events: Falmouth Regatta Week, second week in August. Life Boat Day/raft race mid-August. Gig and Working Boat racing throughout summer

Helford River

Tides
HW Dover +0600. Range: MHWS 5.3m — MHWN 4.2m.
MLWN 1.9m — MLWS 0.6m. Streams attain up to 2kts in
river at springs.

Charts
BA: 147. **Stanford:** 13. **Imray:** Y57.

Waypoint
Voose N Cardinal buoy 50.05.77N. 5.06.90W.

Hazards
Gedges/August Rock, Car Croc Rock, Voose Rock (all unlit).
Bar/shallows within river on north shore. Rough approach in
strong east wind/ebb tide. Beware pot and net buoys.

'When the east wind blows up Helford river the shining waters become troubled and disturbed, and the little waves beat angrily on the sandy shores. The short seas break above the bar at ebbtide, and the waders fly inland to the mud flats, their wings skimming the surface, and calling to one another as they go. Only the gulls remain, wheeling and crying above the foam, diving in search of food, their grey feathers glistening with the salt spray.

The long rollers of the Channel, travelling from beyond Lizard Point, follow hard upon the steep seas at the river mouth and mingling with surge and wash of deep sea water comes the brown tide, swollen with the last rains and brackish from the mud, bearing on its face dead twigs and straws, and strange forgotten things, leaves too early fallen, young birds and the buds of flowers.

The open roadstead is deserted, for an east wind makes an uneasy anchorage, and but for the few houses scattered here and there above Helford Passage, and the group of bungalows about Port Navas, the river would be the same as it was in a century now forgotten, in a time that has left few memories . . .'

S O BEGINS *FRENCHMAN'S CREEK* Daphne du Maurier's bestseller that made the name of the Helford familiar to all, the haunt of the heroine Dona, and hideaway for the Frenchman, and his ship *La Mouette*. Although the numbers of yachts have certainly increased in the roadstead, her words are very true, and large areas in this gem of a river still remain untouched. Overshadowed by the busy harbour at Falmouth, commercially there was never any reason for the Helford to over-develop, it merely served the needs of the surrounding farms and communities, with a few small granite quays dotted along its banks. Apart from the scattered fishing hamlets, it remained *'. . . unvisited, the woods and hills untrodden, and all the drowsy beauty of midsummer that gives Helford river a strange enchantment, was never seen and never known.'*

The few people that did pass along this unpopulated, silent waterway into the depths of rural Cornwall, bounded by high shores, and deep, mysterious woods, were mostly heading for **Gweek,** right at the head of navigation. As the nearest access to the inland town of Helston this was the focal point of waterborne activity, with sailing coasters and barges slowly working their way up on the tide, bringing cargoes of coal, timber and lime, and taking away granite, tin and farm produce, until the advent of rail and motor transport, and gradual silting resulted in its decline at the turn of the century, and the river slipped back into obscurity.

However, another reason for the remarkable natural preservation of the inner reaches of the river is the fact that they are the site of the Duchy of Cornwall oyster fisheries, with large beds in this unpolluted river that reputedly go back to Roman times, a factor which has always inhibited the spread of moorings and other commercial development, This, combined with the limited facilities, means that today the Helford River, even in season, can still, at times, have an almost deserted quality, and a solitude that is increasingly rare, which is fortunately cherished by those who come here to seek it.

Approaching the Helford from the Fal care must be taken to locate the August Rock buoy to seaward of the Gedges, a dangerous shoal that dries at springs

Most of the moorings in the Helford lie in the Pool between Helford Point and Helford Passage on the distant shore

Approaches

Just under four miles from Pendennis Head, the Helford is a regular afternoon jaunt across the bay for many Falmouth boats, perhaps pausing to anchor off a beach or for a quick run ashore to the pub, but as the afternoon draws in, most return home. Although the entrance is well hidden away to the south-west, the various other boats entering and leaving will give a good indication, and as you close Rosemullion Head, August Rock, the green conical buoy to seaward of the Gedges rock will be spotted, and this should be left to starboard, before bearing round into the river mouth as it opens ahead, running to the west; there are no further hazards except very close to the shore, and depths average between 3m and 4m in the entrance. Beating in, there can often be a noticeable funnelling effect within the mouth, but overall, the shelter inside is excellent in anything, except, as we have already learned, easterly winds, when this is a place to avoid. Not only does Falmouth Bay and the approaches kick up a very short steep sea, the swell within the moorings and anchorage, particularly with wind against tide makes for a lot of discomfort, and unless you can tuck yourself away in one of the creeks, you are much better off in the Fal.

Before entering the main estuary of the Helford, on the southern shore is the entrance to **Gillan Creek,** easy to spot by the distinctive hump of Dennis Head across its mouth. This can be a delightful spot in the right conditions, but is really only of interest to shallow draught boats, as it dries for the most part, and the only deep water within its mouth is almost totally taken up with moorings. Car Croc, a particularly nasty rock, drying 1m, sits almost in the middle of the entrance, marked by an east cardinal buoy, BYB, but be warned, it extends further to the south-east than might be imagined so give it a good berth, passing mid-way between it and the south shore

when entering, but also beware of the rocks extending to seawards from Men-aver Point. Ideally, for a first visit, arrive just after LW when all the hazards are easy to see, and feel your way in on the tide, anchoring clear of the local moorings off the houses at Flushing if you can, or go further into the creek to the picturesque hamlet and church at St Anthony, where you will dry out, well tucked away in this hidden corner. Here, on the shingly foreshore is the small yard of Sailaway St Anthony, and it is possible that they might be able to provide a mooring. The densely wooded creek beyond the sandy spit is particularly attractive when the tide is in, perfect for a dinghy trip, or just a walk along the road that follows it inland.

Returning to the main river — in winds between north and west it provides some good anchorages just within the entrance, tucked up in the bight along the northern side. Toll Point is easy to spot with its isolated pine tree, and just beyond there is a gravelly beach at **Porth Saxon,** with depths of 1.6m quite close to the shore, often a quiet anchorage. Landing on the beach walk up over the headland to Mawnan Church, which is set among the trees on the cliff-top overlooking the entrance to the river. This is a particularly lovely spot, and it is not difficult to see why, among the gravestones, you can find those of two eminent yachtsmen, Claud Worth, the grandfather of modern cruising, and his son Tom, who circumnavigated the world in 1953 aboard the Giles designed cutter, *Beyond.* His epitaph is particularly succinct — 'Tom Worth, Who Sailed Beyond'.

The prominent house looking down on the middle of the bay is Glendurgan, a National Trust property, with 40 acres of beautiful gardens, much of it exotic, and a laurel maze, open on Mondays, Wednesdays and Fridays. Just beyond it are a number of moorings off the tiny hamlet of **Durgan,** which is also partly owned by the Trust, where there is another good anchorage. There are no facilities except a phone.

The southern side of the entrance is less hospitable, fringed with rocks, and a couple of small coves, above which can be seen a large house, and, here the locals claim that *this* was the *Manderley* of Daphne du Maurier's *Rebecca,* not *Menabilly* on Gribbin Head, and certainly, Ponsence Cove below it, with a tiny boathouse seems to fit the bill. One thing is certain, there is no doubt where the inspiration for *Frenchman's Creek* came from — just over a mile upriver you can explore it for yourself.

Beyond it lurks the Voose, a drying rock that has snared a surprising number of people in spite of its north cardinal buoy BY, which has replaced the old iron beacon that was there for many years. Approaching the narrows, if the tide is low, keep just over ½ a cable off the steep wooded shore leading up to Bosahan Point, and up towards the large concentration of moorings ahead, avoiding the northern, starboard, shore. Here, shallows extend right up to a cable along the shore with not much more than 0.5m LAT in places, right past the small boat moorings, beach, modern houses and pub at Helford Passage, as far as the green conical Bar buoy. This is often not easy to spot amongst the surrounding boats, and inshore of it at LWS it dries extensively, a muddy bank which stretches as far as the entrance to **Porth Navas Creek,** and is a popular local place for digging

Helford Passage

Steep wooded shores and the unspoiled beauty of the Helford make it unique

cockles. Being easy to reach by road from Falmouth, Helford Passage is the most commercialised part of the Helford River, centred around the Ferry Boat Inn, which has a restaurant as well as bar food, and often live music. There is also a grocery/off licence, showers and launderette, a windsurfing school and a passenger ferry across to Helford Point.

The Pool, which contains the bulk of the Helford moorings, is nearly 15m deep in places, and averages about 6m, extending up the centre of the river. To port is the entrance to Helford creek, but at LWS, this dries extensively, on a line from Bosahan Point to Helford Point, where there is a prominent landing pontoon, and the white buildings of the former Helford Boatyard on the south shore, which became a private residence in late 1987.

In November 1884 the West Briton newspaper revealed that '. . . *the beautiful Helford River has been visited this summer by an unusual number of yachts — as many as five having been at anchor there at any one time.*'

Plus ça change! Inevitably, today, nearly all the available space in the pool is taken up with moorings, and anchoring should not be attempted. However, there are a number of visitors' moorings available, all of which have a green pick up buoy marked Visitors. Either grab one, or contact the Mooring Officer, Jim Stephens, who is sometimes listening on VHF Channel M in his mooring office by the former Helford Boatyard but, more often than not, will be out on the water in an 18 foot white launch, always very helpful and ready to assist. Remarkably there is still no charge for anchoring, and moorings are a very reasonable £3.50 a night, which does not, however, include the voluntary landing fee if you use the convenience of the private pontoon on Helford Point.

The only feasible places to anchor are further upstream off Port Navas Creek, where depths reduce to about 2m LWS, clear of the moorings, or downstream of the Pool, towards Bosahan Point, but clear of the power cable crossing the river, marked by beacons on the shore. Here, an anchor light is advisable as local fishing boats come and go at night. In both places, you will be well away from the normal landing places and it is a good row if the tide is running hard, which it can do, up to 2 knots at springs on the ebb. Shoal draught boats can edge close inshore into Helford creek, or off Helford Passage where they will dry out.

The small village of **Helford** is not really evident at all from the river, just a few houses along the shore which disappears into the narrow creek, and normally it is best to pay the small fee and land at the former Helford Boatyard pontoon to avoid the worry of the dinghy drying out. This and the surrounding area is now privately owned. Please leave a donation in the Honesty Box which pays for the maintenance of the pontoon and do not attempt to berth or land on the quay. A short walk along the point brings you to the Shipwright's Arms, a classic thatched waterside pub, with a strange attraction for thirsty crews, which also has a small restaurant, and a terrace outside. Winding on above the creekside quays and boathouses the

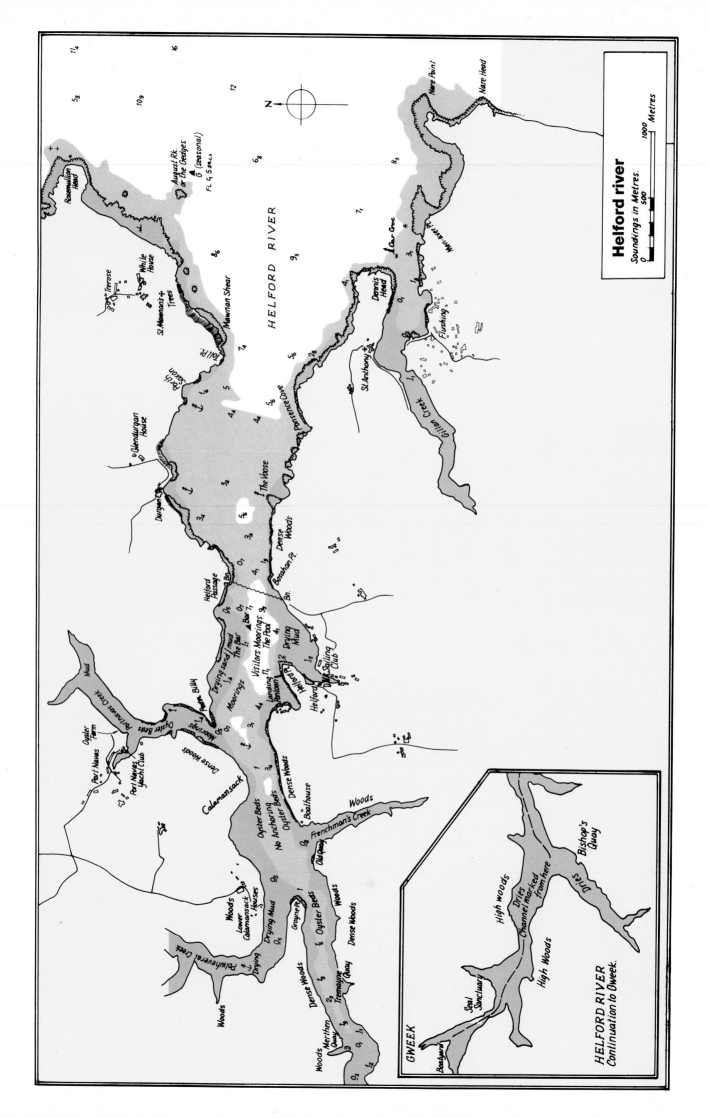

Helford river

Soundings in Metres.

0   500   1000
Metres

HELFORD RIVER

HELFORD RIVER
Continuation to Gweek.

GWEEK

Rosemullion Head

August Rk.
or the Gedges
▲ G (seasonal)
FL G 5 secs

White House
Trerose
St. Mawnan's + Trees
Mawnan Shear
Toll Pt.
Porth Saxon
Glendurgan House

Durgan

Helford Passage
The Voose
Dense Woods

Bosahan Pt.

Car Gee
Dennis Head
St. Anthony
Flushing

Helford River
Nare Point
Nare Head

Gillan Creek

Ponsence Cove

Drying Mud
The Pool
Visitors Moorings
Bar
Drying sand / mud
Moorings
Penn Billy
Landing
Pontoon
Helford Pt.
Helford
Sailing Club

Mud
Porthnavas Creek
Oyster Farm
Oyster Beds
Port Navas
Port Navas Yacht Club
Dense Woods
Calamansack
Oyster Beds
No Anchoring
Oyster Beds
Dense Woods
Boathouse
Woods
Frenchman's Creek
Old Quay
Lower Calamansack
Houses
Woods
Drying Mud
Groyne
Oyster Beds
Woods
Dense Woods
Polwheveral Creek
Drying
Dense Woods
Woods
Merthen Quay
Tremayne Quay
Woods

Seal Sanctuary
High woods
Dries
Channel marked from here
High Woods
Boatyard
High Woods
Bishop's Quay
Dries

narrow lane squeezes past thick walled stone cottages, whitewashed and covered in climbing roses, tiny gardens overflowing with flowers where you can sit and enjoy a cream tea, to the Post Office and general store. At the head of the creek, a bridge and shallow ford lead to another row of equally picturesque cottages following the opposite side of the creek, where you will find the Riverside Restaurant, which, in such an out of the way place, survives on the sort of enviable reputation that enables it to lure its customers from far and wide. However, this is definitely one for a special occasion, and prices are well out of the normal steak and chips range.

That, essentially is Helford village, and fortunately for its residents, cars are banished to a car park during the summer, which you will soon reach if you continue up the hill out of the village. From the car park a track leads down to the Helford River Sailing Club, an impressive Scandinavian style wooden building looking out across the river. Their landing pontoon can be reached an hour or so after LW and the Club is open daily except Mondays, with a good bar, food, showers and laundry available to visitors.

Continuing upstream, just before you reach Pedn Billy point, and the entrance to Port Navas Creek, the large house close to the water's edge is Bar, built by Claud Worth, and for many years his famous succession of yachts, all named *Tern,* were a familiar sight on their mooring off it.

Port Navas is another attractive wooded creek, although the eastern bank did not escape development and has a number of large houses overlooking it. However, just within the entrance, tucked away behind the point is the small, quiet pool at Abrahams Bosom, with just over 2m LWS, now mostly full of moorings, although shoal draught boats might find space to anchor close to the edge; if the wind turns to the east this is one of the few places where you will be completely sheltered. Most of the creek is shallow beyond the pool with extensive oyster beds, which are clearly marked by buoys, and a number of moorings, all of which dry at LWS. However, after half flood it is possible to get up to Port Navas Yacht Club which lies in a smaller creek on the port hand side. Keep in the centre and berth alongside the quay where there is diesel, water and petrol, and the friendly Yacht Club welcomes visitors, with a bar and meals available during normal licensing hours. By arrangement, it is possible to dry out alongside for £3 a night. Overhung with dense woods Port Navas is a very peaceful little backwater, with just a few stone cottages, overlooking the narrow creek. It is, however, the home of the Duchy Oyster Farm, and following the road back towards the mouth of the creek from the Yacht Club you will find their buildings beside the main creek, where nearly 1½ million oysters are processed every year. Should a sudden extravagance overcome you it is possible to buy some, reflecting as they slither down as rapidly as your bank balance that these were once the staple diet of the poor. Mussels, too, are produced by the Farm, so the odds on *moules marinière à la Port Navas* are probably a good bet for tonight. . .

By far the most unspoiled area of the river lies beyond the great rounded woods at **Calamansack,** a clear stretch of water where there are no moorings because of the mussel buoys and oyster beds along both sides of the river. These are clearly marked by buoys and stakes, and anchoring is prohibited. The deeper water lies along the south shore, which is also heavily wooded with low, steep cliffs, but just before Frenchman's Creek, depths reduce considerably to little more than 1m at LWS, and half a mile further on, the river dries extensively. Yet again, this, and the other creeks are ideal for the dinghy, although on a reasonable flood, moderate draught boats can make it all the way to Gweek, which is accessible a couple of hours either side of HW.

It is impossible not be drawn into the romance of **Frenchman's Creek,** where, '. . . the trees still crowd thick and darkly to the water's edge, and the moss is succulent and green upon the little quay where Dona built her fire and looked across the flames at her lover. . .'. The reality is very much as it is described in the book, glistening mud at low tide, where herons and oyster catchers roam, and as the thin trickle of the flood creeps inland again in the dinghy, like the yachtsman in the book, 'the sound of the blades upon the water seeming overloud,' you too can follow its winding course past blackened tree stumps emerging like creatures from the mud, to where the dense trees close in like a tunnel, brushing the incoming tide, and the silence becomes profound.

The atmosphere of Frenchman's Creek is undeniable; at Groyne Point, just a short distance upstream, Polwheveral Creek branches off to starboard, and although just as attractive, somehow has none of the mystery. If you are seeking some real solitude, round the bend beyond the moorings, shoal draught boats can find plenty of space to dry out.

Following the flood up to **Gweek,** the river passes between high wooded banks with mud fringed rocky shores most of the way and the deeper water lies in midstream. It is possible to land at Tremayne Quay, which is owned by the National Trust and there is a lovely woodland walk leading from it. Just downstream of **Mawgan Creek** the orange mooring buoy in the centre of the channel belongs to a local fishing boat, and beyond it the river dries completely at LW. Bishop's Quay on the south shore is private, and opposite the entrance to the creek a large bank fills the centre of the river, the channel swinging to port around it, but fortunately, from here on it is marked with posts; red with square topmarks to port, and green with triangular topmarks to starboard, which meander from one side of the river to the other until you reach the very narrow bottleneck with steep woods on either side just below Gweek. Once through the gap, the head of the river widens, the old coal quay lies to port, and more private quays to starboard, and, almost in the saltings, Gweek Quay is straight ahead where there is a large boatyard, and it is possible to lie alongside, for a brief visit or overnight, which will cost £2.50.

This old, grass covered quay will always be a nostalgic place for me, for here, back in 1973, I came

At the head of the Helford River, the peaceful old quay at Gweek is accessible for a couple of hours either side of high water

across my own boat, *Temptress,* laid up and neglected, and spent many long happy weekends putting her to rights, and dreaming of where we would eventually sail. The atmosphere of Gweek has little changed, and it is still a relaxed and peaceful place, although the yard has grown considerably. Diesel and water are available, chandlery, a 30 ton crane and all normal yard facilities. In the small village close by there is a

well-stocked grocery store, open on Sundays, Post Office, garage and pub, and another couple of cafés; however, the most bizarre thing that Gweek can provide, and one that children particularly adore, is the Seal Sanctuary, where injured and sick seals are looked after before being returned to the sea. It is on the north side of the creek, just downstream from the village, and open daily during the summer.

Port guide — Helford River

Harbourmaster: None. Moorings Officer, Jim Stephens; Mooring Office next to former Helford Boatyard (Tel: 0326 280422). 18 foot open white launch in season

VHF: 'Moorings Officer' Channel M, occasionally. H.R.S.C. Channel M when open.

Emergency services: Lifeboat at Falmouth. Coastguard MRCC Falmouth (Tel: 0326 317575). VHF Channels 16, 67, 73

Customs: Clear at Falmouth. Yacht postbox by moorings office

Anchorages: Off Durgan/Porth Saxon, Gillan Creek, and off Porth Navas Creek. Anchoring in large areas of inner river prohibited because of oyster beds. Drying anchorages in upper reaches/creeks

Moorings/berthing: Visitors' moorings have green pick-up buoys. Drying alongside at Port Navas YC by arrangement, and Gweek Quay Boatyard

Dinghy landings: At former Helford Boatyard jetty, small charge. H.R.S.C. pontoon. Helford Passage, Helford village and Port Navas on tide

Water taxi: None. Passenger ferry from Helford Passage to Helford Point will pick up if hailed

Marinas: None

Charges: Anchoring free. Moorings £3 per night. £2.50 per night alongside at Gweek. Port Navas, £3

Phones: Durgan, St Anthony, Helford Village, Helford Passage, Port Navas, Gweek

Doctor: Nearest at Falmouth

Hospital: See Falmouth

Churches: C of E, Mawnan. St Anthony, Manaccan

Fuel: Diesel and petrol alongside Port Navas YC, HW. Diesel at Gweek Quay, Boatyard, HW. Otherwise in cans

Water: As for diesel, and at H.R.S.C.

Gas: Gweek Quay Boatyard

Banks: None

Post Office: Helford Village, Gweek

Showers/toilets: Helford River Sailing Club when bar is open. Ferry Boat Inn, Helford Passage

Launderette: Ferry Boat Inn (open 24 hours). H.R.S.C.

Provisions: Most basics at Helford Village, Helford Passage, and Gweek. EC Weds

Chandler: Gweek Quay Boatyard (Tel: 0326 22 657). Sailaway St Anthony (Tel: 0326 23 357)

Repairs: As for chandlery

Marine engineers: Gweek Quay Boatyard

Transport: Occasional buses to Falmouth from Helford Passage (Glendurgan) and Gweek

Yacht clubs: Helford River Sailing Club, Helford, Helston (Tel: 0326 23 460). Port Navas Yacht Club, Port Navas, Constantine, Falmouth (Tel: 0326 40419)

Eating out: Pub food/restaurants at Helford village, Helford Passage, Port Navas YC, and Gweek

Things to do: Glendurgan Gardens, NT. Seal sanctuary, Gweek, Maritime Exhibition, Gweek Quay. Magnificent scenery/walks

Passages

The Manacles to Land's End

Favourable tidal Streams
LIZARD POINT: **Bound West: 2 hours before HW Dover**
Bound East: 4 hours after HW Dover

AS THE MOST southerly point of the British Isles, a major headland and tidal gate, the Lizard and the coast to the west of it into Mount's Bay and around Land's End, has a justifiably notorious reputation and should always be treated with respect and caution.

Composed for the greater part of precipitous granite cliffs — a firm favourite with the rock-climbing fraternity — this inhospitable and rugged coast is open to the prevailing winds; it is an area of strong tides, invariably suffers from the long Atlantic ground swell, not to mention concentrated shipping and no absolute harbours of refuge. But don't despair; in reasonably settled weather, with an experienced crew in a well-found boat it can be explored safely, but here, more so than ever, a wary eye should be kept on the weather, and options for shelter always close to mind.

Jack Pender, an old Mousehole fisherman told me

many years ago as I languished there in early September that 'west of the Lizard's no place for a small boat, come the end of August'. I confess to a certain youthful panic and sailed that very night, scurrying back to Falmouth. But his words were born of years of working these difficult waters, and myself a fisherman for several years, I often recalled them as we turned to run for home, the grey sea and sky piling to the west, white crests blowing before it, and the high, dim shore suddenly vanishing to leeward in the gathering gloom. Conditions can deteriorate in a matter of hours, and a contrary tide can produce large, often tumbling seas. It is not difficult to see how this particular coast has claimed so many ships and men over the years.

Beacon	Range (NM)	Frequency (kHz)	Call Sign
Marine beacons			
Lizard	70	298.8	LZ
Round Island	100	308	RR
Aero beacons			
Penzance heliport	15	333	PH
St Mawgan	50	356.5	SM

Coastal Radio
Pendennis Radio, working channel 62.
Land's End Radio, working channels 27, 88, 85, 64.

The Lizard is a bold, rugged headland with a race that should be given a good berth — at least five miles in poor weather

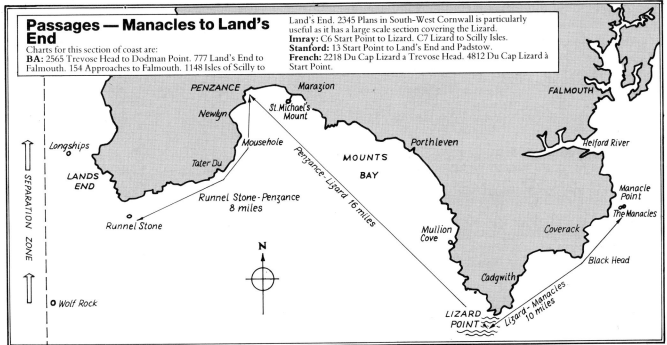

Passages — Manacles to Land's End

Charts for this section of coast are:
BA: 2565 Trevose Head to Dodman Point. 777 Land's End to Falmouth. 154 Approaches to Falmouth. 1148 Isles of Scilly to Land's End. 2345 Plans in South-West Cornwall is particularly useful as it has a large scale section covering the Lizard.
Imray: C6 Start Point to Lizard. C7 Lizard to Scilly Isles.
Stanford: 13 Start Point to Land's End and Padstow.
French: 2218 Du Cap Lizard a Trevose Head. 4812 Du Cap Lizard à Start Point.

Approximate distances — nautical miles

Approaches

Bound west, take full advantage of the ebb tide out of **Falmouth Bay,** which starts to run to the south three hours before HW Dover (three hours after HW Falmouth) and once clear of the Manacle Buoy, east cardinal BYB, a course of 220°T will pass all offshore dangers in the approaches to the **Lizard,** and should be held to a position three miles to the south of the headland to clear the race. Obviously, adequate allowance should also be made for the tidal stream setting to the west which begins about one hour before HW Dover. If bound round **Land's End,** because of the division of the streams into the Irish Sea and English Channel, a favourable tide can now be carried for nearly eight hours. Conversely, the passage east is not so obliging; a vessel carrying a fair tide down the North Cornish coast and round Land's End will invariably run into a foul tide off the Lizard, as from the turn of the tide to the south at the Longships, five hours before HW Dover, only three hours of favourable tide can be carried across Mount's Bay; once round the Lizard the ebb starting from Falmouth Bay will be gathering in strength against you. Bound east from Mount's Bay to Falmouth it is, therefore, advisable to arrive at the Lizard at slack water just over three and a half hours after HW Dover.

At night, the coast is well lit, although once south of the Manacle Buoy (Q(3) 10secs) steering 220°T the Lizard light (Fl 3 secs) will be obscured for five miles until you are in a position a couple of miles south-east of Black Head. Inshore Coverack and Cadgwith show only small clusters of lights. Once clear to the south of the Lizard, Tater Du light (Fl(3) 15secs) will be seen to the north-west on the far side of Mount's Bay, and further west, the Wolf Rock light (Fl 15secs).

Shipping bound down Channel for Land's End converges on the Lizard and this can be a busy stretch of water; many local fishing boats are also likely to be encountered, particularly trawling at night and their movements should be closely watched and avoided; additional confusion is also possible with regular Naval exercises in the vicinity.

Entering **Mount's Bay,** the whole of the northern shore appears as a continuous mass of lights from Marazion to Newlyn, and it is worth noting that both the Lizard and Tater Du lights become obscured in the close approach to **Penzance,** by which time the light on the south pier, (sectored Iso WR 2secs) should be easily visible, and the same will be found for **Newlyn,** with its south pier (Fl 5secs). Low Lee buoy, (Q(3) 10secs) is the only lit buoy in Mount's Bay one mile south-east of Newlyn harbour entrance. Crossing Mount's Bay and proceeding round Land's End, the Runnel Stone Buoy (Q(6)+L Fl 15secs) lies within the red sector of the Longships Light (Iso WR 10secs), and is also covered by a FR light through 060°T to 074°T from Tater Du lighthouse, and it is wise to stand on past the buoy to the westwards until the white sector of the Longships opens before altering to the northwest. Pass well to seaward of the light; the currents in the vicinity run hard, and unpredictably. There is a fine weather passage inshore of the Longships but this should *never* be attempted at night. At this point you enter the inshore traffic zone, and a lot more shipping is also likely to be encountered.

In poor visibility, additional aids to navigation are the fog signals at the Lizard (Siren Mo (N) 60secs); Wolf Rock (Horn 30secs); Longships (Horn 10secs); the Runnel Stone Buoy has a whistle and bell, and the Manacle Buoy a bell. Newlyn harbour entrance has a 60sec fog siren; there is no fog signal at Penzance. Tater Du horn was withdrawn under the 1987 Navaid Review.

However, as enjoyable cruising is the real objective of the exercise, hopefully, you will be sailing this spectacular section of coast in daylight and good visibility when it can be appreciated to the full. In favourable weather, and settled conditions the coastline can for the most part be followed much closer inshore.

From Lowland Point, the land rises to a distinctively flat topped profile, steep-to and rocky with cliffs between 30 and 50 metres in height, and few off-lying dangers. It is interspersed with many attractive coves and bays, so if time permits, or if waiting for the tide, some of the smaller havens of the Lizard peninsular can provide good temporary anchorages and an interesting diversion.

Coverack, the first of these, is easily located by the conspicuous large hotel just south of the clustered houses of the village. Black Head, a mile to the south is the next prominent feature and can easily be mistaken as Bass Point on the Lizard when approaching from the east in poor visibility. The tidal streams can run up to three knots at springs, and in strong southerly winds considerable steep breaking seas will be encountered with wind against tide in the vicinity. If running for Falmouth in such conditions, lay a course several miles to seaward of both Black Head and the Manacle Buoy, where similar poor conditions can also be encountered.

Beyond Black Head the coast falls back to form a wide bay, well sheltered from the west and a one time favourite haunt of the Falmouth Pilot vessels and quay punts waiting for business, and also of a Falmouth tailor's cutter, waiting to put a man aboard homeward bound ships so that the crews could walk ashore in a brand new suit. In its centre **Cadgwith** nestles in a rocky cove, the houses wedged tightly at the mouth of a narrow valley; **Parn Voose Cove** and **Church Cove,** with a small landing slip lie about a mile to the south, and the present Lizard-Cadgwith lifeboat station is spectacularly sited close by in a narrow crevice in the high cliffs at **Kilcobben Cove.** However, special care is needed sailing inshore along this section of the coast and the large scale Admiralty Chart No 2345 is a must. The Craggan Rocks with less than 2m over them lie just over half a mile SSE of Cadgwith, and the Voge Rock, covered by only 1.6m lies two cables east of Church Cove. The yellow buoy further offshore merely marks the end of a sewer outfall. Bass Point is steep and topped by the Coastguard Station with the distinctive white building of the former Lloyds signal station close by.

In Mount's Bay the distinctive pyramid of St Michael's Mount is unmistakable

The Spernan Shoals and notorious Vrogue Rock, covered 1.8m, lies four cables east-south-east of Bass Point, its position indicated by transit beacons ashore, and the passage between the rock and the shore should only be used in settled conditions. Normally, approaching from Black Head without any diversions inshore, your course should be laid well to seaward of Bass Point. With rocks extending over half a mile to the south of the Lizard, and overfalls, severe with wind against tide, it is advisable to give the whole area a good berth in anything but settled conditions, standing off between two and three miles. In poor weather I would advise five miles is not unrealistic, for the seas inshore can be very confused.

Tidal streams are strong, the west-going ebb can run at over three knots at springs, the flood slightly less, and it goes without saying that a fair tide is essential for a sailing vessel with limited power as I have found on several occasions, when I have been forced to give up the unequal struggle. In westerly winds the full force will not be felt until clear of the Lizard, and after spells of weather from that quarter, a considerable ground swell will be encountered.

It is a headland to approach with caution particularly in poor weather or bad visibility; the vast list of vessels lost in the vicinity over the years are an adequate testimony to its natural dangers. Care should also be taken to note shipping movements as they concentrate towards Land's End, the activities of fishing boats, and, yet again, beware of poorly marked pot and net buoys, often without flags, and half-submerged in the tide. One more unusual and peculiar 'hazard'; an encounter that certainly added a few grey hairs recently, was the sudden presence of a totally unmarked rock nearly three miles south of the point, black, and awash with breaking waves, right ahead. The chart confirmed absolutely no existence of such a horror; several minutes of dry-mouthed panic elapsed before it dawned on me that it was an enormous basking shark, a plankton eating summer visitor to Cornish waters and, otherwise, totally harmless.

The Lizard lighthouse is a prominent and distinctive long white building with two octagonal towers, the easternmost topped by the light, its five million candlepower giving a 26 mile range (Fl 3sec). The first light on the headland, and the first in Cornwall, was established in 1619 by Sir John Killigrew, amidst much local protest at the adverse effects on the profits from the wrecking, and Killigrew himself eventually abandoned his light in favour of the more lucrative spoils from the sea. Several other attempts to provide a lighthouse on the headland during the 1700s ensued, notably Fonnereau's twin towers with a fire in each and a cottage between in which an overlooker lay on a couch watching for any relaxation of the firemen's efforts, a blast on a cowhorn 'awakening them, and recalling them to their duty!' The onset of oil lighting in 1813 put an end to such navigational uncertainty, and by the end of the century both an electric light and a foghorn had been established, with a correspondingly dramatic decline in the loss of shipping.

The Boa, a rocky shoal 2½ miles west of Lizard point is the last offshore hazard in the vicinity and although well covered with over 20m it creates a lot of overfalls, and even breaking seas in south-westerly gales. If the Lizard has been given a berth of three miles as recommended, heading into Mount's Bay you should pass clear to the south of the Boa. Its location is usually easy to spot from the concentration of pot buoys.

The western side of the Lizard, exposed to the full force of the Atlantic gales is high, rugged and spectacular for the next five miles as it bears north-west into Mount's Bay. The tall jagged pyramid of Gull Rock and Asparagus Island enclosing the beauty spot of **Kynance Cove** are a distinctive feature, and both Rill Point and Predannack Head should be given a reasonable berth. **Mullion Island** will begin to open as Predannack Head is passed, and in favourable easterly conditions, an anchorage can be found off the small harbour of **Porth Mellin.** Although a passage exists between the island and the mainland, it is not recommended, and the approach is best made to the north of the island.

The character of the coast begins to change considerably as Mount's Bay is entered further. Beyond Pedngwinian Point, the high cliffs recede, and the long sand and shingle beach of Gunwalloe and Loe Bar stretches away northwards. Particularly vulnerable to southerly gales, many vessels struggling to escape round the Lizard from Mount's Bay have come to grief on Loe Bar, including the frigate *Anson* in 1807 when 100 men were lost in the surf trying to reach the shore. Helplessly watching the catastrophe Henry Trengrouse was inspired to invent the rocket line throwing apparatus which is still used by the Coastguards today.

Porthleven, lies at the northern end of Loe Bar, with a conspicuous clock tower by the harbour mouth and should only be attempted in offshore winds and settled conditions, and from here the northern shore of Mount's Bay begins to trend more to the west. Welloe Rock, drying 0.8m lies three miles due west of Porthleven, and the Mountamopus shoal, covered 1.8m is a mile south-west of Cudden Point. Passing to the south of the south cardinal buoy marking this hazard, the distinctive pyramid of **St Michael's Mount** topped by a spire and turrets is unmistakeable, and keeping it on the starboard bow, **Penzance,** 2½ miles to the west is easy to locate, with no further hazards except the Gear, a drying rock marked by a black and red beacon, just under half a mile due south of the harbour entrance. Pass to seaward of the Gear if bound across the bay to **Newlyn.**

Continuing west from Mount's Bay, if leaving from Newlyn, a course can be laid just over a cable from the shore with its extensive quarry workings, inside Carn Base and Low Lee shoals, the latter marked by an east cardinal buoy, and past Penlee Point with its old lifeboat house and slipway. This, and the memorial garden beside it, remain as a sad reminder of the tragic loss of the lifeboat *Solomon Browne* with its entire crew of eight on the 19 December 1981, while attending the wreck of the coaster *Union Star* near Lamorna Cove. It was the last launch from the slipway, and the replacement Penlee lifeboat, a larger Arun, is now kept afloat in Newlyn harbour.

Once past **St Clement's Isle** and **Mousehole** the impressive grass topped granite cliffs form a continuous line, broken only by a few tiny coves and sandy beaches such as Penberth and Porthcurno, and finally the section between Gwennap Head and **Land's End** is particularly precipitous. Stay half a mile offshore until abeam of Tater Du light, when a course is best laid directly to pass just south of the Runnel Stone Buoy, south cardinal, which marks the outer end of a rocky ledge extending nearly a mile southwards from Gwennap Head, with the drying Runnel Stone at its extremity, a considerable hazard to shipping, and the scene of many wrecks. It is not unknown for the Runnel Stone buoy to break adrift in the heavy seas that often run along this most exposed corner. There are, fortunately, two conical beacons inshore on Hella Point, the outer red, the inner black with a lower white band, providing a transit of 352°T over the position of the rocks. When the white base of the inner beacon is also visible above the cliff top you will pass safely to the south of the hazard.

This is, in any circumstances, an area to be navigated with extreme caution. Although the tides in Mount's Bay are weak they rapidly gather in strength towards the Runnel Stone, probably attaining 4-5 knots at springs, becoming increasingly unpredictable as the main tidal streams divide into the Irish Sea and English Channel. As mentioned earlier, this is a very unfairly balanced tidal gate; the north-west stream begins three hours before HW Dover and runs for nearly 9½ hours, the E going stream six hours before HW Dover lasting for a mere three. The Atlantic ground swell is rarely non-existent for the passage 'around the Land' to the north Cornish coast and this, and the coast beyond is an area to take very seriously.

A favourable forecast is essential to attempt Land's End, or the passage to the **Scillies,** and the outlook should also be good, for several days if possible. Bound for the Scillies, it is probably best to push the foul tide out of Mount's Bay and along the coast, leaving about three hours before HW Dover. By the time you reach the Runnel Stone, approximately two hours later, the tide will be with you, running to the south-west for the next three hours which will carry you well clear of Land's End. Wolf Rock lighthouse to the south-west provides a useful point of reference; although the south-west stream will be setting you towards it at this point, further offshore it will be compensating as it turns north-westerly later.

Ideally you should leave Mount's Bay at HW Dover, which is not possible if you are locked in the tidal basin at Penzance, for it will then be just about local LW. Newlyn, or the anchorage off Mousehole are therefore your most likely departure points.

The passage to the Scillies, approximately 36 miles, Newlyn to St Mary's, is likely to take a good seven to eight hours, if not longer, which means that you will be conveniently arriving on the next flood tide, for local HW is exactly six hours before HW Dover.

Bound round Land's End from Mount's Bay, you can comfortably leave later, about one hour before HW Dover; you will then have a favourable tide for the next seven hours and, hopefully, be well on your way.

Coverack

Tides
HW Dover +0600.
Charts
BA: 777. **Stanford:** 13. **Imray:** C6, C7.

Hazards
Small boat harbour dries completely. Manacles. Isolated rocks off Dolor Point (unlit) and to NW of harbour. Fine weather anchorage only and dangerous in onshore wind.

BETWEEN THE MANACLES and Black Head, Coverack is a small, picturesque drying harbour popular with tourists, and still the base for a small fleet of fishing boats, open craft used for potting and handlining and known locally as 'cove boats' or 'toshers'.

In settled weather with offshore wind and an absence of ground swell the bay makes a tenable anchorage although with any indication of a shift of wind to the south or east it is no place to linger.

Approaches

Approaching, the conspicuous large hotel to the south of the village is the easiest landmark to spot, and with the Guthen Rocks off Chynalls Point to the south, and the Dava Rocks extending nearly half a mile from

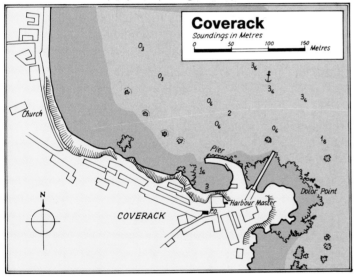

Lowland point to the north end of the bay do not attempt to cut corners. Enter on a westerly course, sounding your way in to the best anchorage in about 8m, a cable or so NNE of the pierhead. The harbour, enclosed by a small, sturdy granite wall dries to beyond the entrance with a clean, sandy bottom but the shore immediately to the west is rocky and very foul. Although there is a minimum depth of 2.4m alongside the pier end at MHWN and it would be possible to dry out, it could only be attempted with the Harbourmaster's permission. Due to the crowding of the local boats which lie on heavy rope fore and aft moorings it is not really a viable proposition. Far better to anchor off and dinghy in, with easy landing at the ladders on the pier or the large slipway across the head of the harbour.

Facilities

Coverack, like so many other Cornish harbours grew with the extensive pilchard fishery, and the old salt store overlooking the harbour is now, inevitably, a gift shop. All the basic facilities are available; provisions, Post Office, several cafés, pub/hotels, including the curiously named Paris Inn, nothing to do with the EEC or *entente cordiale,* but named after the *City of Paris,* an American liner stranded nearby in 1899 when her entire complement of 700 passengers was brought safely to shore by local boats before she was eventually refloated. Early closing Tuesday. Water is available from the Harbourmaster but the nearest fuel is at a garage nearly two miles away. The Old Lifeboat house is now also a gift shop but an inshore boat is still stationed here.

Anchor off Coverack and dinghy ashore to visit this small harbour

Cadgwith

Tides HW Dover +0554.

Charts

BA: 777. **Stanford:** 13. **Imray:** C6, C7.

Hazards

Bow rock (unlit) in entrance. Fine weather anchorage only and dangerous in onshore wind.

'. . . There is a bench from which the whole of the bay can be seen where the fishermen sit in patience, and scarcely turn their eyes from the sea. It really is very exciting to hear the pilchard cry for the first time; visitors rise up and leave their dinner and amusements, and every man who dwells in the village, whatever he may be doing, is called by a strange and terrible cry to come and help in the 'take'. The boats are always ready in the bay, but the real time to see the pilchard take is by moonlight, when the fishes look like living silver . . .'

CADGWITH, IT WOULD SEEM, was popular even as far back as 1885 and although the huge shoals of pilchards vanished in the 1930s, the holidaymakers still descend in their droves. Nevertheless, it is very much a working fishing community, and the traditional atmosphere of the village lingers on among the tight cluster of cottages nestling snugly in a steep green valley at the head of a tiny cove. Almost a bit too photogenic, white painted walls and heavy encrusted thatches contrast sharply with the more familiar granite cottages, and the curious dark green serpentine rock that is local to the Lizard. There is no harbour, and the sizeable fleet of small boats is hauled up the shingle on wooden rollers, a daily spectacle much enjoyed by the visitors. Thumping softly, a magnificent single cylinder Hornsby donkey engine powers the winch; in the cool, dark cellar where it lurks, the surrounding walls are covered with faded paintings, curling sepia photographs, and the sweet aroma of warm oil pervades.

Approaches

Well sheltered from the west, the cove should only be approached in settled weather and offshore winds, and is not recommended for an overnight stop. The houses will be spotted from offshore, forming a break in the flat line of the cliffs, and closing the shore you will find what is effectively two coves, split in the middle by a low rocky outcrop called the Todden. The extension of this, a group of rocks — the Mare — extends to seaward, and it is advisable to sound in and anchor off them in about 2-3m. Do not proceed any further into the cove as the Bow is a dangerous rock right in the centre which covers at quarter tide, and the entrance is also in frequent use by the local boats. Landing is easy anywhere on the shingle beach, but make sure you take your dinghy well clear, to avoid obstructing the winching operations.

Facilities

There are limited provisions, a Post Office and pub/hotel/café, and a pleasant walk up on to the cliffs

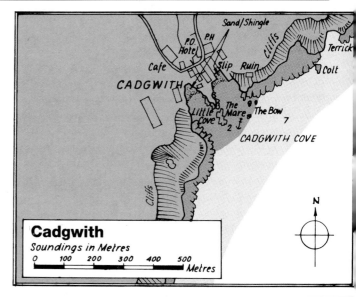

Cadgwith is a steep sided cove where local fishing boats are hauled up on the beach

overlooking the cove, past some lovely cottages to a small black hut, high on the headland. It was here that those fishermen used to sit waiting and watching, and once the cry of 'Hevva, Hevva!' sent them to sea, from this high vantage point the 'huers' would direct the boats towards the shoals by a series of special hand signals and wild shouts through a large tin speaking trumpet.

Huers' huts can still be seen in many places along the Cornish coast abandoned after the strange demise of the pilchard and the herring. The huge shoals that were once the livelihood of so many small villages like Cadgwith began to dwindle mysteriously in the mid-1930s, and after the war they were never found again, a phenomenon that has never really been explained. Today, the fleet of cove boats works nets, pots and handlines, rock hopping along this beautiful but at times very wild stretch of coast.

Mullion

Tides HW Dover +0552.
Charts
BA: 2345, 777. **Stanford:** 13. **Imray:** C7.

Hazards
Mullion Island, many rocks close inshore. Fine weather anchorage only and dangerous in onshore wind.

THIS SMALL DRYING harbour three miles north-west of the Lizard, spectacularly situated in a magnificent stretch of coast, provides another interesting stop in favourable conditions of offshore winds and settled weather, and is also convenient if waiting for a fair tide eastwards round the Lizard.

Approaches

The approach is straightforward: both **Mullion Island** and the conspicuous Mullion Cove hotel high on the cliffs above are easy to see. Although there is a narrow channel between the island and the mainland used by local boats it is not recommended and the northern end of the island should be given a good berth to the northwards, entering the anchorage midway between it and the harbour wall which will be easily seen. Now owned by the National Trust, **Porthmellin** harbour was built in 1895, a somewhat lethargic response to the disastrous loss of the cove's entire fishing fleet when a sudden gale descended over fifty years earlier. Today there are only a few local small boats based here, for the years have done nothing to change its disadvantage of being very exposed to the prevailing wind and sea. Although there is a berth alongside the western wall as long as it is not being used by the fishing boats it is not recommended as there is frequently a considerable surge in the harbour which is, incidentally, closed to fin keel boats, and no overnight stays are permitted in any craft.

Anchorages

The anchorage between the harbour and Mullion Island is, therefore, for me, now the only option, well sheltered to the north and east with good holding on a sandy bottom in 7m midway between the harbour entrance and the northern end of the island. It is now an unusually remote spot, well off the normal track, but has not always been so . . . Writing in September 1868, R T McMullen, anchored here in a north-easterly gale aboard his *Orion*, counted sixty-four vessels sheltering, and commented, '. . . *I was surprised to see how regularly they were arranged according to their ability to work offshore if the wind were to fly in. The Orion was first in line with three pilot cutters, then came*

The anchorage off Mullion is good in offshore winds; let go midway between the island and the harbour mouth

the sloops and yawls, and a brig-rigged steamship. Next schooners and ketches, then brigs and barks; those in the first division were almost still on the water, the second were rolling perceptibly, the third decidedly uneasy, and the last, having no protection at all from Mullion Island, were rolling miserably.'

Facilities

Dinghy ashore when the tide allows to land on the slipway at the head of the cove. There are just a few houses beside the harbour, and a café, and away from the main tourist track it is a particularly unspoiled little corner with some magnificent views and excellent walks along the cliffs in both directions. Most normal provisions are available at Mullion village just over a mile away, and the Mullion Cove Hotel above the cove is open to non-residents with meals available in the bar. Owing to the potentially exposed nature of the anchorage I would not, however, recommend leaving your boat unattended for any length of time, and to leave with any sign of a shift of wind to the south.

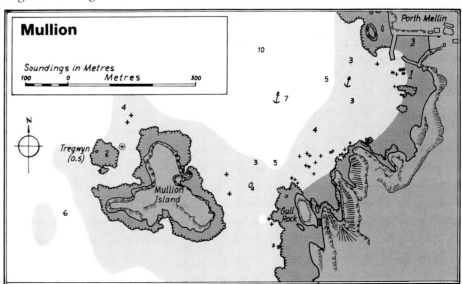

Mullion

Soundings in Metres

Metres

Tregwyn (0.5)

Mullion Island

Gull Rock

Porth Mellin

Porthleven

Tides
HW Dover +0551.
Charts
BA: 2345, 777. **Stanford:** 13. **Imray:** C7.

Hazards
Harbour dries. Deazle rocks, Little and Great Trigg rocks (all unlit) to west and east of entrance. Dangerous to approach in onshore winds.

I ALWAYS FEEL rather sorry for **Porthleven,** for it is certainly a magnificent example of the harbour builder's art, a long protective entrance leading to a fine basin enclosed by massive granite walls. However, its chequered history reveals that it never really enjoyed much success. There has been a chapter of disasters, starting right from the beginning when a group of speculators obtained an Act of Parliament ostensibly to build a harbour of refuge in 1811. Disagreement and squabbling dogged the venture and the harbour was not completed until six years later, surviving for another six before it was devastated by a storm, a fact that did little to encourage shipowners to use it. Although it was rebuilt and greatly improved in the mid-1800s, its fundamental failing was the fact that it dries completely and the narrow entrance faces right into the prevailing south-westerlies, rendering it frequently unapproachable, and forcing its closure with large baulks of timber in heavy weather.

Today, Porthleven is mostly used by pleasure craft, and a small but diminishing fleet of fishing boats. However, as with all the other small harbours of the Lizard, with offshore winds and settled conditions it makes another interesting place to visit off the regular cruising track, and a feasible overnight stop providing you don't mind drying out.

Porthleven has a large inner basin which dries completely

Facilities

A popular place with holidaymakers, Porthleven provides a curious contrast of old fishermen's cottages and converted net stores, and a long row of typically bold Victorian semi-detached houses that completely dominate the entrance. All normal facilities are available, Post Office, banks, fuel and water at the garage at the north-west end of the harbour or through the Harbourmaster. There are a number of cafés, pubs and restaurants, including the inevitable *Ship Inn* overlooking the harbour entrance, and an interesting walk can be had along the great shingle sweep of Loe Bar as far as Loe Pool, a large freshwater lake, formed when the bar sealed off the estuary of the River Cober that was once navigable as far inland as Helston. It is part of the large Penrose Estate, and now owned by the National Trust. There are some delightful walks through the woods along its banks.

Approaches

The harbour mouth lies at the northern end of Loe Bar, a long shingle beach that begins just over two miles north of Mullion Island, the houses on the hillside easily visible on the cliffs, and the south pier, with a prominent clock tower at the landward end should be closed on a bearing of 045°T. The harbour dries right to the entrance at MLWS, but is accessible sensibly from half-tide onwards, and if waiting for water, anchor in 5m, 200m due south of the pier. Care must be taken to avoid the submerged Little Trigg rocks off the pier end though there are no further hazards once past the old lifeboat house on the north shore. Pass through the outer entrance and into the inner basin where the local boats mostly lie on fore and aft moorings with heavy ground chains running north-south up the harbour. Visitors are advised to berth by the entrance on the east quay and seek out the Harbourmaster John Vaughan if he has not already spotted you. His office is in a white building midway along the western quay, and he will advise on the most suitable berth. The south quay with a crane at its end for lowering the timber baulks is used by the local fishing boats and should be avoided.

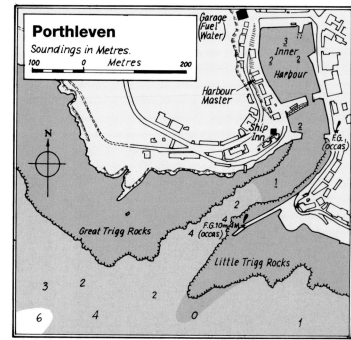

Penzance

Tides
HW Dover +0550. Range: MHWS 5.6m — MHWN 4.4m.
MLWN 2.0m — MLWS 0.7m. Tidal dock gate manned every
tide from 2 hours before to 1 hour after HW.

Charts
BA: 2345. **Stanford:** 13. **Imray:** C7.

Waypoint
South Pier Head 50.07.02N. 5.31.62W.

Hazards
Gear Rock (unlit). Outer harbour dries, tidal wet dock.
Harbour approach very dangerous in strong southerly
weather. Pot and net buoys in Mount's Bay. Keep clear if
RMS *Scillonian* or other commercial shipping entering or
leaving.

WHEN McMULLEN PUT into **Penzance** in
1868 it was still in its busy commercial heyday
and he moaned bitterly about the state of the quays,
*. . . which are allowed by the Corporation to be in so
offensive a state, encumbered with coal dust that nothing
short of real distress will drive me into the nasty harbour
again.'*

The coal has long vanished from the quays of
Penzance but so, too, has most of the waterborne
trade. Now a busy centre for tourism, the town's
development and prosperity was founded around the
export of tin, reaching its peak in the mid 1800s, when
nearly half of the mineral mined in Cornwall passed
through the port, stacked in 300 lb ingots on the
quayside for shipment to places as far afield as Russia
and Italy. Also a major centre for the export of salt
herring and mackerel, there are records of a
prosperous trading and fishing village here as early as
1300, but the major extensions to form the present day
harbour were made in 1745-72 when the Albert Pier
was built, with further improvements during the
nineteenth century. A dry dock was established in
1814, and Holman's still operate one here today.
Penzance was also the first proud possessor of a
lifeboat in Cornwall in 1803, but the station was not
particularly successful and discontinued in 1917, its
place taken by the Penlee lifeboat which is now based
in Newlyn. Trinity House has maintained a base here
since the early 1800s, and their distinctive black, white
and buff vessels have long been a familiar sight in the

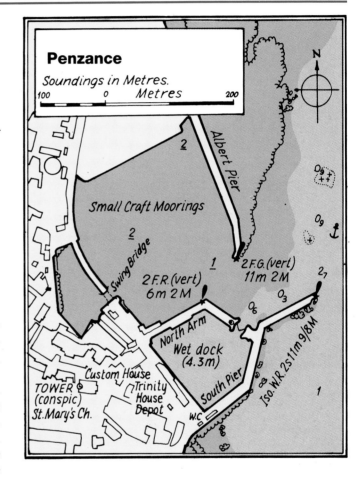

Penzance has a drying outer
harbour full of local boats,
and a tidal basin where
visitors can berth. If waiting
for the tide into the inner
basin, lie temporarily on the
south pier in the ferry berth
which is usually empty
during the day. Once locked
inside, the Penzance tidal
dock is secure in any
weather

bay, with buoys sitting rather incongruously beside the harbour road outside their depot.

I have to confess that I always rather thought of Penzance as a strictly commercial port and tended to pass it by; the additional tidal disadvantages are that the main outer harbour dries almost completely at LAT and the floating wet dock, entered through a hydraulic gate, is only accessible for two hours before HW until one hour after HW. However, a recent forced visit changed my attitude considerably, when unable to get round the Lizard in a fresh north-easterly we decided to admit defeat, and turned *Temptress* back towards this hitherto unvisited corner. It turned out to be a decision that proved far from disappointing.

As the outer harbour dries almost completely at LAT and is given over to a large number of local moorings on fore and aft trots visitors normally use the tidal wet dock where there is ample berthing for up to fifty yachts, afloat at all times in total protection. A small amount of commercial traffic still uses the basin, and it has become popular for steel conversions, refits and repair work. It is, perhaps, not the most attractive place, but the warm and helpful welcome extended by the dock staff and present Harbourmaster, Martin Tregoning, more than makes up for the surroundings. A keen yachtsman himself, a lot of genuine effort has been made towards encouraging visitors, and this is certainly reflected by their increasing numbers. As a base to explore west Cornwall, and the rugged Land's End peninsular it is ideal, with good bus services and cars for hire; boats can be left unattended without worry for a few days or even longer at a very reasonable rate.

Approaches

Approaching from the east, pass to the south of Mountamopus Shoal, least depth 1.8m (South Cardinal), holding the unmistakeable bulk of St Michael's Mount on your starboard bow. The conspicuous tower of St Mary's Church provides a good landmark to locate Penzance. Gear Rock, which dries 1.8m lies 4.5 cables almost due south of the harbour entrance and is marked by an unlit black and red beacon with a topmark of two black balls, not particularly hazardous when arriving from the east but right on the approach from the south-west. Penzance Harbour lighthouse, a white tower, displays a red and white sectored light (Iso WR 2secs, red sector through 159°-268°T, white sector through 268°-345°T 8 miles). The white sector safely clears Gear Rock, and if approaching from the Low Lee buoy steer a north-easterly course until the white sector opens. There are lights displayed vertically from the Berthing Master's Office by the north side of the dock gate to indicate whether it is open or closed: a red over a green means that it is closed; red over red for open.

Accessible with safety in winds from south-west to north, Penzance should be not considered as a harbour of refuge in bad weather, particularly with winds from the east through to south, when heavy breaking seas can build up in the shallowing approaches, often breaking over the south pier, and making the whole entrance highly dangerous. In these conditions, Newlyn is the only place to contemplate, an approach to be attempted with extreme caution and as near to HW as possible. However, in reasonable weather, and offshore winds a temporary small craft anchorage can be found just over two cables NNE of the end of the Albert Pier, in about 1.2m LAT, or further offshore depending on your draught, ensuring that you are clear of the fairway into the harbour entrance, or alternatively anchor two cables due south of the south pier head. The Harbour Office monitors VHF Ch 16 during working hours, works on 12, and will advise when the tidal dock is likely to open. Although the outer harbour is full of moorings, it is sometimes possible to dry out alongside the Albert Pier with the Harbourmaster's permission.

A feasible alternative to anchoring off while awaiting the tide is to moor on the inside of the South Pier in the berth used by the Isles of Scillies ferry RMS *Scillonian III*, which is normally empty Monday to Friday from 0930 to 1830, and is only otherwise occupied on summer Saturdays from 1130 to 1400, and all day Sunday when there is no sailing. At low water keep tight to the south pier as the water shoals rapidly on the northern side of the entrance, but between the convenient ladder half way along the wall and the lighthouse a depth of 1.8m will be found even at LAT. You can lie alongside the large floating fenders — be warned, though, if you clamber on to them they roll instantly, and the noticeably polluted water is probably not the best to swim in. If VHF contact has not already been made with the Harbour Office check in with the Harbourmaster once berthed, and I would not recommend leaving the boat totally unattended. Do not obstruct the stone steps by the entrance to the wet basin as this is in constant use by local boats taking fishing trips.

As I mentioned earlier, the dock gate is manned two hours before HW every tide, day and night, and opened soon afterwards. Once in the basin, the Berthing Master will allocate a berth alongside, and he will also issue a very useful key to the locked toilets and shower situated beneath the berthing office in the end of the large white building nearest to the lock gate. The public toilets on the south pier should only be considered in the direst of emergencies. The Berthing Master can also arrange for water and small quantities of diesel if required; petrol you have to fetch yourself from the nearest garage which is close by the railway station. By arrangement with the berthing master, vessels can be left unattended in complete safety in the wet basin.

Facilities

Ashore, just about everything is available in Penzance, from sailmaker to cashpoints. It is a very busy and popular tourist spot, an interesting old market town with many fine buildings. The outer harbour was once much larger but half filled in to provide a huge car park, and the road beside it leads to the main bus and railway station, the terminus for the main line to London. Avis car hire and the new tourist information centre is also located here. The main shopping centre, the curiously named Market Jew Street is derived from the Cornish 'Marghas de Yow' meaning 'Thursday Market' and it climbs away up the hillside towards the impressive granite Market House, with its ionic pillars and domed roof, which also houses Lloyds Bank. In front of it there is a statue of Penzance's famous son, Sir Humphrey Davy, best known for his invention of the miner's safety lamp. Behind the station, on the road out of town, there is a good launderette open seven days a week, 0900-1930, and a bit further on, a large Shell Garage. Bennetts, at the bottom of Market Jew Street, are the main Calor and Camping Gaz suppliers and they are also able to repair and install gas equipment. Continuing up the hill there are supermarkets, chemists, newsagents and the main Post Office half way up on the left. It is the largest town in the far west and just about all normal requirements will be found. For eating ashore there is a reasonable selection of options, from Indian to fish and chips. There are several good pubs in the area, most notably the *Turks Head* with a separate restaurant and reasonably priced pub food although it's usually very crowded; the *Admiral Benbow* is a lot more up-market with a very comprehensive menu for those intent on a real gastronomic night ashore. Chapel Street, the main tourist area that leads back down from the top of Market Jew Street towards St Mary's church and the harbour, has a number of fine listed buildings, many of them gift shops, and also the bizarre Egyptian

House, restored by the Landmark Trust and now the local premises of the National Trust. In the narrow adjoining streets there are several smaller bistros and pubs, interesting exploration in itself.

Shopping and eating out of the way, there are a variety of other things to do ashore. If time permits a trip inland and across the north coast or to Land's End is well worth the effort, and there are regular bus services to St Michael's Mount if you decide against a visit by sea. If the weather has put paid to plans to sail to the Scillies, by way of a consolation you could consider whetting your appetite with a day trip to the islands. The RMS *Scillonian III* sails daily; there are also frequent helicopter flights from Penzance Heliport.

In Chapel Street there is the Nautical Museum, a private collection of fascinating artefacts salvaged from local wrecks, open daily May to September with a charge for admission, and a small, town Museum located centrally in the Penlee Memorial Park. Apart from history and old photographs of the harbour, it is also the home of the town's permanent collection of the Newlyn Painting School. They provide a romanticised glimpse of the final years as a simple working port, just before Brunel's Great Western Railway wiped out the isolation of the far west, and the first large hotels began to rise along the new promenade at the shingly head of the bay. There's nothing like a bit of nostalgia; conveniently we tend to forget all that coal dust.

Port guide — Penzance

Harbourmaster: Captain Martin Tregoning, The Harbour Office, Wharf Road, Penzance TR18 4AB (Tel: 0736 66113 (night 61119) or 62341 ext. 294). Office manned Mon-Fri 0830-1200, 1300-1430; Sat 0830-1230; closed Sunday

VHF: Channel 16 monitored during working hours. Working channels 12 and 9 (Penzance Pilots)

Mail drop: Harbour office will hold mail

Emergency services: Lifeboat at Newlyn (Tel: 0736 60666)

Customs: Clearance available on request (Tel: 0736 63366) or contact Harbour VHF in advance

Anchorages: In fair weather 500 ft to ENE of Albert Pier, clear of fairway, or two cables to ENE of South pier

Mooring/berthing: Tidal wet dock available two hours before HW to one hour after HW, ample alongside berthing within, afloat at all time. Anchor off, or berth on inside of South Pier in Isles of Scilly ferry berth if available, to await gate opening

Dinghy landings: Steps on inside of Albert Pier; public slipway by Sailing Club

Marinas: None

Charges: 14p per foot per night plus VAT. Every third night free

Phones: Harbour office in emergency. Nearest public phone on promenade opposite bathing pool

Doctor: Port Medical Officer, Dr Mike Hersant (Tel: 0736 63886)

Hospital: West Cornwall Hospital, 24 hour casualty dept (Tel: 0736 62382)

Churches: All denominations

Local weather forecast: Displayed at Harbour Office Mon-Sat

Fuel: Diesel by arrangement with berthing master. Petrol from local garage

Water: See berthing master

Camping Gaz/Calor: Bennetts, close to railway station

Tourist information office: At railway station

Banks/cashpoint: All main banks in town have outside cashpoint facilities, also TSB and Abbey

Post Office: Market Jew Street

Rubbish: Skip on quay

Showers/toilets: Key available from berthing master

Launderette: Near railway station

Provisions: Plenty of shops, some close Weds pm but not main supermarkets. Newsagents only on Sundays

Chandler: Limited selection at Matthews, New Street (Tel: 0736 64004). Penzance Chandlers, Wharf Road (Tel: 0736 67851). R Curnow (Albert Pier). Two good chandleries in Newlyn

Repairs: Limited facilities. Drying out on Albert Pier slipway by arrangement with Harbourmaster in emergency. Crane available for up to 8 tons

Marine engineers: Albert Pier Engineering (Tel: 0736 63566). R&D Engineering (Tel: 0736 60253). Manta Marine Services, St Buryan (Tel: 0736 72265). Quay Engineering (Tel: 0736 69996)

Electronic engineers: Curnow Marine Electronics (Tel: 0736 68606)

Sailmakers: Matthews, New Street (Tel: 0736 64004)

Transport: Bus and rail

Car/bike hire: Car hire at railway station

Car parking: Large car park close to harbour

Yacht club: Penzance Sailing Club, Albert Pier

Eating out: Pub food, fish and chips and several up-market restaurants, but not much choice in between

Newlyn

Tides

HW Dover +0550. Range: MHWS 5.6m — MHWN 4.4m.
MLWN 2.0m — MLWS 0.7m. Main harbour dredged to 3m
MLWS

Charts
BA: 2345. **Stanford:** 13. **Imray:** C7.

Waypoint

South Pier Head 50.06.15N. 5.32.50W.
Hazards

Low Lee Rock (lit). Gear Rock (unlit). Busy fishing harbour,
beware vessels in narrow entrance. Approach dangerous in
strong southerly weather, heavy swell sets across entrance.
Pot and net buoys in Mount's Bay.

W ALK THE STREETS of **Newlyn** at your peril! Large articulated refrigerated lorries, fork lift trucks and continually spraying hoses form an assault on all sides, leaving little doubt that this is a very busy fishing port, alive with colour, boats and activity. In contrast with its declining neighbour Penzance, Newlyn has seen considerable commercial expansion in recent years, particularly with the opening of the new Mary Williams Pier in 1980, and further major development during 1988.

The port is dredged to an average depth of 2m at LAT, and is accessible at all states of the tide, providing the only real harbour of refuge in Mount's Bay. However, in strong south or south-easterly winds a heavy sea builds up in the shoaling water at the head of the bay, particularly at LW causing a considerable run within the harbour entrance. This factor should be carefully considered if running for shelter, and entry is best attempted as close to HW as possible.

Approaches

Approaching from the east the run across Mount's Bay is straightforward, passing to the south of the Mountamopus shoal, (south cardinal buoy unlit) and well clear of Gear Rock, three-quarters of a mile to the north east of the harbour entrance, which dries 1.8m and is marked by a black and red beacon with a topmark of two black balls. From the west, Low Lee shoal, least depth 1.5m LAT, is marked by an east cardinal buoy (BY Q(3) 10secs), but Carn Base shoal three cables to the north-west is unmarked, has a least depth of 1.8m, and breaks in heavy weather. However, once St Clement's Island off **Mousehole** is abeam, a course should be held just over a cable from the shore which will lead inside all the shoals, past Penlee Point with its former lifeboat house, and the conspicuous quarry buildings from where the white lighthouse on the end of the south pier (Fl 5sec) is easy to spot against the town which rises up the hillside overlooking the harbour. The northern side of the entrance which is 47m wide displays a FWG sectored light, green 238°-248°T. The only other hazard to consider, particularly at night, is the considerable intensity of pots along this stretch of coast, and also the large numbers of small craft that will be found working them; as always, fishing craft restricted by gear should be given a generous berth, and your intentions made obvious at an early stage.

In offshore winds it is possible to anchor a cable SSE

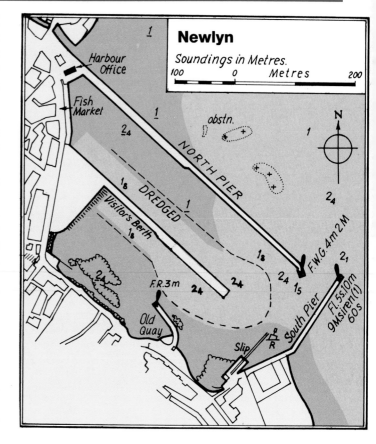

of the harbour entrance, sounding in to about 3m, or alternatively a similar distance to the north-east in Gwavas Lake. Owing to the frequency of fishing boat movements, a riding light is essential. Newlyn itself provides no specific facilities for yachts, and at one time they were positively discouraged. As in all busy fishing harbours remember that commerce takes precedence over pleasure. Sailing and anchoring is prohibited anywhere in the harbour except in emergency, but the berthing situation has been helped considerably by the fact that short stay visitors will usually find space alongside the fishing boats on the west side of the new pier, which tends to be occupied by local vessels that are laid up for refits or work aboard. Consequently there is less daily movement on this side of the pier in contrast to the continual comings and goings elsewhere in the harbour where the fleet lands daily to the largest fishmarket in Cornwall.

As well as breast lines to your neighbour, bow and stern lines should be led ashore if intending to stay overnight, and with the boats often five or six deep this will involve quite a scramble. The best bet is

Newlyn's central pier has been extended a further 90m since this photograph was taken in 1987. Visitors should berth on the western side.

to moor temporarily, and check with the Harbourmaster, Mr Munson, whose office is at the head of the harbour by the north pier, up a flight of steps next to the fish-merchants' offices. He is very helpful, and will endeavour to point you to a spot where you are not likely to be disturbed. However, yachts on passage, or sheltering from weather are tolerated on a strictly day to day basis. At one time they were not allowed to be left unattended at all, and it is still advisable to let the Harbourmaster know if the entire crew has to go ashore for any length of time. There are no facilities for leaving a yacht in Newlyn — the wet dock in Penzance is the nearest place where this can be done.

Facilities
Ashore, Newlyn is a bustling working town, the fishmarket central to its life, and early risers, providing they keep out of the way of the very serious business in hand, can spend a fascinating hour or two watching the landings and daily auction which starts at around seven in the morning Monday to Saturday. The old town, a pleasant meandering sort of place, climbs up the hillside in tight rows of sturdy granite cottages, sheltered courtyards and narrow alleyways. It has been a fishing harbour since medieval times, and the magnificent remains of the original pier, a gently curving wall of huge granite blocks, weathered and mottled with orange lichens can still be seen forming part of the small inner basin beneath the cliff on the west side of the harbour.

The present harbour was built between 1866 and 1888, and was the centre of the huge mackerel and pilchard fishery in the nineteenth century. In 1896 this was the scene of the infamous riots when the devout local fishermen ran amok, angered by visiting east coast boats landing fish on Sundays, and hurled their catches back into the sea, a bloody disturbance that was only eventually put down by military intervention. The magnificent luggers that once packed these west Cornish ports have for the most part vanished forever, but fortunately *Barnabas,* a fine example of a St Ives lugger restored and owned by the Maritime Trust, is at present based in Falmouth where she can often be seen sailing during the summer months. These powerful double-ended vessels between 30 and 50 feet in length evolved from the wild conditions in the Western Approaches and were renowned not only for their sea-keeping qualities but also for their speed.

The present day fleet has grown considerably in recent years, and ranges from large beam trawlers and scallopers that venture as far afield as the North Sea and the Irish Sea to the smaller pot and net boats that work the tricky inshore waters round Land's End and fish for mackerel in winter.

Although small, the town provides most necessary provisions, catering as it does for the fishing fleet, and it is particularly convenient as supplies can be obtained on Sundays from Caddys close to the harbour, as most of the fleet puts to sea on Sunday evening. Anything not obtainable in Newlyn can usually be found a mile away in Penzance, a pleasant walk along the promenade, or by bus every fifteen minutes. There is no sailing club but hot showers, for both men *and* women can be obtained at the Royal National Mission for Deep Sea Fishermen.

This part of Cornwall has a long tradition of

123

Yachts must lie with the fishing fleet in Newlyn's busy harbour, and stays of more than a couple of days are not encouraged

popularity with artists, in particular the famous Newlyn School of the 1890s, highly realistic paintings which have enjoyed a great resurgence of interest with fishing and fisherfolk one of its central themes. Today, cultural diversion can still be found at the Newlyn Orion Art Gallery on the seafront with regular local and visiting exhibitions; gastronomic activity is well catered for, with several fishermen's cafés, fish and chips (very fresh!), a Chinese takeaway, some good pubs with food, notably the *Tolcarne*, and the *Smuggler's* which overlooks the harbour with an adjoining restaurant. There are also several more up-market bistros, with, predictably, a good choice of seafood.

Port guide — Newlyn

Harbourmaster: Mr A T Munson, Harbour Office, Newlyn (Tel: 0736 62523). Weekdays 0800-1700

VHF: Channel 16 monitored during office hours. Working channels 12 or 9

Mail drop: Harbour office will hold mail

Harbour patrol: Harbour launch white 19 ft open boat

Emergency services/lifeboat: Penlee lifeboat stationed in harbour (Tel: 0736 60666)

Customs: As for Penzance

Anchorages: In fair weather to NE of harbour entrance in Gwavas lake, or to SE of entrance. Anchoring prohibited within the harbour

Mooring/berthing: Alongside fishing boats on the west side of the Mary Williams (inner) pier. Contact HM on arrival

Marinas: None

Charges: 8p per foot plus VAT

Phones: By Harbour Office and on Fish Market

Doctor: See Penzance

Hospital: See Penzance

Churches: All denominations

Local weather forecast: At Harbour Office

Fuel: See Harbourmaster for diesel; any quantity available. Petrol from filling station

Water: Available on quay

Tourist information office: See Penzance

Banks/cashpoint: Barclays and Lloyds open 1000-1230 Mon-Fri. All banks, normal hours in Penzance, and full cashpoint facilities

Post Office: By Harbour Office

Rubbish: Skips on quay

Showers/toilets: Available at Royal National Mission to Deep Sea Fishermen, north pier. Public toilets on quay

Launderette: On road towards Penzance

Provisions: Supermarket, butchers, newsagent, no half day closing, and Caddys Central stores also open Sunday mornings

Chandler: Good selection at Cosalt, Harbour Road (Tel: 0736 63094) opposite fishmarket, and also at Westrens, The Bridge (Tel: 0736 62413)

Repairs: Large slip for commercial craft; Penzance recommended for yacht repairs except in emergencies, drying out by arrangement with the Harbourmaster

Marine engineers: C K Jones on North pier, Ford Agents. See also Penzance

Electronic engineers: Kernow Marine Electronics (Tel: 0736 68606)

Sailmakers: Matthews — see Penzance

Transport: Regular buses to rail connection at Penzance

Car hire: See Harbourmaster

Car parking: Near Fish Market

Yacht club facilities: None

Eating out: Pub food, fish and chips, and several good restaurants

St Michael's Mount and Mousehole

St Michael's Mount: HW Dover +0550.
Charts: BA 23445. **Stanford** 13. **Imray** C7.
Hazards: Harbour dries. Hogus rocks, Outer Penzeath rocks and Maltman rock (all unlit).

Mousehole: HW Dover +0550.
Charts: BA 2345. **Stanford** 13. **Imray** C7.
Hazards: St Clement's Island (unlit). Harbour dries.

St Michael's Mount

THERE IS NO PROBLEM identifying **St Michael's Mount,** Cornwall's own mini version of the famous Mont St Michel in Normandy, a dramatic tidal island which rises like a fairy-tale castle into a distinctive 300ft pyramid in the north-east of Mount's Bay. Topped with the towers and buildings of the home of the St Aubyn family who have lived here since the mid-1600s. Although they continue to do so, the island was presented to the National Trust in 1954 by the present Lord St Levan. During the summer months, the Mount and parts of the castle buildings are open to the public on weekdays, 1000-1700; there is a charge for admission.

As a contrast to the larger Mount's Bay ports of Penzance and Newlyn, in the right conditions, St Michael's Mount and the old fishing harbour of **Mousehole,** in the south-west of the bay provide an interesting alternative. Both harbours dry completely at LAT but are normally accessible after half flood. For the whole of Mount's Bay local HW is about 6 hours after HW Dover.

Historically, the tiny harbour on the northern side of the Mount was once the most important in Mount's Bay, a major centre for the export of tin dating back as far as the first century BC, when the ore was sensibly brought overland from the mines on the north coast to avoid the treacherous journey around Land's End. A Benedictine monastery was established here in 1135, making it an important place of pilgrimage, but this was dissolved by Henry VIII during the Reformation, and during the Civil War the Royalists held the Mount for four years, a vital siege as the fortress was an ideal place for the import and stockpiling of arms and ammunition brought in from France.

In 1727 the modest harbour was rebuilt and extended, and by the early 1800s it prospered considerably, with over fifty houses on the island and a population of about 300. As you will see from the many pictures and prints if you visit the castle, large numbers of vessels regularly lay here, anchored in the bay or crammed into the tiny harbour, discharging timber from Scandinavia, coal and salt, before loading the return cargoes of copper, tin and cured fish that was exported in considerable quantities all over Europe. It was, however, the new harbour at Penzance that eventually sealed the fate of the Mount, and by the turn of the century it had lost all the trade to its larger rival.

Facilities

Today, it is the focal point of a very different kind of industry — tourism, and as one of its major attractions, at times it is almost overrun by the hordes who stream across the low tide causeway from **Marazion,** or pack the continuous fleet of small ferries that run during the summer months when the tide is in. In spite of it, the small harbour, with its simple row of neatly restored cottages is well worth a visit. Despite the dire warning that the climb to the castle should not be attempted by those suffering from any kind of heart condition, it is not as steep as it looks and provides spectacular panoramic views across Mount's Bay. In the evening, when the crowds have gone this is once again, for a few brief hours, a peaceful and tranquil place. There is a restaurant, café and gift shop by the harbour when the Mount is open; most normal

Great Hogus rocks

Anchorage

Visitors' berth

Marazion

Causeway at low tide

Harbourmaster's office

The small harbour at St Michael's Mount provides an interesting diversion if the weather permits

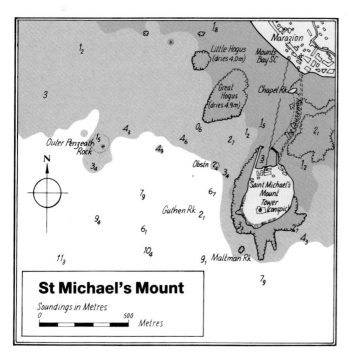

St Michael's Mount

Soundings in Metres

0   500

Metres

towards the anchorage where about 2m will be found at LW, over a firm sandy bottom between the Great Hogus reef, which dries 4.9m and the western pier end. After half-tide, the harbour is accessible to average draught boats — stay a reasonable distance from the pier heads and beware of the constant stream of ferry boats. Known locally as the 'hobblers' they operate from the steps on both sides of the entrance continuously as soon as the tide covers the causeway and should not be obstructed in any way. Berth between the ladders on the western wall and report to the Harbourmaster whose office is the opposite side of the harbour as soon as possible, if he has not already directed you into the berth. A small charge will be made for a night's stay, well worth it for the peace and quiet.

Mousehole

MOUSEHOLE IS IN MANY ways similar to St Michael's Mount, for this is another picturesque honey pot around which the tourists swarm. Available from half tide, this small, oval harbour with massive granite boulder walls is the epitome of a Cornish fishing village, though long past its commercial heyday in the mackerel and pilchard fishery. The residue of the fishing fleet once based here is now kept in Newlyn but a few local pot, net, and angling boats lie here on fore and aft trots and there are a number of small pleasure craft, too.

From early November until the end of March the harbour is closed completely with heavy wood baulks across the mouth and few winters pass without some damage to the seemingly impregnable walls as the south-easterly gales roll into Mount's Bay. Privately administered by its own Harbour Commissioners, the unfortunate dominance of car parking on the quays and beside the harbour does pay for its upkeep, and the small charge for visiting yachts contributes to it too. In appropriate settled conditions, the harbour, or the anchorage off it provides a worthwhile diversion for an overnight stay, or just a daytime visit.

Approaches

St Clement's Isle, a distinctive, low rocky outcrop with a small obelisk on its highest point lies close to the east of the harbour entrance and between it and the

provisions, Barclays and Lloyds bank, phone and Post Office and several pubs will be found at Marazion.

Approaches and anchorages

The best anchorage for a visit to the Mount is just to the north-west of the harbour entrance; alternatively it is possible to lie alongside in the harbour where you will dry out on hard sand. The approaches have a number of rocks and shoals and should only be considered in fine weather, offshore winds, and a rising tide. Do not attempt a visit at night, and under no circumstances should an approach ever be made to the east and north of the Mount where there are extensive rocky shoals. Coming from Penzance, although there are a number of unpleasant reefs across the head of the bay, Western Cressar Rocks and Ryeman Rocks, both marked by a beacon (YB) with south cardinal topmark, a course towards the southern extremity of the Mount will lead clear of these and the Outer Penzeath rock, awash LAT and unmarked. Closing the Mount, approach on a north-easterly course keeping a good 300m from its steep western side to avoid Guthen Rocks, a shoal patch with just over 2m LAT, due west of the castle. Sound in

Always popular with the tourists, Mousehole is becoming increasingly visited by yachts which can dry out alongside the harbour walls

shore there is a convenient anchorage, rolly at times, but particularly handy if waiting for sufficient tide to enter. Approach can be made to the north of the island towards HW and local fishing boats use the inshore passage regularly, but there are rocks on both sides and a very narrow channel at LW. For the little extra distance involved the approach from the south of the island is far wider and safer, entering mid-way between the island and the shore on a north-westerly course, sounding in to a point roughly between the middle of the island and the south pier head where a depth of 3m will be found at LW. There are many pot buoys around the island and along the shore — be particularly wary in the approach.

Anchorages

After half-tide there is plenty of water inside the harbour; on the outer corner of the northern wall there are a number of horizontal concrete ledges and if the top three are showing there will be a good eight feet inside the outer ends of both harbour walls where you can dry alongside on a firm sandy bottom. The northern arm tends to be the better spot, with three convenient ladders. On both piers there are stone steps which should not be obstructed as these are used by the local boats for landing fish and crews. Alternatively, bilge-keelers can anchor fore and aft if space can be found among the local boats where they will dry out. However, the possibility of fouling the moorings does make the quay the better option providing you don't mind becoming an inevitable object of constant fascination to the passing holidaymakers. There is no harbour office, and the Harbourmaster, Frank Wallis, will probably wander down in the evening to collect his dues.

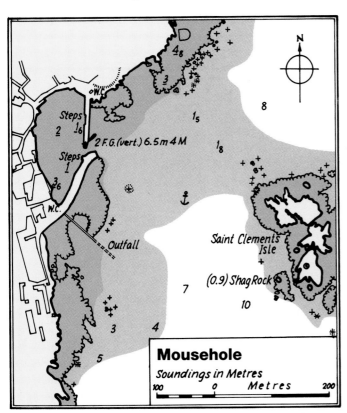

A bustling, colourful place where visitors bravely compete with the traffic trying to squeeze through the narrow streets, Mousehole's unique charm has not only survived the onslaught of recent years but also considerable mayhem in the Middle Ages when the village, then the most important port in Cornwall, was raided and burnt to the ground by marauding Spaniards. It enjoys a certain fame today as the home of Dolly Pentreath who died in 1777, reputedly the last person to speak Cornish as her native tongue, and a commemorative plaque can be found on the wall of her cottage close by the harbour. Perhaps she would have been able to provide the answer (although presumably none of us would have been able to understand it . . .) to the village's curious name for which there seems to be no definitive explanation. Remember, though, that it is always pronounced as 'Mowzle', and never, never as Mouse Hole!

After Dolly Pentreath, the other singular notoriety that Mousehole enjoys is Tom Bawcock's Eve, a celebration on 23 December of the time when this fabled local fisherman put to sea in desperation after weeks of gales, returning with a fine catch of seven different kinds of fish and a Christmas feast for the village. Hopefully, you will not be visiting by sea at this time of year — not only will you find the baulks down, but you will also be confronted by the infamous Starry Gazy Pie, a hideous creation with the heads of the seven varieties of fish poking through its crust.

Facilities

Starry Gazy apart, most other basic provisions are available in the village: groceries, off-licence, Post Office, butcher and newsagent. Just about everything else is obtainable in Penzance and there is a regular bus service; for the more energetic, bikes can be hired just outside the village on the Newlyn road. There are several cafés; the *Ship Inn*, in spite of the tourism has managed to retain a distinctively village pub atmosphere, and though present throughout the village, the tragedy of the Penlee lifeboat particularly lingers here as the former landlord of the pub was one of her crew. There is a small reasonably priced restaurant adjoining, but for those with more expensive tastes and wanting a bit of *cordon-bleu*, the *Lobster Pot* overlooking the harbour has a worldwide reputation for its food. Whether you need to work up an appetite or not, the fine walk along the cliffs to the south of the village towards Penzer Point and the beautifully named Lamorna Cove should not be missed.

Mousehole, like many of its counterparts in Cornwall has a singing tradition and possesses a renowned male voice choir. If you are lucky, on one of those increasingly rare, balmy summer's evenings, sometimes they assemble on the quayside, soft Cornish voices drifting in a strangely haunting harmony across the natural arena of the harbour into the gathering twilight around the bay. It will be one of those particularly evocative moments that you, like me, will never forget.

Passages
Land's End to Pentire Point

Favourable tidal streams

LAND'S END Bound West: 1 hour after HW Dover
Bound East: 5 hours before HW Dover

As a cruising ground there is, sadly, little to recommend the North Cornish coast. In the prevailing winds from a westerly quarter it presents an exposed and rugged lee shore with just a few drying harbours that cannot be guaranteed as places of refuge — an unwholesome combination and a natural deterrent for pleasure boating. Bound round Land's End, and up the Irish Sea your course will soon take you well away from the coast, an offing that you should endeavour to maintain.

Although I am anxious not inadvertently to promote any real cruising potential for this dangerous stretch of coast it has become increasingly used by yachts on passage to and from South Wales and the Bristol Channel to the Scillies and the West Country during the summer months. Most would, I'm sure, agree that it is an area they try to pass through as quickly as possible, waiting for the right conditions, and completing it in one leg. However, it is for such boats on passage that this briefer section is included, as there will obviously be occasions when circumstances can dictate a need to put in somewhere, or, just possibly, in very settled weather and an offshore wind, a little bit of cruising *can* be contemplated.

Land's End is not a particularly distinctive headland, somewhat lost against the rest of this stretch of cliffs of pinkish grey granite rising to over 70m; one of the most spectacular sections of coast in Southern England. The large white hotel building is part of the privately owned Land's End tourist complex, and further to the north the famous 'First and Last House' in England perches high on the cliff top.

A mile offshore, the infamous **Longships** reef has claimed many ships, the tidal streams strong and unpredictable in their vicinity, but overall, the north going flood, begins one hour after HW Dover, but does not turn north-east along the north Cornish coast until two hours later attaining over 2 knots at springs. Five hours before HW Dover, the ebb begins to run south-west back along the coast.

There is an inshore passage between the Longships (Iso WR 10secs) and the mainland but this should only be attempted in settled conditions and good visibility and never at night. Pass a quarter of a mile to seaward of Land's End, from where the Brisons, two conspicuous rocky islands to the north provide the best transit. The highest point of the highest island (27m) should be kept just open to the west of the highest point of the low island (22m), a bearing of 001°T. Kettle's Bottom, the most inshore rock of the reef dries 5.2m, and Sharks Fin, the most northerly dries 3.2m. If passing to the west of the Longships, give the whole area a good berth, and bound up the coast maintain a course well north of east for just over a mile to clear the Sharks Fin. At night, the north-eastern red sector of the Longships covers all hazards along this section of coast and should not be entered until Pendeen light (Fl (4) 15sec) opens. With jagged rocks and breaking water to seaward, and the

Beacon	Range (NM)	Frequency (kHz)	Call Sign
Marine beacon			
Round Island	100	308	RR
Aero beacon			
St Mawgan	50	365.5	SM
Coastal Radio			
Land's End Radio, working channels 27, 88, 85, 64.			

Passages — Land's End to Pentire Point

Charts for this section of coast are:
BA: 2565 St Agnes Head to Dodman Point. 1148 Isles of Scilly to Land's End.

1149 Pendeen to Trevose Head. 1156 Trevose Head to Hartland Point. 1168 Harbours on the North Coast of Cornwall is particularly useful.
Imray: C7 Lizard Point to Trevose Head. C58 Trevose Head to Bull Point.
Stanford: 13 Start Point to Padstow.
French: 2218 Du Cap Lizard a Trevose Head.

tall, lonely finger of the lighthouse with its precarious helicopter landing pad this is a menacing stretch of water where you will probably feel little inclination to linger.

The large sandy sweep of **Whitesand Bay** forms a break in the cliffs, and the village and tiny harbour of **Sennen Cove** will be seen at its southern end with its lifeboat house, the most south-westerly station in England. There is a fair weather anchorage in offshore winds just off the village, inside the Cowloe Rocks, but this is very exposed and not recommended. Passing to the north of the Brisons the tidal streams run strongly past **Cape Cornwall,** a distinctively conical shaped headland. The cape has two claims to fame — it is the only cape, and it is also the most westerly point in England. Topped by a conspicuous ruined mine chimney, it is one of the first indications of the extensive mining operations that covered this stretch of coast, and ruined pumping houses, chimneys and other buildings line the cliffs for the next ten miles. The workings extended far beneath the sea bed, in places over a mile out into the Atlantic.

The Vyneck is an isolated rock three cables northwest of Cape Cornwall — from here onwards a course a mile to seaward will clear all hazards except the overfalls which extend westwards from Pendeen Head, a bold headland. On it, the squat white lighthouse of Pendeen Watch looks out over the Wra, or Three Stone Oar, a group of small rocky islands, just under a half mile offshore. The coast follows a north-easterly direction from here on, a continuous unbroken line of impenetrable granite cliffs and one of the major sea cliff climbing centres in England. Along it, and in the approaches to **St Ives Bay** a good lookout should be kept for pot and net buoys; in spite of the exposure of this coast it is much worked by local boats.

Guarding the northern end of the bay, close inshore,

There is a fine weather inshore passage between the lurking reefs of the Longships and the high cliffs around Land's End

Although Godrevy Island lies close to the land, the Stones, a dangerous reef extends nearly a mile further offshore

is the lighthouse (Fl WR 10sec) on Godrevy Island. From its inception in 1859 this was always a controversial siting for it gives little indication of the notorious reef, the Stones, which extends nearly a mile to the north-west. A lightship or lighthouse on the outermost rock was the favoured option but turned down because of the cost. An area of strong currents, and drying rocks, many awash at HW, their outer limit is marked today by a north cardinal BY (Q), and the area is covered by the red sector of the Godrevy light 101°-145°T. The Sound, the inshore passage between Godrevy and the Stones is half a mile wide and should only be used in fair weather with a favourable tide; there are overfalls, particularly with wind against tide, and there is the additional hazard of numerous pot buoys — this is no place to be caught with a fouled propeller if motoring. If in doubt, pass to seaward of the whole area. Bound north from St Ives Bay the flood begins about two hours after HW Dover, two hours after local LW. Bound south, ideally leave around local HW, which will entail pushing the tide for the first hour, but will ensure a fair tide round Land's End and into Mount's Bay.

From the Stones buoy it is just over 17 miles to the next possible harbour at **Newquay,** along an impressive but unwelcoming stretch of coast, mostly high, crumbling cliffs, averaging between 40 and 75 metres in height. Along them there are numerous sandy coves and bays such as **Porthtowan** and **Perranporth,** holiday resorts, particularly popular with surfers, the almost perpetual ground swell producing ideal conditions for the sport. Numerous small rocky islets lie close inshore, but with the exception of Bawden Rocks, two small islands a mile north of St Agnes' Head there are no off-lying dangers. Unless heading for **Newquay,** the direct course to Trevose Head, the next lighthouse, (Fl 5secs) a prominent white tower on a steep headland with two large rocks to seaward, just over 22 miles to the north-east, takes you safely 2-3 miles offshore. Inland,

high ground runs parallel to the coast, and a very conspicuous feature is the large obelisk on the skyline south east of Portreath.

With no shelter in winds between south-west and north-east if the weather deteriorates and a blow looks

Trevose is a bold headland with a prominent light

likely, particularly from the south-west, the advice in the Admiralty Pilot to seek a good offing is probably as sensible as you will get. **Padstow** is the only place where complete shelter will be found once inside, but this has the disadvantage of being a tidal harbour with a dangerous bar, and the temptation to run for it in deteriorating conditions should be considered very carefully, particularly with regard to the state of the tide, aiming to arrive between half-flood and HW. With any ground swell, once the ebb commences, the shallow waters of Padstow Bay can become very hazardous, and unapproachable in strong winds and sea from the north-west.

In fog or poor visibility additional aids to navigation along this section of coast are foghorns on the Longships (Horn 15secs), Pendeen (Siren 20secs), Stones Buoy (Whistle), Trevose Head (Horn (2) 30secs).

Although protected from the west, St Ives can be very exposed in winds from the north

St Ives

Tides HW Dover −0605
Charts
BA: 1168. **Stanford:** 13. **Imray:** C7.

Hazards
Harbour dries, exposed in onshore winds. Hoe Rock, and
green buoy to NE (both unlit), Carracks rocks to SE (unlit).

FROM A DISTANCE St Ives Head looks like an island and entering the bay this should be given a good berth to avoid Hoe and Merran rocks on its north-eastern side, which both dry. A green conical buoy marks the end of the ruined outer pier and should be left to starboard. Smeaton Pier, the eastern arm, has an old white lighthouse at its end, at night this is marked by (2 FG vert) and the west pier (2FR vert), enclosing a harbour which dries completely at LAT, but is normally accessible after half flood. It has a firm sandy bottom, and there is a fleet of quite large fishing and pleasure boats based here during the summer months which lie on heavy fore and aft drying moorings or alongside the quay. Shelter is good in south and westerly weather, but anything further north can send a considerable sea into the bay and a heavy swell within the harbour. In favourable conditions, anchor about 100m south-east of the harbour entrance in about 3m, but watch out for the large number of buoys marking the keep pots towards Porthminster beach. Deep keel boats can only really berth inside the outer end of Smeaton Pier, where they will dry, but this is not the most comfortable place as there is often a surge, and there is also a lot of commercial activity. However, bilge keelers, or boats able to take the bottom are well catered for with eight drying visitors' moorings in the harbour just off the prominent Woolworths store on the waterfront. Charges in both cases are £4 per night including VAT. Local HW is HW Dover −0605, range in the entrance MHWS 4.5m to MHWN 2.6m.

During the season the town reels under the assault of the tourists, its picturesque narrow streets and alleyways, harbour and wide sandy Porthmeor Beach on the seaward side of St Ives Head, providing all the essentials of a seaside holiday. In spite of a certain amount of inevitable commercialism, it retains much of its unique atmosphere, a factor that has made it a popular haunt of artists for many years.

Eric Ward the Harbourmaster will help with any problems, and can provide small quantities of diesel but petrol has to be fetched in cans from the garage nearly a mile away. His office (Tel: 0736 795018) does have a VHF but no constant watch is kept and he suggests that vessels wishing to make contact should call 'St Ives Coastguard' Channel 16, who are on watch 1000-2000 in the summer. There is fresh water on the piers, Calor and Camping Gaz from the Fishermen's Co-operative, and there is a very convenient new toilet and public shower block in the car park just behind the harbour front. All other normal requirements can be found, banks, Post Office

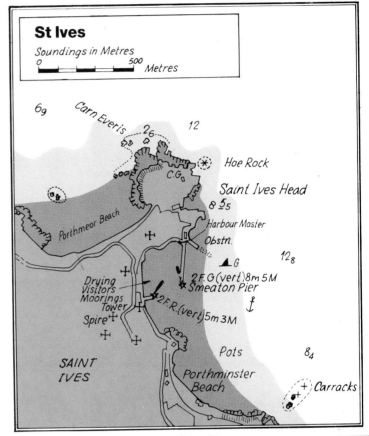

Most of St Ives harbour dries at low water but visiting boats can sometimes find a berth on the outer end of the pier

and provisions, and there are many cafés, pubs and restaurants. There are road and main line rail connections. A lifeboat is also stationed at St Ives, launched on a trailer across the beach.

St Ives bay stretches away to the north-east backed by the extensive sand dunes and beach of Hayle Towans. **Hayle,** in the south-eastern corner is a run-down, tidal harbour used by a few local fishing boats, approached over a dangerous bar and tricky entrance channel through a large expanse of drying sands that is not recommended for visitors.

Newquay

Tides
HW Dover −0604.
Charts
BA: 1168. Stanford: 13. Imray: C7.

Hazards
Small harbour dries beyond entrance. Heavy surge in onshore winds and dangerous to approach. Old Dane and Listrey rocks to N (both unlit).

IN FAIR WEATHER AND, ideally, offshore winds and daylight **Newquay** is a pleasant small drying harbour that is certainly feasible for an overnight stop. Midway between it and Godrevy, St Agnes' Head is prominent, 91m high, with steep cliffs, and inland the isolated St Agnes' Hill (200m) covered in heather and gorse is surmounted by a beacon. This was another site of intensive tin mining activity in the 1800s, and several prominent ruins can be seen along the shore. Just north of St Agnes' Head, Trevaunance Cove is a testimony to the destruction of the elements along this coast, one of several small ports built to export the tin and copper that was rebuilt time and time again between 1700 and 1920 as gales relentlessly swept away the massive granite walls.

Closing the land, East and West Pentire Points form the entrance of the curious Gannel, a very shallow silted-up river mouth, which forms a fine sandy beach, and, Fistral Bay, renowned for surfing, leads up to Towan Head, the entrance to Newquay Bay. With a large hotel prominent at the highest point, the land falls away to a long, low rocky promontory which projects northwards. Although there are no off-lying dangers, overfalls occur up to half a mile offshore, and it is wise to give it a reasonable berth before turning into the Bay, when the eastern extremities of Newquay, extensive hotels and houses will come into view along the skyline right down to the cliff fringed beaches.

The harbour lies in the south-eastern corner, hidden behind a headland. On it stands the huge Atlantic Hotel, and also an old white painted huer's hut. East-north-east of this, 1½ cables offshore are the Listrey Rocks, least depth 0.5m and 1.2m, which should be carefully avoided before heading in towards the harbour walls as they come into view. The whole of the inner part of the bay dries at LWS and the harbour is normally only accessible for average draught boats three hours either side of local HW which is at HW Dover −0604. If waiting for the tide, anchor off in the bay, which is well sheltered from the south and west, but very exposed in northerly winds

Newquay is usually full of fishing boats but a drying berth will be found on the south pier if the weather is suitable for an overnight stay

Newquay although an attractive harbour should only be considered in settled offshore conditions

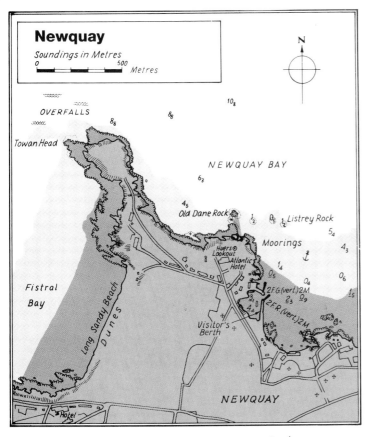

Newquay

Soundings in Metres

0   500

Metres

OVERFALLS

Towan Head

NEWQUAY BAY

Old Dane Rock

Listrey Rock

Moorings

Huers Lookout

Atlantic Hotel

Fistral Bay

Long Sandy Beach

Dunes

2F.G.(vert.)2M

2F.R.(vert.)2M

Visitor's Berth

NEWQUAY

Hotel

maintaining a VHF watch on Channel 16, working on 14, and will be able to advise you (Tel: 0637 872809).

Inside the harbour, visitors normally lie alongside the outer end of the south quay, where there is a clean, hard sandy bottom, and you will dry at LW clear of the local fishing boats which lie on fore and aft moorings on the west side of the harbour. The Harbourmaster's office is the building on the south pier, charges are 15p per foot per night, and water and diesel are available from him on request. There are public toilets close by, and also the licensed clubhouse of the Newquay Rowing Club, where temporary membership is available for visitors, which saves the trek up into town for a pint. This dedicated bunch of enthusiasts own several of the beautifully restored Scillies pilot gigs including *Newquay,* the oldest one still afloat, built in 1812. In recent years the racing has become a fast growing sport in Cornwall with intense rivalry between clubs at Newquay, Cadgwith, the Scillies and Falmouth; a spectacular but horribly masochistic activity for the six oarsmen that man these 30ft boats, which can be regularly seen pounding around the bay.

The main town of Newquay is a few minutes walk from the peaceful harbour and when you reach it you will probably wish you had not bothered for it is the largest holiday resort in Cornwall, the surfing capital of Britain and the unabashed commercialism clearly reflects it. Brash, noisy and very busy, there is no shortage of pubs and restaurants, and all normal requirements are available; Post Office, banks and provisions, launderettes, road and rail connections.

and ground swell which creates a surge making the harbour very uncomfortable, and entry through the narrow pierheads dangerous. In the bay, there are several moorings used by local fishing boats, and it may be possible to lie on one of these. Captain Sampson, the Harbourmaster, is very helpful and is usually around from 0830-1930 in the summer,

Padstow

Tides

HW Dover −0550. Range: MHWS 7.3M — MHWN 5.6m
MLWN 2.6m — MLWS 0.8m. Streams attain over 2 knots in
channel off harbour entrance at springs

Charts

BA: 1168. **Stanford:** 13. **Imray:** C7, C58.

Waypoint

North Pier End 50.32.48N. 4.56.10W.

Hazards

Gulland, Newland, Gurley, Chimney and Roscarrock Rocks
(all unlit). Wreck west of Stepper Point (unlit). Doom Bar and
large area of river and harbour dries. Buoyed channel (lit) but
liable to frequent change. Approach very dangerous in
onshore wind and sea. Busy tidal fishing port. Beware pot
buoys.

IT IS ANOTHER thirteen miles from Newquay to the mouth of the River Camel, and **Padstow** lies two miles upstream. This is a most attractive estuary, a spectacular area of golden drying sands, with a shoreline of low cliffs, fine beaches and sand dunes providing some lovely walks. However, the mouth of the river is almost choked by the Doom Bar, a massive drying sandbank. During strong onshore winds, or a heavy ground sea this lives up to its melancholy name, particularly near low water, when the sea breaks right across the entrance — conditions that are not always obvious from seaward. With care, though, in reasonable and settled weather the Camel is not a difficult river to enter and yachts of normal draught will be safe enough from half-flood onwards.

The approach to the River Camel from the south is unmistakable as Trevose Head, four miles to the west, is a steep headland, 80m high, which rises higher than the surrounding hinterland to give it the appearance of being a separate island from a distance. In addition, the Bull and Quies, prominent large rocks, extend a mile further to the west, making it a distinctive landfall from north or south. The lighthouse is on the north-western corner of the headland, a fine prominent building dating from 1847, and on the north-eastern side of the headland is the Padstow lifeboat station, re-sited here after the original station in the river fell prey to the increasing silting up of the

Doom Bar, which according to local legend was created by a mermaid shot by a local man who thought she was a fish. Cursing him with her dying breath she threw up a handful of sand which turned into the Bar, vowing that 'henceforth the harbour should be desolate!'

Tidal streams run strongly off **Trevose,** over two knots at springs, particularly between the rocks and the headland and you should keep to seaward of the Quies before heading up into Padstow Bay, passing inside Gulland Rock, a prominent rocky island 28m high. There are several isolated hazards further inshore; Gurley Rock, least depth 3m, and Chimney Rock, 2.3m, not normally a problem to boats of average draught but worth remembering near low water, particularly if there is any ground swell running. Stepper Point, a bold, rounded grassy headland footed with cliffs forms the south side of the river mouth, and is easily identified by the large stone daymark, like a truncated factory chimney. There is a Coastguard lookout at its eastern extremity, manned only in bad weather, and a light on an iron pillar (LFl 10secs). Three cables west-north-west of the daymark there is a dangerous wreck, almost awash at LW, so give the headland a wide berth and head up towards Pentire Point, the north-eastern arm of the bay, another bold headland with the distinctive island of Newland, a pyramid 35m high, half a mile to the

Viewed from St Saviour's Point at low water the channel to Padstow harbour mouth holds close to the shore and almost dries completely

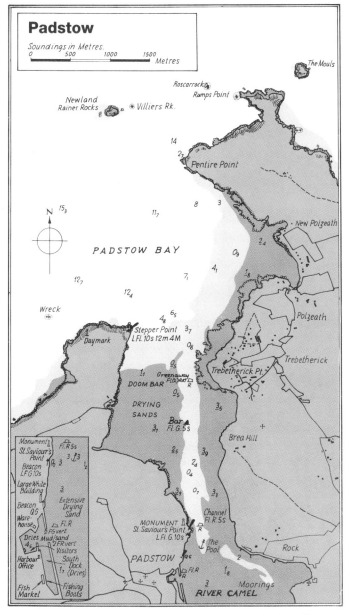

Padstow

Soundings in Metres.

0   500   1000   1500   Metres

PADSTOW BAY

Newland
Rainer Rocks

Villiers Rk.

The Mouls

Roscarrock

Rumps Point

Pentire Point

New Polzeath

Polzeath

Trebetherick

Trebetherick Pt.

Stepper Point
L Fl. 10s 12m 4M

Daymark

Wreck

Greenaway
Fl.(2) R.10s

DOOM BAR

DRYING
SANDS

Bar
Fl. G. 5s

Brea Hill

Monument
St Saviour's
Point

Beacon
LFl.G.10s

Large White
Building

Beacon
QG

Ware-
house

2FR vert

FLR

Extensive
Drying
Sand

Dries Mud/sand

Visitors

Harbour
Office

South
Dock
(Dries)

Fish
Market

Fishing
Boats

MONUMENT
St Saviour's Point
L Fl. G. 10s

Channel
Fl.R.5s

The
Pool

PADSTOW

Rock

Moorings

RIVER CAMEL

Looking from Rock towards Padstow, at low water large areas of the River Camel become drying banks of golden sand

north-west. Approaching from the north, it is best to keep well to seaward of Newland, as Roscarrock, a rock with least depth of 0.8m lurks three cables west of Rumps Point, the north-eastern corner of Pentire.

Enter the river on a flood tide, no earlier than 2½ hours before local HW (HW Dover −0550) and do not attempt it in any ground swell from the north-west, or if breaking water can be seen. The Doom Bar, a large area of drying sand fills the south-western corner of the river mouth, and opposite, the houses of **Trebetherick** sprawl along the low cliffs. These are fringed with rocky ledges, and the channel between them and the sands runs due south on a line from the western end of Pentire Point, a useful back bearing. Depths reduce quickly from 3m to a least depth of 0.8m LAT two cables north of the first channel buoy 'Greenaway' a red port hand can (Fl (2) R 10secs) and Doom Bar, two cables further south, is a conical green starboard hand buoy (Fl G 5secs). At low water the channel is a cable wide and depths vary between 2m and 0.4m LAT as far as St Saviours Point, known locally as 'Ship-me-Pumps', a quarter of a mile downstream of the harbour. There is a prominent monument on this low rocky headland and another port hand red can (Fl R 5secs) off it. Here the channel

divides, the main stream bearing away towards the village of Rock on the eastern shore, and the approach channel to Padstow which dries almost completely at springs holds very tightly to the western — starboard hand — bank. However, just south of the buoy, there is 'The Pool' with an average depth of 3m and a number of local moorings in it. It is possible to anchor clear of them, although at springs the tide can run strongly, between 4 and 5 knots at times on both the flood and ebb.

A large area of drying sandbanks fills the centre of the river and the narrow Padstow channel passes close to two green beacons with triangular topmarks on the shore, the first (L Fl G 10secs) and the second (QG). Just short of the harbour entrance is another port hand can (Fl R), and the outer pier ends are marked with (2FR vert) and (2FG vert) port and starboard. No sailing is allowed in the final approach channel. Proceed under power and watch out for the movements of the large number of fishing boats particularly in the harbour mouth, where the main stream runs strongly at right angles to the entrance. South Dock, the commercial harbour, lies immediately to port, a long narrow basin, but visitors should continue straight ahead through the entrance to the inner harbour. During the winter of 1988/89 a flood prevention scheme created a tidal barrage across the entrance to the Inner Harbour, with a hydraulic bottom hinged gate. At the time of writing it had not been decided whether this gate will be closed in future over low water to keep vessels afloat in the Inner Harbour, or whether it would only be used occasionally in anticipation of tidal flooding. Berth alongside the south quay, where it is best to assume that, as before, you will dry out completely in soft mud.

The Harbour Office is close by on the quay and is open 0830-1730 weekdays, and 2½ hours before to 1½ hours after HW, on every tide, and you should report after arrival. Previously exposed to south-easterly winds the new gate will mean that the inner harbour will now be much more sheltered, but visitors are still requested not to leave vessels unattended for any length of time without consulting the Harbour Master. The Harbour Commission sometimes has a

At Padstow visiting yachts can dry out in the attractive inner harbour

few visitors' moorings in the river for vessels up to 12m; either call 'Padstow Harbour' on VHF Channel 16, working Ch 14 when the office is manned, phone ahead for availability, or enquire on arrival.

A small, unspoilt town, with attractive and colourful old buildings lining the quayside, although popular with holidaymakers Padstow has managed to avoid much of the overt commercialism of some of the other north Cornish resorts. Formerly a vital port for north Cornwall exporting tin, copper, slate, granite, china clay and grain, and importing coal, salt and timber, it was also important as a shipbuilding centre. By the beginning of this century, however, commercial trade had dwindled steadily with the silting of the Doom Bar and the advent of road and rail transport and it would seem that the mermaid's wish had been fulfilled, for little more than a small fishing fleet remained. However, in recent years this has grown considerably, with a new fish co-operative and market, evidence of the resurgence in prosperity. Pot and net boats land large quantities of shellfish here, as a look in the large wet tanks on the Fish Quay will reveal, and there are also large beam trawlers now working out of the port. Coasters occasionally discharge cargoes of fertiliser and roadstone and there is a sand dredger working in the river.

Facilities include Midland, Lloyds and Barclays (none of which have cashpoints), provisions, launderette, chandler and water; diesel is available through the Harbourmaster, but there is no petrol. There are several pleasant pubs, a number of restaurants, and the walks out towards Stepper Point are a delightful way to work up an appetite. It is unlikely that you will be in the area as early as 1 May when the famous 'Obby Oss' festivities take place when a strange creature dances through the streets to celebrate the coming of summer, but you might coincide with the annual regatta during August. There is also a small museum in the centre of town, and Padstow Sailing Club on the quay.

However, most of the sailing activity in the estuary is centred on **Rock,** on the opposite shore, where there are several deeper pools and a large number of local moorings, and some drying Harbour Commission moorings also available for visitors, although these tend to be hired on a weekly basis for people holidaying in the area. A much quieter little village, with many holiday homes, Rock is linked by a regular ferry to Padstow, and is home of the Rock Sailing Club which has a fine clubhouse, an old converted grain warehouse on the quay with excellent facilities. Visitors are welcome to use the bar and showers, and snack meals are also available. The sand dunes and clean beaches running to seaward from Rock towards Brea Hill are most attractive, and it is a particularly fine area for dinghy sailing.

The Camel, once a busy waterway, is still navigable as far as **Wadebridge,** about five miles inland, on a good tide, but this is definitely only with local knowledge as the channel is tortuous and unmarked.

Port guide — Padstow

Harbourmaster: Mr E M Wakelin, Harbour Office, Padstow PL28 8AQ (Tel: 0841 532239). Office manned 0830-1730 weekdays and 2½ hours before to 1½ hours after local HW, every tide

VHF: Call Sign 'Padstow Harbour' Channel 16, works 14

Lifeboat: At Trevose Head

Coastguard: Contact MRCC Falmouth (Tel: 0326 317575)

Customs: Custom House, Padstow (Tel: 0841 532313)

Anchorage: The Pool, quarter mile downstream of Padstow Harbour. Drying, clear of moorings off Rock

Mooring/berthing: Visitors normally dry out in inner harbour. Moorings in river sometimes available from Harbour Commission, also drying moorings off Rock

Charges: Harbour dues 12p per foot per day plus VAT, 50% surcharge for multihulls. Extra for moorings depending on size

Doctor: (Tel: 0841 532346)

Hospital: East Cornwall Hospital, Bodmin (Tel: 0208 77771)

Churches: All denominations

Fuel: Diesel from Harbourmaster. Petrol, Padstow Garage 1 mile or at Rock

Gas: Calor, Camping Gaz, Rigmarine Yacht Chandlers, South Quay (Tel: 532657)

Water: On quay

Banks: Barclays, Midland, Lloyds. No cashpoints

Post Office: In town, Duke Street

Rubbish: Bins and skip on quay

Showers/toilets: Public toilet on quay. Showers at Rock Sailing Club

Launderette: In town, Church Street

Provisions-half day: Most normal requirements. EC Wednesday

Chandler: Rigmarine Yacht Chandlers, South Quay, (Tel: 532657 or 532386)

Repairs: Westerly Boats, Rock (Tel: 020 886 3439). A J G England (Tel: 0841 532418). Chapman & Hewitt (Tel: 020881 3487)

Marine engineers: Reynolds Marine, Treverbyn Road (Tel: 532528). Padstow Auto Marine (Tel: 0841 532766). G B Smith & Son (Tel: 020886 2815)

Electronic engineers: None

Communications: Buses to Bodmin to connect with main line railway

Yacht Clubs: Padstow Sailing Club, The Quay, Padstow Rock Sailing Club, The Quay, Rock, Wadebridge PL27 6LB (Tel: 020 886 2709)

Eating out: Pubs, cafés and restaurants in both Padstow and Rock

Things to do: Museum in Padstow. Excellent beaches and good walking

Coastal and harbour views

The following pages are intended to provide quick 'at a glance' reference to supplement the main text, arranged for the most part in the same east-west sequence. The first section, Passages, covers major headlands and other useful features; section two, Harbours, contains additional approach shots, details of berthing and anchoring facilities and other views of general interest

Passages

Viewed from the north, Berry Head forms the southern limit of Torbay, and its long flat top, heavily quarried cliffs and prominent Coastguard station make it easy to identify (p16)

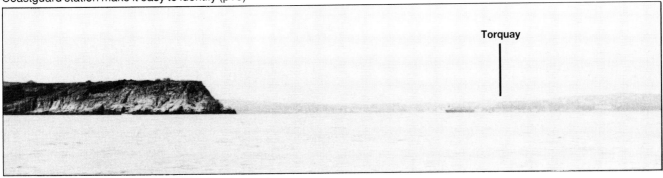

Berry Head from the south-east, with Torbay beyond

It is not difficult locate the River Dart when approaching from the north-east as the high, conspicuous daymark inland, the jagged Mewstone and the Eastern Blackstone to seaward of Inner Froward Point are all distinctive marks (p17)

Viewed from the north-east, Start Point is a bold, rugged headland topped with a string of rocky outcrops along its prickly spine (p17)

Passages

From a position east of Start Point, Peartree Point is precipitous, the Sleaden Rocks lie to seaward, and Prawle Point is visible three miles to the west (p47)

Approached from the west Start Point is just as distinctive, with Start Rocks to seaward

Entering Salcombe from the south-west, Bolt Head is a spectacular sight, with the Great Mewstone close to its base, the Little Mewstone further to seaward, and Prawle Point away to the east (p47)

To the east of Bigbury Bay the cliffs between Bolt Tail and Bolt Head provide an uncompromising stretch of coast. The houses of Hope Cove, an anchorage sheltered in easterly winds, can be seen just west of Bolt Tail (p47, p58)

At the western end of Bigbury Bay Hillsea Point has a Coastguard lookout on its summit and Bolt Tail is visible away to the east (p48)

From the east, the Great Mewstone is a useful offshore mark for the entrance to the River Yealm and the approaches to Plymouth beyond (p47)

The Draystone Buoy lies in the western approaches to Plymouth and Rame Head to the west has a distinctive profile, topped with a ruined chapel (p48)

Gribbin Head has a large red and white striped daymark, and to the south-east the Cannis Rocks are clearly marked by a south cardinal buoy (p77/78)

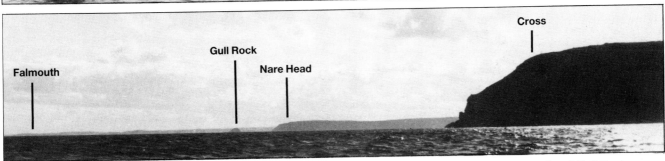

The Dodman is a bold, rounded headland with a white cross at its summit. Looking to the west, Nare Head and Gull Rock can be seen clearly (p78)

Viewed from south-west, the Dodman is just as impressive.

Passages

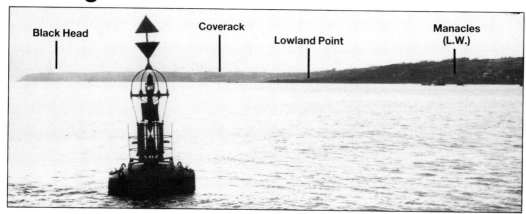

Heading south from Falmouth the treacherous Manacle Rocks are marked by an east cardinal buoy. Coverack lies beyond the aptly named Lowland Point, and Black Head is prominent in the distance (p112)

Near LW rocks extend to seaward from Black Head. Bass Point on the Lizard can be clearly seen to the south-west (p112)

Surmounted by the former Lloyd's signal station, Bass Point lies to the east of the Lizard Lighthouse (p112/113)

Lizard Lighthouse has two distinctive towers (p113)

Looking west beyond the Lizard at LW, the sinister Stag Rocks extend to well seaward. Rill Point is open in the distance, and Asparagus Island is visible against the cliffs (p113)

From south of the Lizard, Bass Point lies to the east and Black Head is open to the north-east

Land's End from the south-west. The tourist complex and hotel stand high above the Armed Knight Rock, and the 'First and Last House' is prominent on the headland beyond (p128)

From a position north-west of Land's End the Armed Knight Rock lies clearly to seawards (p128)

From the inshore passage at half-tide the jagged Longships reef is a sombre sight. Kettle's Bottom Rock can be seen clearly (p128)

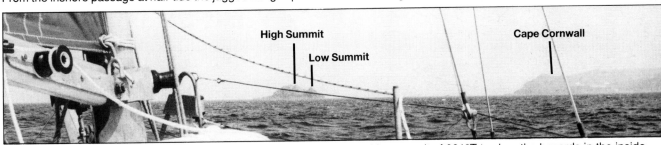

The two rocky islands of the Brisons south-west of Cape Cornwall provide a transit of 001°T to clear the hazards in the inside passage between the Longships and Land's End. Keep the slightly higher summit just open to the west of the low one (p128)

Pendeen Head lies in the distance and the distinctive pyramid of Cape Cornwall is seen here framed between the Brisons, which must be passed to seaward as dangerous reefs extend from them south-east towards the shore (p129)

The entrance of the approach channel to the River Exe lies to the SSW of the low cliffs on Straight Point (p19)

The clearly marked channel into the Exe runs parallel to the Exmouth shore inside the drying Pole Sands, and Holy Trinity Church Tower is a conspicuous landmark (p19)

A prominent row of hotels lines the Exmouth seafront, and beyond the river narrows between the Docks and the low sandy promontory of the Warren, on the western side. Do not cut the corner but hold close to the Docks until the entrance is almost open (below) before turning to the west. Beware of the strong tidal streams and other vessels emerging (p21)

The channel runs west between the Warren and Bull Hill Bank, then northwards beyond No 13 buoy through the Bight. The boat on the extreme left is anchored just off Salthouse Lake, where she will just dry towards LW (p21)

Turf Locks is a popular local watering hole, where it is also possible to enter the Exeter Canal (p24)

Approaching Topsham Quay, where there is a prominent brick built warehouse, a clear fairway leads through the moorings from the final No 18 port-hand buoy (p24)

For a small charge visitors can lie alongside Topsham Quay and dry out in soft mud. There are few ladders and bollards, however, and ingenuity is needed to get ashore at LW (p24)

Looking downstream from Topsham nearing LW, the fairway is clear. Trout's Boatyard lies on the left (p24)

The upper reaches of the Exe are very shallow when seen at LW, but boats of moderate draught can reach the Retreat Boatyard two hours either side of HW, the only place on the river where diesel can be obtained alongside (p25)

Approaching Teignmouth from the north-east, St Michael's Church tower is prominent and the land rises high above the Ness on the south side of the river mouth (p27)

From the east the Ness is a bold sandstone bluff. The bridge across the estuary can be seen in the distance and Den Point lies between it and the row of hotels on the extreme right (p28)

The houses of Shaldon are beyond the coaster in the channel, with Den Point to the right of it (p28)

Above left: at LW Philip Lucette beacon is perched on top of a training wall, with Den Point and beacon just across the river (p28) Above right: the transit of 334°T to clear the Ness Rocks is provided by a grey stone tower and a tall black pole in front of the hotels (p28)

The current runs hard round Den Point and the fairway leads past the moorings to the docks in the distance (p28)

Torquay

Approaching from the south-east the many large hotels make Torquay easy to locate. Although the harbour entrance is not immediately apparent, the large cluster of masts and the Torbay Seaways ferry give a good indication as to where to head! (p31)

Closer to, the harbour mouth is soon evident, and vessels entering must pass to port of the conical green buoy and keep to starboard between the pierheads (p31)

Within the harbour there is a clear fairway and Torquay Marina lies straight ahead...(p32)

...where the marina visitors' berths are clearly indicated along the eastern side

145

Victoria breakwater light

Approaching across Torbay from the north, Brixham is easy to locate a mile west of Berry Head (p34)

Victoria breakwater end

From the east Brixham's long breakwater and the former quarries on the far side of the harbour are easy to distinguish (p34)

The entrance to Brixham is wide and easy to enter in all conditions, but keep a wary eye out for the many fishing boats that use this busy harbour (p34)

Due to open in the spring of 1989, the new Prince William Marina was still under construction when this photograph was taken earlier in the year, although its limits and location is clearly defined by the outer lines of piling opposite the fish quays. The white building in the foreground is Brixham Yacht Club (p34)

Brixham's picturesque inner harbour dries extensively and is used by local craft, including a 'replica' of Drake's Golden Hinde which is always popular with younger crew members (p34)

The steep cliffs fall back to reveal a memorable approach to the River Dart from the east (p36)

Approaching across Start Bay from the west, the elusive entrance to the River Dart would be difficult to spot without the prominent daymark (p36)

Seen from the 'Range', Dartmouth and Kingswear Castles guard the deep and narrow entrance to the river, where the high surrounding hills can often produce very fluky conditions (p37)

With commanding views over the entrance, Dartmouth Castle on the western shore is well worth a visit while staying in the Dart (p37)

Within the wide inner river, Darthaven Marina lies to starboard and Dart Marina can be seen further upstream to port (p39)

Harbours

The DHNA visitors' pontoons on the embankment are very popular and convenient for the town. Further upstream the larger Town Jetty has visitors' berths inside the lower end, and between 1700 and 0900 the outside can also be used (p39)

On the Kingswear side of the river, just below the higher ferry, the other DHNA visitors' pontoon is less convenient for the town but much quieter, although you will have to be around early in the season to see it this empty! Dart Marina lies across the river (p39)

Dart Marina fuel berth

One of the few anchorages in the Dart lies just downstream of the Anchor Stone on the western shore which shelves steeply, and care should be taken to avoid swinging inshore over the shallows of Parson's Mud (p41)

Although anchoring is prohibited, there are a number of convenient and clearly marked DHNA visitors' moorings off Dittisham, although usually you will have to raft (p41)

Sharpham House is one of the features of the peaceful upper reaches of the Dart, which is navigable to the attractive town of Totnes on a rising tide (p43/44)

Approaching Totnes, the ferry landing lies to starboard and visitors' berth to port alongside the far quay (p44)

Drying completely at LW in level soft mud, the snug berth at Totnes suffers only from a notable lack of bollards and ladders, and improvisation is needed to get ashore! (p44)

To the south, Salcombe is flanked by the dramatic heights of Bolt Head, which can often produce fierce down-draughts. Limebury Point, on the eastern side of the entrance, can be seen in the distance (p50)

From offshore, the leading marks are sometimes difficult to spot at first and can be more easily located below the left-hand side of the prominent twin gabled red brick house on Sandhill Point (p52)

Salcombe entrance looking to seaward near LW. The Blackstone, Wolf Rock buoy and beacons are clearly seen, with Bolt Head beyond (p52)

The first row of visitors' buoys in Salcombe lie to port below the large Marine Hotel (p52)

You can anchor off the fine sandy beach at East Portlemouth just upstream of the ferry, but deeper keel boats should check the depths carefully as the shallow bank extends well out before dropping away steeply! (p53)

Looking upstream from the beach at East Portlemouth towards the Bag showing the anchorage and visitors' moorings at Ditch End (p53)

The sheltered area of water known as the 'Bag' opens out above Snape's Point, and here there is a very handy visitors' pontoon off the western shore (p55)

The Salcombe Harbour Authority visitors' pontoon in the Bag is far quieter than the lower moorings and much more comfortable in a blow. Beware, however, of weed washing downstream on spring tides, and check your propeller before getting under way (p55)

Delightful to explore on a rising tide, the peaceful upper reaches of the Salcombe estuary has a well marked channel right up to Kingsbridge, a busy country town with good facilities for shopping (p57)

Hope Cove lies just north of Bolt Tail, a pleasant anchorage in easterly weather just WSW of the small drying harbour. Landing is easy and there are basic provisions, Post Office, and two pubs in the village, with a fine walk up on to Bolt Tail for the more energetic (p58)

The shallow river of the Avon should only be approached in settled offshore conditions, and if waiting for the tide to enter, a good anchorage will be found just east of Murray's Rocks (p58)

Looking south-west from Lower Cellars Point at LW, the entrance to the River Avon dries almost completely, with breakers right across. Burgh Island, in the distance, is joined to the mainland by a sand bar at LW (p58)

Beneath Mount Folly, the inner reach of the Avon is narrow but deeper and the stream runs fast (p58)

Within the river the channel swings sharply back into the deeper pool by Lower Cellars Quay and its quaint thatched boathouse (p58)

Wembury Church, on a bearing of 010°T, clears the outer hazards in the approach to the River Yealm (p61)

Mouthstone Point has a conspicuous Speed Warning notice upon it. The outer leading marks in line (088.5°T) clear Mouthstone Ledge, which extends west of the point (p61)

Closer to the Bar buoy can now be seen to port, and the beacon to starboard which clearly marks the passage between the end of the sandy bar and the rocky eastern shore. (P.61)

The outer leading marks lose their alignment as you pass to the east of the Bar buoy. Cellar Bay, dead ahead, is a popular daytime anchorage in settled offshore weather (p61)

Steer 047°T for the single leading mark on the opposite shore (p61)

As soon as Misery Point is abeam to starboard turn into the inner reach, where the first moorings will come into sight (p61)

The largest visitors' moorings lie on the port side of the channel approaching Warren Point. The first houses of Newton Ferrers can now be seen (p61)

Entering the Pool do not cut inside the small Spit buoy. There are visitors' moorings immediately to starboard, and the main visitors' pontoon lies ahead (p61)

The Pool, looking to seawards, showing the landing pontoon and anchorage (p62)

Entering Plymouth from the east, one of the few hazards, the Shagstone, is clearly marked with a white beacon (p65)

Visitors to the Mayflower International Marina should berth on the clearly marked reception area on the outer pontoons unless a berth has already been arranged on the VHF (p67)

Quiet and self-contained with all facilities, the Mayflower International Marina has a deservedly high reputation (p67)

Barn Pool is one of the few feasible yacht anchorages in Plymouth; attractive and well sheltered in westerly weather but far from most amenities (p67)

Approaching Sutton Harbour, Fisher's Nose lies to port, and the prominent piling wall to starboard is the breakwater surrounding Queen Anne's Battery Marina (p68)

Private finger berths form the bulk of Queen Anne's Battery Marina and visitors normally lie along the inside of the breakwater (p68)

Close to the visitors' berths at Queen Anne's Battery, the smart Marina building houses the reception office, bar, showers, toilets, and is also the new home for the Royal Western Yacht Club (p69)

Sutton Marina; the fuel pontoon and visitors' berths are of easy access on the outside of the marina area (p69)

St Germans Quay

The empty upper reaches of the St Germans River dry almost completely at LW, but the winding channel is clearly marked and St German's Quay can be reached on a flood tide (p71/73)

The upper reaches of the Tamar provide plenty of opportunity for exploration and many peaceful anchorages like Cargreen, where there are limited facilities and a pub (p73)

The impressive viaduct at Calstock is about as far as most boats are likely to penetrate inland on the Tamar; diesel and visitors' moorings are usually available from the boatyard (p73)

Well sheltered to the south and west, the wide bay at Cawsand is a very pleasant anchorage in the western approaches to Plymouth (p65)

A perfect natural daymark, Looe Island lies just south and west of the harbour (p76)

The houses at Looe climb high up the surrounding hillsides, and the harbour mouth lies at western end of the beach (p80)

From the anchorage in Looe Bay the harbour mouth is clearly visible, with whitewash on the end of the Banjo Pier and the rock opposite, which even has 'Looe' painted upon it just in case you're in any doubt! (p80)

Protected by the Banjo Pier, the entrance to Looe is long and narrow and dries completely at LW springs (p80)

Within the entrance Looe Harbour widens, and the only visitors' berth is clearly marked on the west side, where you will dry out. Beware of the numerous self-drive hire boats, which, it can be safely assumed, are not aware of the Rules of the Road! (p81)

Approaching from the south, the houses of Polperro appear in a narrow cleft among the high cliffs (p82)

Give jagged Peak Rock a reasonable berth to avoid the Ranny Rocks which lie just off it (p82)

It is only safe to approach Polperro in settled offshore weather, and then it is sometimes possible to lie to one of the fishing boat moorings just outside the harbour (p82)

The harbour dries completely at LW and the only two visitors' berths are along the eastern wall. Note, too, the harbour gate which is closed in heavy weather (p82)

Approaching Fowey from the east, a hazy Gribbin Head lies away to the west and the entrance to the harbour is just beyond the steep headland with a prominent Coastguard lookout (p77)

Although Fowey is still hidden, the conspicuous white house is a clear indication that you are almost there (p77)

A Coastguard lookout guards the eastern side of the entrance to Fowey, a popular stop for cruising boats and a busy commercial port that handles over 850 ships a year (p85)

As Fowey Harbour opens, St Fimbarrus Church and the town come clearly into view (p84)

Punch Cross clearly marks the rocks on the eastern side of the entrance; the only other hazard, Lamp Rock, is also marked by a beacon (p84)

Polruan Fort guards the narrowest part of the harbour entrance (p84)

Beyond the Fort, the harbour widens and the bulk of the moorings off Polruan come into view (p84)

Visitors' moorings lie opposite the town along the eastern shore upstream of Pont Pill, inside the big ship berths. Note, too, the floating rubbish skip, a useful facility (p86)

Extremely convenient for shopping or topping up the water, the Fowey Harbour Commission short-stay visitors' pontoon at Albert Quay can be used for up to two hours at a time (p86)

Above Wiseman's Point the river is peaceful and wooded. Although this former anchorage is now completely taken up with moorings, they are sometimes available for visitors through the Harbour Authority (p88)

The narrow entrance to the historic china clay port of Charlestown dries completely at LW, but visitors can sometimes lock into the inner tidal basin (below) for a longer stay (p90)

The inner harbour at Mevagissey dries completely and its use is restricted to local boats, although visitors may enter on the tide to take on fuel and water (p91)

Close to the Dodman, Gorran Haven is a delightful anchorage in settled offshore conditions (p91)

Approaching the River Fal from the east, St Anthony's lighthouse peeping from behind the headland is always a welcome sight, with Pendennis Castle and the cranes of the Docks beyond (p92)

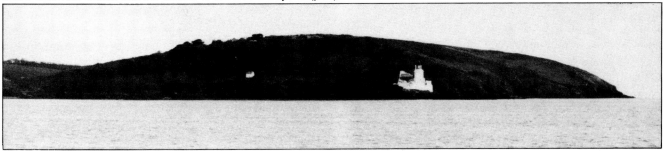

Looking east to St Anthony Light

Black Rock Beacon, right in the centre of the entrance to the River Fal, is unlit. Do not cut too close to it either, as shallows extend 200m north and south. Beyond it, the entrance to Falmouth Harbour lies around the Docks' eastern breakwater (p92)

Rounding the Docks' eastern breakwater keep a good lookout for commercial shipping as you approach the northern arm (p94)

Clearing the northern arm, Falmouth town and waterfront opens ahead (p94)

Close to the centre of Falmouth, the Visitors' Yacht Haven is a popular facility with a convenient fuel barge (p94)

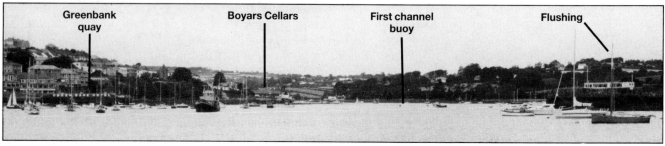

Looking towards the Penryn River from Falmouth harbour, Greenbank Quay lies to port and Flushing Sailing Club is on the quay to starboard. Falmouth Marina is out of sight, but a ship can be seen berthed at Boyars Cellars in the distance (p97)

Approaching Falmouth Marina, the wharf at Boyars Cellars is a prominent feature to port. The houses and quay at Penryn lie upriver in the far distance (p97)

Visitors usually lie in the outer basin at Falmouth Marina which caters for most cruising requirements and has a very friendly reputation (p98)

St Mawes Castle guards the approach to this pretty village. Lugo buoy lies to the right of the nearest boat (p99)

The peaceful wooded upper reaches of the River Fal provide plenty of scope for exploration and a few surprises too - sizeable ships can usually be seen laid-up in King Harry Reach (p101)

From Sunny Corner the channel bears west again past two red cans towards Lighterage Quay (p103)

Above Lighterage Quay the channel meanders toward the distant spires of Truro Cathedral (p103)

At Truro Town Quay the river divides; the Harbour Office is to port and the best berth for visitors lies to starboard (p103)

Truro - looking downstream at LW. Visitors should berth by the steps, where the soft mud is reasonably level (p103)

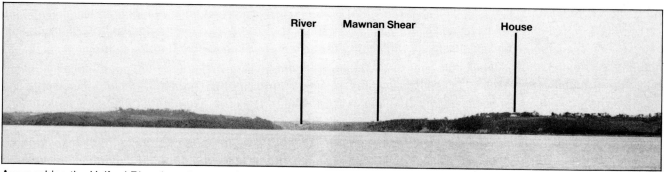

Approaching the Helford River from the east, the isolated white house is useful for locating the entrance (p106)

The drying Gedges Rocks lie inshore of the August Rock Buoy, which should be left to starboard (p106)

Once past Mawnan Shear, the river opens ahead, with Toll point to starboard and Bosahan Point in the distance to port (p106)

Porth Saxon, just inside Toll Point, is a pleasant anchorage in settled conditions (p106)

Beyond Bosahan Point drying Helford Creek opens to port; the anchorage and visitors' moorings lie off it in the 'Pool' (p107)

Helford Passage, on the northern shore, has a pub/restaurant, showers, launderette and basic provisions; dinghy over from the moorings or hail the ferry from Helford Point (p107)

Looking to seawards from the Pool towards Bosahan Point and Toll Point in the distance, the Helford River is very open to the east

From the Pool the most convenient dinghy landing place is at Helford Point, where a private pontoon is maintained by voluntary donations from visitors (p107)

Looking upriver from the Pool to Calamansack Woods, Pedn Billy Point conceals the entrance to Port Navas Creek on the northern shore (p109)

Upriver, the unspoiled Helford River owes much of its uncluttered beauty to the fact that most of it is given over to extensive oyster beds. Moorings and anchoring are not permitted, and it is a delightful stretch of water to explore gently on a rising tide (p109)

Viewed from St Saviours Point at LW, the Doom Bar chokes most of the mouth of the River Camel, with waves breaking almost right across the channel, which is deepest close to low-lying Trebetherick Point (p135)

Looking towards Padstow from the beacon at St Saviour's Point at LW springs, the harbour approach channel holds tightly to the western shore and dries almost completely (p135)

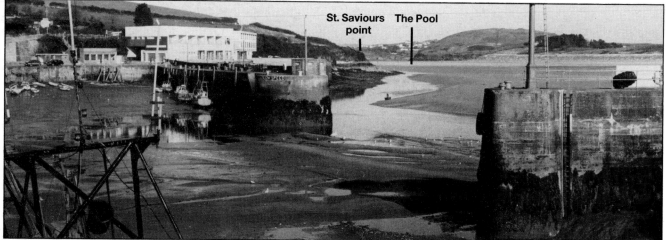

Looking to seaward from the outer harbour mouth at LW, St Saviour's Point and the Pool in the distance (p135)

Visitors' berth in the inner harbour at Padstow. Although a new hydraulic flood prevention gate has now been built, it had not been decided (early 1989) whether this would also be used to retain water and provide floating berths in this normally drying harbour (p135)